EDDY ARNOLD

His Life and Times

Don Cusic

Brackish Publishing
P.O. Box 120751
Nashville, TN 37212

Cover Design & Layout: PricelessDigitalMedia.com

Production Coordinator: Jim Sharp, Sharp Management

BOOKS BY DON CUSIC

The Beatles and Country Music (2015)

James Weldon Johnson: Songwriter (2013)

Roger Miller: Dang Him (2012)

Elvis and Nashville (2012)

Dressed in Grey & Blue (Novel) (2012)

Sharecropper's Son (Novel) (2011)

The Cowboy in Country Music (2011)

Encyclopedia of Contemporary Christian Music (Editor) (2010)

The Trials of Henry Flipper: First Black Graduate of West Point (2009)

Discovering Country Music (2008)

Gene Autry: His Life and Career (2007)

Johnny Cash: The Songs (2004)

Baseball and Country Music (2003)

It's the Cowboy Way: The Amazing True Adventures of Riders In The Sky (2003)

Merle Haggard: Poet of the Common Man (2002)

Saved By Song: A History of Gospel and Christian Music (2002)

Eddy Arnold: I'll Hold You in My Heart (1997)

Music in the Market (1996)

Willie Nelson: Lyrics 1957-1994 (1995)

Cowboys and the Wild West: An A-Z Guide From the Chisholm Trail to the Silver Screen (1994)

Hank Williams: The Complete Lyrics (1993)

Hank Williams: The Singer and The Songs

The Poet As Performer (1991)

Reba: Country Music's Queen (1991)

Randy Travis: The King of the New Country Traditionalists (1990)

Sandi Patti: The Voice of Gospel (1988)

PREFACE

By Shannon Pollard

As a rule, most American teenagers do not want to spend much time with their grandparents. I was a typical American teenager, but as I moved into my early twenties, I realized that since my paternal grandparents had long passed away and I had not known them very well, I did not want to make the same mistake with my maternal grandparents, Eddy and Sally Arnold. Sure, I had grown up knowing that my grandfather was a country music legend, but in our small family, he was an everyday sort of person and we were not regularly subjected to the "music industry."

At the time of my revelation, circa 1996, my grandfather happened to be the subject of a soon to be published biography of his life by Dr. Don Cusic. By 1997, my grandparents were very active and relatively healthier than most people decades younger than them and it was a relatively calm period because he was consciously slowing his career down. Lucky for me, my grandfather had taken an interest in my future and enlisted his friend and aforementioned biographer, Dr. Don Cusic, to give me some career/life advice, I am eternally grateful for their interest because it forever shaped my life and allowed me the opportunity to spend a lot of quality time with my grandfather.

Whenever I could, I accompanied him to many of his legendary daily lunch gatherings at various meat and threes, tagged along (or drove) on road trips and sat in his office listening to records and to his stories from the road. When he passed on May 8, 2008, I was 34 years old. My grandmother had passed away less than two months earlier, so for a good portion of my adult life, I was fortunate to have them in my life. My two children were able to know them as well, which brought great joy to all parties.

As executor of the Eddy Arnold estate, and grateful grandson of Eddy and Sally Arnold, I hope you enjoy this updated biography Dr. Don Cusic has prepared. Eddy Arnold lived a rags to riches story. He is an American icon, often overlooked, but if you read this book, you will quickly realize his importance in the history of county music and, hopefully, get a sense of his wonderful personality. My only wish is that you could have known his laugh, which I still miss on a daily basis.

CHAPTER 1

In Tennessee, it's not a long way from Chester County to Nashville if you only measure the miles. But if you look first at a poor farm boy and then at a world famous entertainer who's voice reached millions, the distance seems immeasurable. Eddy Arnold was that penniless farm boy who made the journey to country music superstardom, but his story is not his alone. It is also the story of country music's journey from the rural south to acceptance in big cities. In many ways, the stories of Eddy Arnold and country music run parallel; both started out poor and a bit backwards but, in the end, reached from Tennessee to the ends of the Earth.

Tennessee is a long, narrow state, about 500 miles from the northeast city of Bristol to Memphis in the southwest corner. Traveling west from the Smoky Mountains on the eastern border, Tennessee first becomes hilly through the Cumberland Plateau and then gets flatter as the traveler gets closer to Memphis and the Mississippi River, which serves as the western border. Nashville is located near the middle of the state; Memphis sits about 200 miles west of Nashville. Jackson, Tennessee is about halfway between Nashville and Memphis or about a hundred miles away from Nashville. By the time you get to Jackson, the land has gotten flat with a few rolling hills while the dirt has grown dark and rich.

South of Jackson about 20 miles is the small town of Pinson; turning east near the Pinson Mounds you enter into Chester County, whose county seat, Henderson, is about 15 miles further south. In 1918 the roads were not paved and there was no electricity; it was mostly small farms while the towns of Pinson and Henderson consisted of a handful of stores and a school, although Henderson also has a Courthouse sitting on a hill.

In May, 1918 American soldiers were in Europe fighting World War I. Under General John J. Pershing, most American forces were in France on the Western front, digging trenches and trying to break the back of the German army. President Woodrow Wilson had abandoned his promise to "keep America out of the European War" and joined the Allies, Great Britain and France, to defeat Germany. This was the first War in the air and Eddie Rickenbacker downed 26 enemy planes over France. Sergeant Alvin York, a farm boy from the mountains of Jamestown, Tennessee, became a national hero for capturing 132 Germans single handed. Later that year, in the November elections, the Republicans took control of both houses of Congress.

At the beginning of 1918 President Wilson proposed a 14-point peace plan. Daylight savings time was put in motion on March 31 to help the war effort by cutting electricity needs in the nation. Throughout the summer about a million American troops were fighting in "The Great War." On November 11 the Armistice was signed, ending the War and on December 4 President Wilson sailed to the Versailles peace conference, where he presented his idea for the League of Nations to the Europeans.

Out on a 240-acre Tennessee farm about half-way between Pinson and Henderson in Chester County, Richard Edward Arnold was born on May 15, 1918. Both parents had been married before and widowed. Will C. Arnold's first wife, Mary Etta, died on April 7, 1905; they had nine children. On September 4, 1906, Will Arnold married Georgia Wright, who had two surviving children from her first marriage to J.D. Ingle. Will and Georgia had five children of their own: a daughter, Patty, then two sons, W.D. and John, a daughter who died at 18 months, then the son they named Richard Edward Arnold. Edd, as he was called, was born when his Dad was 58 and his mother was 44. "I must've been quite a surprise for them," Arnold observed. In the combined two families, Eddy Arnold was the youngest of fourteen children born to Will Arnold and the youngest of sixteen when the families of both parents were combined.

Edd's dad, Will C. Arnold, was a farmer and entrepreneur. Their farm was located beside a dirt road and had a creek running through it. The adjoining farm belonged to the Lathams and Edd and the Latham boys spent countless hours playing in the fields and ravine between the two houses. Edd showed an early interest in music; around 1928 he received a harmonica, which gave him his first taste of playing music, and he obtained a guitar when he was ten. He had music in him, "in his bones," as country folks say, because his father played the fiddle and his mother sang. His mother, who played the guitar and sang around the house, taught Edd his first guitar chords. His Grandfather Wright encouraged him with his music, although he was often told to "keep quiet" in the house because his father was sick and couldn't stand the noise from a young boy trying to learn to play the guitar. But learning the guitar was a labor of love and young Edd kept clanging away.

In addition to his farm, where he grew cotton, peas, corn, hay, potatoes and some livestock, Will C. Arnold had a grist mill and sawmill. He was a successful, respected man in the community and people often came by to talk and get advice. Will Arnold had high blood pressure and, as Edd was growing up, his Dad grew sick. On Edd Arnold's eleventh birthday, May 15, 1929, as he was playing at a nearby farm in a field with the Latham boys across the ravine from his house, he heard the dinner bell ringing in the late afternoon. As soon as he heard it, young Edd Arnold knew his father had died.

The boyhood days of fun and frolic were forever changed. The next day, May 16, was Edd's brother W.D.'s birthday and the day after that their father was buried on a little knoll in a graveyard beside the white clapboard Friendship Baptist Church. As friends and family gathered for the funeral, young Edd thought his heart would break and couldn't imagine how times could be tougher or something could hurt deeper.

Problems arose immediately. On April 24, 1924, Will C. Arnold had borrowed $1,980 from D.S. Parker and gave a deed of trust for the loan. The loan had been partially repaid but when Will Arnold died, Parker came to collect all his money. A series of documents were filed in court to sell the 167 acre farm where the family lived as well as two other 35-acre tracts owned by Will. After a series of delays, the farm was auctioned at the Henderson Court House on October 25, 1930 to Parker, who bought the three tracts for a total of $1,745. Then, in December, the Arnold's neighbors, the Lathams, purchased the land from Parker for $2,344; a week and a half later the Lathams sold the land to A. A. Arnold, son of Will C. and Mary Etta and Edd's half brother. Allan A. Arnold let Georgia and the three boys who remained at home--W. D., John and Edd--live on the farm as sharecroppers.

Out in the country, there's a big gap between being a land owner and a sharecropper. A land owner has social status, respect and prestige. Owning land means owning something, having some control of your destiny, having a connection to the earth and a stake in the community. Being a sharecropper means having no status or prestige--you're just a short step away from hired help. Being a sharecropper puts you on the bottom rung of the economic ladder, subject not only to the normal pitfalls of farming--too much or too little rain and crops that sometimes fail--but also the whims of the landowner. It helped a little that the landowner was Edd's half-brother, but it was still a big come down for the Arnold family to go from being a family headed by a respected landowner to a family of sharecroppers. The loss of self-respect that comes from not owning your own land was even bigger than the loss of the farm implements and animals the Arnolds had to watch auctioned off.

There was a great deal of turmoil during the years 1929 and 1930 for the Arnold family; legal papers were filed and family members had to appear in court. For young Edd it turned his world topsy turvy; there was a roiling cauldron of emotions because he didn't know if the family would remain on the farm or not. An eleven year old boy is left out of the loop when family decisions are made; the eight older half-brothers and half-sister (one half brother had died in 1927) were heirs to the property in addition to the four Arnold children. It was a disturbing time.

During the auction in October, 1930, much of their personal property was sold to clear the debt; Edd remembers they were allowed to keep a couple of cows, some pigs, two mules, and some farm equipment, but he had to watch as the rest of their belongings were sold to others. He felt a deep sense of loss as well as a personal emptiness; he did not know what was going to happen to him or his family and this turmoil was wrenching. Sixty-five years later he could close his eyes and still recall those feelings that day.

The purchase of the land by Allan Arnold kept Georgia Arnold and her three boys from being evicted, but also created conflict within the Arnold family, who were relegated to tenant status.

The year 1929 was a particularly formative one for Eddy Arnold. First, his father died and he had to face growing up without a Dad. Eddy Arnold felt a deep gap in his heart and soul his entire life because he didn't grow up with a Dad.

As a young boy he had been learning to play the guitar during the year his father died and was often told to "keep quiet" because his father was ill and the playing bothered him. After his father's death, Edd felt a great deal of guilt because he had not realized just how sick his father was, or that somehow his boyish guitar playing had been partly responsible for his father's death.

In December of that year, his blind grandfather Wright, who regaled the family with stories from the Civil War (he'd been a soldier in that conflict) and who encouraged young Edd in the boy's efforts to learn to play the guitar, also died. Finally, he watched the family's farm and the family's possessions sold and this left him with a deep, abiding fear that one day all he owned might also be lost. Never a wealthy family, the Arnolds plunged into poverty in 1929. It caused Eddy Arnold to scrimp and save his whole life, to be careful with his money and, even when he was making more money than he could spend, always carry in the back of his mind that it could all be gone tomorrow.

The one bright spot in 1929 was a phonograph that Edd's sister Patty brought home with her from St. Louis at Christmas. It was the first time Edd Arnold had seen a phonograph, and he sat enthralled as he listened to the records. As he got older, Edd's family bought a phonograph and he ordered records from the Sears catalog; his favorite artist was Gene Autry and the first Autry song he fell in love with was "When Jimmie Rodgers Said Good-Bye."

CHAPTER 2

When you grow up poor on a farm out in the country you spend a lot of time alone with your dreams. While some farm boys immerse themselves in the day to day activities of farming, planting crops, worrying about the weather, and feeding the livestock, others let their minds wander to wonder what life would be like without the day-to-day chores of farming.

Farming is a hard way to make a living. First, there are enormous risks involved; there are no guarantees that once you plant a crop the rains will come at the right times or that, when a crop is ready for harvest, a storm won't come along and wipe out a whole year's work. Next, the farmer is at the mercy of the buyer for the price he gets for his crop; he must take what he can when he delivers it because there's no way to drive a bargain when your whole crop will rot if it isn't sold quickly.

Many boys who grow up on a farm want to get away from farming. Farming might sound glamorous and appealing to city folks--fresh air, in touch with the land and all that--but the truth of the matter is that it is never-ending hard work. Some boys move off the farm and go into town for a job in a store, or with some factory or manufacturing company. Edd's brother, W. D. went to barber school, then set up a barber shop in Jackson.

Making a living is only part of life. To some, it is the major part and so they try to get a job as soon as possible, get married, have a family and try to pay the bills. But some boys have dreams that are bigger. They want to matter, want to go beyond just making a living to making a mark in this world. Edd Arnold was such a boy.

What could a farm boy do in the 1930s? Jobs were scarce--it was, after all, the Great Depression--so most people stayed put if they had a job at all. With farming, at least you could grow your own food. Most boys never finished high school--Edd Arnold dropped out after the ninth grade--because they couldn't afford to stay in school. Besides, if you were a hard worker you were more likely to get hired by somebody than if you were smart. People needed hard workers.

A boy could stay on the farm, or go into town and look for a job in a store or office. But if you could sing, the whole wide world was open to you. It was almost like being paid to have fun, or being paid to do what you'd be doing anyhow, and you could receive recognition and attention in the community. People would know who you are so you would not be just another struggling nobody; if you could sing on the radio you could be somebody. Edd Arnold wanted to be somebody.

CHAPTER 3

Eddy Arnold remembered hearing early Jimmie Rodgers records and reading about Rodgers death in 1933 in the newspaper (Arnold had just turned 15 when Rodgers died). The following year, 1934, Edd Arnold had four music "lessons" when a traveling musician drew some chord diagrams on the school house blackboard and demonstrated the fingering to Arnold; those four lessons cost 75 cents each.

When Eddy Arnold was 16 he went on a school trip to visit the radio station in Jackson and knew when he walked in the door that singing over the airwaves was the life for him. Things were starting to click in his own mind; singing was a way to get off the farm and out into the world at large and he could sing pretty good. Arnold remembered the impact that radio station had on him at the time: "I want to do that!" Arnold said. The radio station in Jackson, "looked so big to me, to see an engineer in there turning the knobs. I didn't know what he was doing, but I knew it was something important." The wheels were turning: "I'm saying all the time in my mind, this is what I want to do--sing on the radio!"

When Edd Arnold was 16, he was picked by his school to sing at the Madison County Fair; he sang "If You'll Let Me Be Your Little Sweetheart." Later, he played at house parties for

$1 a night. The school choir, with Edd Arnold as a member, sang at a county fair and the radio station came down and broadcast it. It might not have been the big break of Edd Arnold's career, but it was one more step toward seeing his dream of becoming a singer on the radio come true.

Another step came from a salesman.

"One day I was down on the farm," remembered Arnold. "You work in the morning and come in at 12 and have dinner and I'd clang on my guitar. Eat and strum the guitar. Sometimes I'd sit out on the front porch. One day a man came selling subscriptions to The Jackson Sun in Jackson, Tennessee and they owned radio station WTJS. He was trying to sell us a subscription and I was sitting there with the guitar and he said, 'Why don't you come down and I'll get you an audition.' So I did."

Arnold quit school when he was sixteen, after he'd finished the ninth grade. At that time, it was rare to find someone who did finish high school, especially in the rural South. Farm work needed strong young men and, besides, schooling really didn't help you all that much at the time; hard work did. If somebody had a strong back and was willing to work hard, they could make a way in life, support their family, and even climb the ladder of success. Hard work and experience were what counted and the sooner you got some experience, the better off you were.

Another turning point occurred for Arnold when he was 16. After his father died, W. D., his eldest brother, took young Edd under his wing, was good and kind to him, and became a father figure. But John, Edd's other brother, who was seven years older than Edd, was a different story. The two fought constantly, or rather, John beat up the younger, smaller Edd constantly. They just couldn't get along, possibly because John was a bit jealous of the attention Edd got from W. D., possibly because that's what older brothers do, or maybe just because that was the way John was.

When Edd was 16, strong as a horse with lots of stamina, the tables turned. John had been plowing with some mules and Edd came out to help; the mules were tired and sweaty and Edd thought they should be given a rest. John was adamantly against that and told Edd to keep on plowing. Then John reached down, picked up the single tree from the plow (a piece of wood about a foot and a half long that connects the mules to the plow) and hit Edd over the head with it, drawing blood. Edd lit into him with his fists, leaving bruises and a black eye. Their mother was upset, especially after seeing John's condition. John kept his distance from Edd for the next several days; it was the last time John ever beat up on his young brother.

Edd sang around the house, in the fields and walking along the road. His older brother W. D. taught him how to cut hair and young Edd would go to the local store, set up a soft drink crate and cut hair for extra money. He sang while he was at the store, too. Soon, he began playing at neighborhood gatherings, house parties and square dances. He learned that when he sang people took notice and gave him compliments; it was easy to get some money and the attention of girls if you were a singer.

CHAPTER 4

Bill Westbrooks was a struggling singer who'd landed a job with the Hunt Brothers Furniture Store in Dyersburg, Tennessee. Part of that job involved appearing on a radio program sponsored by the store and traveling around on a small, flat-bed truck to sing and advertise the store. Soon Westbrooks moved to Jackson, where the Hunt Brothers opened another furniture store. The store sponsored a radio program for Westbrooks and also provided a truck to travel and sing to advertise the furniture store.

Because Eddy Arnold was attracted to music he came and listened to Bill Westbrooks sing and hung around the radio station in Jackson where Westbrooks performed. According to Westbrooks, he first met Arnold when "I went to a homecoming--a gathering out kind of near his home... we started calling him Smiling Eddy Arnold. You could hear him laugh above five-hundred people...directly he come to where I was by the sound truck and we got to talking--and so I told him we was fixing to have a talent show. Hunt Brothers was fixing to have it on Sunday afternoon. Anybody from anywhere around there could appear on our broadcast. And we was going to run it for thirteen weeks. And the one that won out on the top got to be on the program--for free. ...I asked him, 'Eddy, don't you want to enter this talent contest?'...and he said, 'Yeah, Bill, I believe I would'...And so Eddy was on the talent show--but Eddy didn't win. But anyway, I said, 'Eddy, I'd like to have you work with me.' And he said he'd like to work with me 'cause him and his mother and his brother John...were pretty poor. He kind of wanted to get out of that country, and plowing them mules. He was getting tired of them mules!"

On the radio program, Arnold appeared with Bill and his wife Vera (known as Arizona Lou), Al "Happy Jack" Goebel (accordion), Jimmy Allen, Val Morris (steel guitar), Buddy Tucker and Angelina Palozola (accordion). Morris taught Eddy Arnold new guitar techniques and chords.

Bill Westbrooks needed a fiddler in his group and Eddy recommended Howard McNatt, who Arnold knew from musical gatherings; the two often played together before Arnold joined Westbrooks. McNatt's family owned a general store and Howard took classical violin lessons in Memphis during his high school years at Henderson High School. Right after McNatt graduated, he joined Westbook's group and he and Eddy took a room at a boardinghouse. McNatt taught Arnold how to read music and the two wrote songs together.

McNatt's nickname, "Speedy," came from Eddy because McNutt was habitually slow to arrive at the radio station and local shows.

The Westbrooks group performed on 250-watt WTJS at noon each day and Arnold sang Gene Autry songs like "Silver Haired Daddy" and other ballads while McNatt played fast, lively tunes like "Red Wing" and "Boil Them Cabbage Down." They worked "the kerosene circuits" where they'd go to a school house, charge ten or fifteen cents admission, and play for the farmers. Eddy Arnold didn't make much money, but at least he was on the radio. By 1936 radio was mass entertainment in the United States and families sat around their home sets in the evening and listened to President Roosevelt's "Fireside Chats," drama and comedy shows and the big bands coming out of New York and Chicago. Since radio stations broadcast over the AM band, and those radio waves could bounce off the ionosphere, even people living out in the country could pick up a number of distant radio programs. That's how country music was heard coming from Chicago over WLS on "The National Barn Dance," from WSM's "Grand Ole Opry" in Nashville and other "barn dances" in neighboring states. Eddy Arnold listened and soaked it all in.

In addition to his job on the radio, Arnold landed a job with the George A. Smith Funeral Home, on East Main Street in Jackson, driving the hearse, which also served as an ambulance. Many small cities did not have an ambulance service so funeral homes usually answered emergency calls. This is how Edd Arnold learned how to pick up an injured person with the least amount of pain or damage and get them to a hospital. Because he drove the ambulance, Edd had a room at the funeral home. This meant he was near when an emergency call came in; also, he helped the funeral home when a pallbearer was needed.

The Westbrooks group did well on WTJS and, wanting to move up, auditioned for a spot on WMPS, a thousand watt station in Memphis. Eddy Arnold had decided to accept an offer from George Smith for a full time job at the funeral home when Westbrooks' group was notified WMPS wanted to hire them; Edd elected to go with Westbrooks. On January 3, 1938, the Westbrooks group made their debut on WMPS. Each group member made $10 a week; they performed each day at six in the morning and 12 noon as well as a weekly Friday evening show, "The Family Program." However, on January 15, station manager George Engleton, disappointed in the group's ragged performances, fired them.

The Westbrooks group auditioned for Memphis station WMC at the Hotel Gayoso; the program director liked them but his talent line-up was full. Eddy and Speedy made their first recordings when the WMC program director asked them to record some songs for future reference; they recorded "Nighttime in Nevada," "Four or Five Times," "St. Louis Blues" and the 1937 pop hit, "Merry-Go-Round Broke Down."

Westbrooks decided to go back to Jackson but Arnold and McNatt chose to try their luck in St. Louis. "I had a sister, two half-brothers, and two uncles in St. Louis," remembered Arnold, "so we took off." They caught the bus over, arrived Sunday morning, January 16 at 6 a.m. and moved in with Patty Burns, Arnold's sister, at 23 Euclid Avenue.

The next day, Arnold and McNatt made the rounds at radio stations, auditioning for a job. St. Louis was a

entertainer and even did some "rube comedy" in outlandish outfits. He allowed decisions to brew within him and didn't make many false moves.

Arnold practiced constantly in St. Louis and learned new songs; the duo did pop songs like "In the Mood" and "The Woodpecker Song" as well as western numbers such as "Rose of the Rio Grande" and "Leaning On That Old Top Rail."

"I always had a quiet confidence," said Arnold. "I was always aggressive in a quiet way. I knew where I wanted to go because I couldn't go back. There wasn't anything to go back to." After two years in St. Louis he felt it was time to move on but wasn't entirely sure where his next step should be. However, he had become a seasoned entertainer, knew he wanted a crack at the Big Time, and felt he was ready for it.

Speedy McNatt did not want to push for the Big Time; he was homesick and returned to Jackson where he joined Gabe Tucker's band, the Musical Ramblers. Eddy continued to perform in St. Louis with other musicians. Now and then Eddy came back to Jackson and sat in with the Tucker group when they played local dates.

CHAPTER 5

Sometime in late 1939 Eddy Arnold drove his 1932 Coupe from St. Louis to his hometown of Henderson to visit his mother and perhaps sit in with the Musical Ramblers. It was around nine in the morning and the car radio was tuned into WSM, the powerful 50,000 watt station from Nashville that broadcast the Grand Ole Opry every Saturday night. Opry star Pee Wee King had a morning program on the station and Arnold was listening to it. He had met King for a brief handshake around 1936 while he was performing on the Jackson radio station and followed King's career. He knew King had a singer named Jack Skaggs as a regular, but that day he did not hear Skaggs.

Arnold wondered if King was looking for a male vocalist and when Arnold returned to St. Louis he sent a hand-written letter and picture to King in Nashville, asking if King would consider him as a male vocalist. King's manager (and father-in-law) J. L. Frank replied to Arnold and requested a transcription. Since this was before the era of tape, all recordings were made on transcriptions, a large, thin disc that looked much like an over-sized record. Arnold talked with KXOK Program Director Blaine Coldwell, who recorded one for Arnold at the radio station, and the singer sent it off. Frank and King listened, liked what they heard and a few weeks later sent for Arnold. Hired for $3 a show with a guarantee of $15 a week, Arnold convinced Frank and King to hire Speedy McNatt as well and the two became members of King's group, the Golden West Cowboys.

It was an opportune time to be on the Grand Ole Opry. In January, 1939, the Opry attracted a major sponsor, "Prince Albert" tobacco, through the Esty advertising agency. In October, through the efforts of Dick Marvin, a key executive of Esty, the Opry went on the NBC network on Saturday nights with a 30-minute segment sponsored by Prince Albert. The Opry was organized and run by George D. Hay, "The Solemn Ole Judge." Other key executives at WSM were Program Manager Jack Stapp, who joined the station in 1939 after a stint with CBS in New York, and Harry Stone, who was General Manager of the station.

The time in Nashville on the Grand Ole Opry was short-lived for young Eddy Arnold; he performed with the Golden West Cowboys starting in January, 1940 and the group played in and around Nashville throughout most of the Spring, then moved to Louisville, where they performed on WHAS on a daily morning show at 9 a.m. sponsored by Dr. Coldwell's Syrup of Pepsin. It was a time of professional growth for Arnold and the first time he'd toured extensively and played major vaudeville houses in front of large audiences. It was also the first time he saw the role of a manager and how the business of country music worked.

The key figure behind the career of the Golden West Cowboys was J. L. Frank, one of the most powerful executives in early country music. He had been the manager and booking agent for Gene Autry and Smiley Burnette when Autry was in Chicago appearing on the "The National Barn Dance" on WLS. Frank helped Autry obtain a spot on the WLS program and then used the exposure to book Autry for personal appearances.

King first met J. L. Frank in 1932 when Autry's band, the Range Riders, was involved in a car accident in Wisconsin while on tour and couldn't perform. Frank and Autry heard King's band on the radio while they were getting their car repaired at a service station and Frank called and asked if the group could help Autry fill in a scheduled date. King agreed; later, in the early fall of 1932, King was hired by Autry to play accordion. He appeared with Autry on WLS in Chicago for about a year, then moved with Autry and J. L. Frank to Louisville, Kentucky, where Autry obtained a position on WHAS for a show.

Autry had been trying to get into the movies and in 1934 made his first appearance in a Hollywood western, Ken Maynard's *In Old Santa Fe*, and then in a serial, *The Phantom Empire*. After those two films, Autry came back to Chicago, then to Louisville before he moved to Hollywood in 1936 to star full time in singing cowboy westerns.

When Gene Autry moved to Hollywood, J. L. Frank remained in the Midwest and promoted live country music shows, one of the first show promoters in the nation to do so.

When Eddy Arnold joined the Golden West Cowboys he joined a well-organized group that influenced his own career.

First, Pee Wee King and the Golden West Cowboys were not a traditional "hillbilly" group; they came out of vaudeville and theaters in the mid-West and their organization was based more on the Big Band model where a group had an owner, a manager, and the musicians had different roles. Second, the Golden West Cowboys were the first Opry group to have a manager, which meant the group was not so dependent--or obligated-- to WSM executives for advice, guidance, commitments or career decisions.

Musically, they were smooth and more "pop" sounding than traditional string bands such as the McGee Brothers, Missouri Mountaineers, the Delmore Brothers or Uncle Dave Macon. Visually, they eschewed the bib overall look of mountain folk for the Western apparel of the singing cowboys; they were sharp dressers and presented an attractive visual image.

Pee Wee King was an unlikely Opry star, if you believe the traditional story about the Opry only representing true southern folk music. He was born Frank Julius Anthony Kuczynski in Milwaukee, Wisconsin and grew up in Abrams, near Green Bay. He learned the accordion and joined his father's polka band, then struck out on his own at 15 after taking the name "King" from his idol, Big Band leader Wayne King. His first group was the Farm Hands, organized around 1932; he then formed the King's Jesters, which played mostly Western music, heavily influenced by the Western music heard on WLS's Barn Dances.

CHAPTER 6

During the time Autry performed in Louisville, there were three band members named "Frank" so Frankie King became "Pee Wee," with the name given to him either by J. L. Frank or Autry.

In the summer of 1935 Pee Wee King and J. L. Frank moved to Louisville where King joined Frankie More's Log Cabin Boys on WHAS. The following year, 1936, J. L. Frank organized a group he named The Golden West Cowboys, put Pee Wee in charge, and found a sponsor, Crazy Water Crystals, a laxative company, for a show on WHAS. During personal appearances, the Golden West Cowboys were sometimes teamed with a group from WNOX in Knoxville, Roy Acuff and his Crazy Tennesseans.

By 1937 The Golden West Cowboys consisted of Pee Wee King on accordion, Abner Simms on fiddle, Milton Estes on banjo, Curley Rhodes on bass, Curley's sister Texas Daisy on vocals, and Cowboy Jack Skaggs on guitar. This was the group that auditioned for David Stone, Harry Stone, and engineer Percy White for the Opry. The group was hired and on June 4, 1937, made their Opry debut; however, J. L. Frank made Archie Campbell, then going under the name Art Bell, the head of the group when they first joined the Opry. Frank and Pee Wee King insisted that his band members be allowed to join the musicians union; at first the union objected but, with Frank's and King's persistence, the union relented and King's Golden West Cowboys were among the first individuals in a country music group to become members of a musician's union, which gave them access to network exposure.

The Golden West Cowboys were not the first Opry group to dress in Western clothes (that honor belongs to Zeke Clements) but they dressed well and brought the cowboy image to the Opry. They even went to Hollywood in 1938 and appeared in Gene Autry's movie, *Gold Mine in the Sky* (billed as "J. L. Frank's Golden West Cowboys").

During his time with the Golden West Cowboys, Eddy Arnold joined Texas Daisy as the group's main vocalist. Arnold, Pee Wee King, Milton Estes and Curley Rhodes did group numbers for Sons of the Pioneers' songs as well as love songs. In addition to Arnold, the Golden West Cowboys added fiddler Redd Stewart in 1940 in Louisville.

The time in Louisville was a great learning experience for Eddy Arnold as a professional but it was also important for Eddy Arnold's personal life. While in Louisville, Arnold met Sally Gayhart, who worked at the lunch counter in the Woolworth store. They met after she was in the audience for one of the Golden West Cowboy shows. She stopped him and asked for an autograph; he was happy to oblige, but quickly realized she did not have a pen or paper.

Pretty young Sally Gayhart was from LaGrange, Kentucky, just outside Louisville, and came to the city after her father died. She was dating a boy who played piano at the radio station, which is why she was in the radio audience when she met Eddy. The two began dating between Arnold's appearances. By July 29, 1940, shortly after Eddy Arnold left Nashville for Louisville, the Opry was on 40 stations and reached all the way to the West Coast. During that year Hollywood became enamored with the Opry and filmed a movie, The *Grand Ole Opry*, which starred Roy Acuff and Uncle Dave Macon. The movie company was Republic, known for their "B Westerns" and singing cowboy movies; this is where Gene Autry and Roy Rogers rode the studio range.

In the summer of 1941 (probably mid-to-late July) the Golden West Cowboys moved back to Nashville and the Grand Ole Opry. Fiddler Redd Stewart was drafted soon after they moved; King hired Chuck Wiggins and Shorty Boyd, who performed trio numbers with him while Eddy Arnold sang two songs solo during their shows.

Within weeks after the Golden West Cowboys moved back to Nashville, J. L. Frank met with Dick Marvin, the executive at the Esty Agency responsible for purchasing radio advertising, and Harry Stone, general manager of WSM. On that August day, Frank, Stone and Marvin agreed to organize a "Camel Caravan" to be sponsored by the R. J. Reynold's Company through the Esty Agency. Stone made a commitment to the Agency that the Opry would not accept any competing tobacco sponsors and waivec the requirement that Opry acts had to return to Nashville every Saturday night for the weekly broadcast. This allowed King's group to tour constantly from November, 1941 until December, 1942.

"The Camel Caravan" was originally a popular radio show hosted by Vaughn Monroe. When the touring show was organized, the Esty agency decided to have groups from Hollywood, New York and Nashville on the road. Since R.J. Reynolds had been a sponsor of the Grand Ole Opry since January, 1939, it was in a position to convince the Opry to provide performers for this patriotic tour. The Camel Caravans played at military bases all over the United States and were a mixture of business and patriotism.

The tour carried a patriotic theme. All military personnel in uniform were admitted to the concerts free and many concerts were held on military bases where, during the show, "cigarette girls" passed out free samples of Camel cigarettes to military personnel in the audience.

King's group consisted of himself on accordion, Redd Stewart on fiddle, singer and guitarist San Antonio Rose (Eve McColl) and singer/emcee Eddy Arnold. In addition to King's group, other performers included comedienne Minnie Pearl, 18-year old pop vocalist Kay Carlisle, dancer Dollie Dearman, a trio of girl singers (Mary Dinwiddie, Evelyn Wilson and Alcyone Bate Beasley) as well as four female dancers in short skirts known as "The Camelettes" who passed out free Camel cigarettes to the soldiers. Master of Ceremonies for the show was Opry regular Ford Rush, although Arnold emceed King's segment. Others who performed on the shows during the 19-month tour were Chuck Wiggins (Cowboy Joe), Joe Zinkan, Gene Widner, and Curley Rhodes (Cicero the Comedian).

The tours began in late summer and were held at military bases close enough to Nashville to allow them to return to the Grand Ole Opry on Saturday nights. The troupe traveled in five red vehicles, which each had the Prince Albert logo painted on the side. Pee Wee King's car pulled a trailer that served as a dressing room for outdoor shows. A truck carried the instruments; the sides of the truck dropped down to create a stage. On those early shows, Eddy Arnold opened the show with "I'll Be Back in a Year, Little Darlin'," a popular song for those who had been drafted.

Eddy Arnold could see he was making headway in his career: only two years before he was in St. Louis with Speedy McNatt on a radio station; now he was touring with a top name group and appearing on major radio shows. Life in Nashville was looking up: he was on the Grand Ole Opry with their network connections and about to embark on a national tour with the Camel Caravan. But he was in love with a girl back in Louisville, Kentucky and missing her nearly drove him crazy.

While appearing in Charlotte, North Carolina, Arnold went to a pay phone and called Sally Gayhart long distance and proposed to her; she said she would think about it. Soon she accepted and came to Nashville where the two were married on November 28, 1941. The day after their wedding, Eddy Arnold left his wife with his mother in their small apartment on Pinnock Avenue and departed with the Camel Caravan. "It wasn't really fair to Sally," he remembered. "As soon as we got married, I left." But he'd married the girl of his dreams and life looked good. It wasn't until after they were married that Sally learned she earned more money at her job at the Woolworth's soda counter than Eddy Arnold made as a performer.

On Sunday, December 7, 1941--only nine days after Eddy and Sally were married--the Camel Caravan was in San Antonio, Texas. It was an off day for them; they were scheduled to perform at Kelly Field, Randolph Field and Fort Sam Houston the next day. During the early afternoon, an announcer came on the radio with the news that the American Naval base at Pearl Harbor had been bombed by the Japanese. The next evening the troupe sat and listened to President Roosevelt tell the nation the date would "live in infamy" and that war was being declared on Japan.

A few days later the United States declared war on Germany as well. And so the year 1941 ended with the United States part of World War II, embarked on a mission that would change the country and change the world.

CHAPTER 7

In 1939 the Great Depression still hung over America; there were eight million unemployed in the nation of 131.6 million people. Prices were low but this was deceiving because incomes were also low and money was scarce.

At the beginning of 1939 you could buy a good used car for around $500 (or less!). The well-dressed executives at WSM could purchase a tailored suit for $18.95 with top of the line wing tip shoes for $5. Newspaper ads touted off the rack suits for $14.95-17.95 with topcoats costing around $20. Shirts cost from $1-1.65, sweaters $1.95-3.95 and pants $1.95-3.95.

A young couple setting up a household could purchase a three piece bedroom suite for $39.50 or a rocking chair for $3.89--with credit terms of 25 cents down and 25 cents a week. A 50 piece kitchen set--including a cabinet, silverware and glassware—cost $39.95. For dinner, roast beef cost 15 cents a pound, a round steak cost 29 cents a pound, potatoes were 5 cents a pound and Red Snapper was extravagant and expensive at 30 cents a pound. For the bathroom or outhouse, toilet paper was 4 cents a roll.

Nashville was surrounded by farms and if a farmer needed overalls it would cost him 87 cents; if his wife needed a flannel nightgown, that would be 47 cents. Although those prices sound unreasonably cheap, the plain fact is that 87 cents was a lot of money for farmers; most farmers earned less than $100 a year.

The year before, in 1938, President Roosevelt announced the South was the nation's top economic problem, putting the entire nation at risk with its severe poverty. The annual wage in the South was around $865, compared to $1,291 in the rest of the country.

During the nine months between January and October, 1939, when major changes were happening at the Opry, there were also earth shaking changes in the world at large. Newspaper headlines throughout the year talked about Hitler and the war developing in Europe. The previous year Germany annexed Austria; on March 15 the German army entered Prague and quickly destroyed Czechoslovakia.

On the home front, President Franklin Roosevelt was still creating jobs with his various federal programs, although Congress was concerned about deficit spending. On January 30, 1939 the Tennessee Valley Authority won a victory in the United States Supreme Court, which ruled that the utility was constitutional. The suit was brought by the Tennessee Electric Power Company, which argued that the federal government should not compete against private enterprise. The Tennessee Valley Authority played a major role in bringing electricity to one of the poorest regions of the country.

On April 30, 1939, the New York World's Fair opened and it was a marvel of electric lights and the wonders that technology and science could bring to the world. It was the last great World's Fair, held at a time when a World's Fair allowed people to see all the modern advances in science and technology. That World's Fair introduced television to America and President Roosevelt became the first President to appear on TV with an appearance from the Fair. Not many watched this event on TV; there were less than 400 sets in the entire United States.

The Fair was lit gloriously and called "The World of Tomorrow." The message was that the World of Tomorrow would be brightly lit, no longer a slave to the sun for light. But this World of Tomorrow was mostly confined to cities. In 1935 only two out of 100 farms in the middle Tennessee region had electricity and most families had incomes of less than $100 a year. Private utility companies refused to wire rural areas, arguing that it was cost prohibitive and that farmers wouldn't pay their bills. In 1937 Congress passed the Rural Electric Act which required companies to wire rural areas.

On September 1, 1939 Germany invaded Poland, bringing a Declaration of War from Great Britain and France. The United States declared its neutrality amid cries from the country to "keep us out of war."

Radio came of age during the 1930s and WSM and the Grand Ole Opry were in the right place at the right time. By the end of the decade there were an average of 6.6 soap operas on every day; popular shows included "Burns and Allen," "Our Gal Sunday," "Search for Tomorrow,"

"The Jack Benny Show," "The Shadow" and "Captain Midnight."

WSM received 50,000 watt clear channel status in 1932. This meant that it had the maximum power allotted to an American radio station with no other station at 650 on the dial. Nashville was situated in a geographically advantageous location; virtually anyone within a 200 mile radius could hear the Grand Ole Opry by tuning their AM radios to 650.

The Opry's success depended on it being carried on AM radio, whose waves bounced off the ionosphere at night, enabling listeners hundreds of miles away to tune into the broadcast. If the Opry had been on FM, the signal would have been cleaner and clearer, but it would have been limited to Nashville and the immediate area. Instead, the crackling, popping sound of AM radio airwaves carried the Opry to much of the United States and even into Canada.

There were changes in the music world at large which would have a direct affect on Opry performers and country music in general. Those changes affected publishers and songwriters.

In 1939 the American Society of Composers, Authors and Publishers (ASCAP) decided to raise the fees they charged radio stations for the right to play their songs. This performance rights organization, founded in 1914, was the force that made songwriting a profitable profession because it "licensed" songs for play; i.e. by paying ASCAP, a club, radio station or concert hall could perform any song it wished while ASCAP collected the money and distributed it to their songwriters and publishers. For twenty-five years it was virtually the only game in town, and the years of having a monopoly bred arrogance within its ranks and resentment outside the fold.

The attempt to dramatically increase the fees in 1939 led to a counter-move by broadcasters, who formed a new performance rights organization, Broadcast Music, Inc. (BMI), which opened its doors on April 1, 1940.

The possibility of country music publishers and songwriters earning significant money from their songs changed dramatically on January 1, 1940 when a ten-month radio boycott of ASCAP songs began. Opry performers had to find songs that were Public Domain or else write their own. Pee Wee King's group in Louisville stopped using "Night Time in Nevada," their regular theme song, and began using the "No Name Waltz," a tune composed by fiddler Redd Stewart. Later, Stewart and Pee Wee King took that basic melody and added lyrics to create "Tennessee Waltz."

When, BMI opened its office in New York, and let it be known they'd sign songs from anyone--there was no requirement that a songwriter had to be "elected" by its current members, which was the requirement at ASCAP. That's why most early country music songs are registered with BMI, which built a great deal of its early success on country music. The benefits ran down a two way street; for the first time, country music songwriters and publishers had access to a performance rights organization that collected money for them for public performances. This meant that as country music was increasingly played on radio, there was a way for country songwriters and publishers to get paid for this exposure. This eventually brought Big Bucks into country music's songwriting and publishing coffers.

The call to arms was strong; American anti-war sentiment practically evaporated after Pearl Harbor and, a few days later, Germany's Declaration of War against the United States. Thousands of young men enlisted in the Armed Forces and those who didn't enlist knew they would soon be drafted. Indeed, 75 percent of young American men born between 1918 and 1927 served in World War II. Although the draft induced many to serve, the intense feelings of patriotism and the belief that Hitler must be defeated in order for the world to be safe was paramount in the country. Bond drives, rationing and victory gardens became part of everyday life. Entertainers also felt the call to serve, some at home and some abroad.

At Melody Ranch in Hollywood was Gene Autry, the most popular singing cowboy during the 1930s. The success of the singing cowboys meant employment for a number of songwriters who had to come up with songs for Autry and the other singing cowboys that followed, such as Tex Ritter, Roy Rogers, and others. Autry generally required five to eight songs for each of his movies and always insisted on quality songs. One of the best songwriters for supplying

Autry material was Fred Rose, a pop songwriter who had written hits such as "Deed I Do," "Red Hot Mama" and "Honest and Truly" during the 1920s. Rose had moved to Nashville in 1933 to appear on WSM on an afternoon show, "The Freddie Rose Song Shop"; while in Nashville he had married.

Rose moved to Hollywood in 1938 to work on the Gene Autry movie *Gold Mine in the Sky*. He stayed and worked on a number of Autry movies, writing "Be Honest With Me" and other songs for Autry. During the summer of 1942 Autry entered the Armed Forces as a pilot and Rose moved back to Nashville because his wife wanted to return home. Rose was popular at WSM and quickly landed an afternoon show on the radio station. He was approached by Roy Acuff about starting a publishing company because Acuff wanted to keep the rights to his songs (he reasoned that "if the New York and Chicago publishers wanted to buy them, they must be worth something") and because the songbook business was extremely profitable but also a burden. He needed someone to handle that part of his business.

Fred Rose was in a unique position. He knew the people at WSM and the Opry, had learned about the market for country music--and the money involved--through his work with Autry and the singing cowboys in the movies, and was a pop songwriter who came to Nashville as country music was changing from a folk based music into a major commercial music. Rose played a major role, introducing the pop song format with country topics to replace the folk song format.

This had already been done with western music for the movies, most of which was composed by Tin Pan Alley writers who used pop song structures with western themes. Fred Rose took that same process to Nashville and applied it to southern-based country music.

CHAPTER 8

The Camel Caravan Tour of Opry performers ended at Christmas, 1942; by this time the troupe had traveled over 50,000 miles, performed 175 shows in 19 states at 68 Army camps, hospitals, air fields and naval and marine bases. In March, 1942 it left the United States and performed in the Panama Canal zone.

When it was over, the Camel Caravan had done as much as anything to introduce country music to servicemen all over this country. It had also done a great deal for Eddy Arnold, who gained a wealth of experience and national exposure as he traveled around the country and performed for a wide variety of audiences.

Most Opry performers were tied to the Saturday night Opry shows and this prohibited Opry acts from extensive touring. Even though Opry performers played shows during the week, they could never venture too far away because they had to be back in Nashville on Saturday night. The performers on the Camel Caravan had no such restrictions; Eddy Arnold experienced extensive touring during 1942 and performed before a wide variety of audiences--not just for those who heard him on the Opry. Although the Opry's Camel Caravan had Opry members, it wasn't strictly a "country music" show in the style of the mountaineer image and sound of Roy Acuff. King's group was more pop oriented and the diverse audiences on this tour demanded a style of music beyond the traditional string band sound.

There were memorable adventures along the way. The troupe was stranded in Guatemala for about a week and had to idle away each day, not knowing when they would be able to return. Finally, they got to Texas and Eddy Arnold hitched a ride in the back of a truck, braced against the freezing air, all the way back to Nashville. The traveling was a heady experience for the young singer, who became worldly wise with the traveling and met a large cross-section of people, from dignitaries to conscripts.

The Camel Caravan performances also brought Eddy Arnold to the attention of key executives and decision makers. WSM General Manager Harry Stone visited some of the shows and was impressed by Arnold's smooth vocals. He was also impressed by Arnold's stage introductions and by the fact that the singer was an ambitious, level-headed young man. Stone and Arnold engaged in conversations during the Camel Caravan tour and got to know each other.

Eddy Arnold had a secure position with Pee Wee King's Golden West Cowboys; he made $20 a week but knew his future was limited as a band member. He agonized over breaking away from King and striking out on his own. Sally encouraged him to leave King and go solo when he came back in Nashville after the tour ended and the Golden West Cowboys returned to the Opry. Arnold went into Stone's office one day in late December and told him he wanted to pursue a solo career and asked if Stone could use him in that capacity. Stone looked at Arnold and said, "I don't see why not." Eddy Arnold then submitted his resignation to Pee Wee King.

Harry Stone hired Eddy Arnold for a variety of musical jobs at WSM in 1943, made him a member of the Grand Ole Opry and gave him several daytime radio shows during the week where Arnold performed with just his guitar.

"The Tennessee Plowboy" was the name given to Eddy Arnold by Judge George D. Hay when most performers had a "handle" in which to advertise themselves; Roy Acuff was "the Smoky Mountain Boy" and Uncle Dave Macon was "The Dixie Dewdrop." Eddy Arnold became "The Tennessee Plowboy," an accurate description for billing him at the time.

Throughout 1943 and 1944 Eddy Arnold stayed busy performing on WSM during the day, the Grand Ole Opry on Saturday nights, and personal appearances throughout the South. The Opry sent out a number of "tent" shows in the Southeast where several performers set up a tent near the edge of town, put up posters, alerted the media, and hoped a crowd showed up to buy tickets. Generally, a single performer undertook the financial risk of buying (or leasing) a large tent, having promotional materials drawn up and paying the other performers. The Opry allowed its name to be used and collected a 15 percent commission from ticket sales in exchange for use of its name.

Eddy Arnold performed on a tent show tour organized by Jamup and Honey, two black-faced comedians. During a tent show performance in Arkansas, advertising executive Charles Brown watched Eddy Arnold and was impressed with Arnold's voice and stage demeanor.

In January, 1943 another national sponsor bought time on the Opry. The Ralston Purina Company, maker of feed for farm livestock, purchased a thirty minute segment, called the Purina Grand Ole Opry, which was broadcast over the NBC network in the South and Southwest.

During the War years the Opry continued to hold performances. By October 1943 it was on 125 stations on NBC's national network. In addition, there were transcriptions sent to radio stations all over the country and broadcast on Armed Forces Radio.

In Nashville there was a huge influx of servicemen. The South was chosen as the site for a number of Armed Services training camps because of the large amount of cheap, undeveloped land that could be turned into bases. In Nashville the Aviation Manufacturing Corporation of California (later AVCO) established an airplane manufacturing plant, Vultee Aircraft; the plant opened in May, 1941 and employed 7,000 workers. The Nashville Bridge Company, on the Cumberland River in East Nashville, built submarine chasers and mine sweepers for the Navy; the Kerrigan Iron Works made pontoons, Allen Manufacturing manufactured stoves for the Armed Services, the Tennessee Enamel Company manufactured shell and torpedo parts, the DuPont plant made parachutes, General Shoe manufactured military footwear, Werthan Bag manufactured sandbags, and Phillips & Buttorff made pontoons. Military airplanes were manufactured by Tennessee Aircraft while military uniforms were made by Washington Manufacturing, Southern Manufacturing, and the O'Bryan Brothers. A hospital for wounded soldiers, Thayer General, was built in Nashville; it would treat 13,000 soldiers. On Thompson Lane an Army Air Classification Center was constructed that classified numerous recruits for the flying service; later it served as a hospital and then a demobilization center.

In Clarksville, northwest of Nashville, Camp Campbell was constructed in the summer of 1941; it joined Camp Forrest in Tullahoma and the Smyrna Air Field as military training bases just outside Nashville.

On weekends Nashville was filled with servicemen with weekend passes; during 1942 over one million soldiers visited the city and many of them saw the Grand Ole Opry. Jack Stapp left WSM to serve in London and some of the musicians and performers also left, but a number of key performers stayed home and kept performing. Opry performers and National Life insurance salesmen were engaged in War Bond drives, which raised a substantial amount of money and contributed to positive public relations for country music and Nashville.

CHAPTER 9

The Ralston Purina Company began advertising on WSM's Grand Ole Opry in January, 1943; advertising executives Charles and Bill Brown, in charge of the account at the Gardner Advertising Company in St. Louis, soon broke off and formed their own agency, the Brown Brothers, with the Purina account. Charles Brown decided to make Eddy Arnold the "star" or host of the "Checkerboard Square" segment of the Opry. There was some grumbling among the Opry troupe when Arnold obtained this plum spot; some muttered he was too young and inexperienced for such a slot while others felt that because they were seasoned, loyal Opry performers it was their turn and they should have been given the spot. Arnold didn't say much; he just went about his business of hosting the show, but he heard the whispers and felt the envy.

The Brown Brothers also sponsored a one hour show from the Andrew Jackson Hotel with a large cast and a big band led by Owen Bradley, with Eddy Arnold as the host. It was a mammoth job. The daily show, broadcast over the Mutual Network, lasted about a year.

During the early morning hours, before WSM switched over to NBC programming at 9 a.m., WSM featured a number of live music shows. Eddy Arnold appeared several mornings a week on shows with the John Daniel Quartet and Paul Howard's Arkansas Cotton Pickers. *The Southern Agriculturist* magazine sponsored a show at noon each day that featured Eddy Arnold. Dean Upson, head of WSM Artists' Service Bureau played a role in placing Eddy, Pee Wee King and WSM staff musician Owen Bradley on a syndicated show sponsored by Black Draught laxative, owned by the Chattanooga Medicine Company.

During the summer of 1943 Eddy Arnold, who had performed either solo or backed by the Georgia Peach Pickers, formed his own band. He hired 16-year old steel guitarist "Little Roy" Wiggins, his old friend Speedy McNatt on fiddle, Herbert "Butterball" Paige on electric lead guitar and Gabe Tucker on bass. Tucker also served as the comedian. He was booked by the WSM's Artists Service, the Opry's booking agency, headed by Dean Upson.

Little Roy Wiggins (named "Little Roy" because of his size and age) played with Pee Wee King's group until Clell Summey returned from the service. Inspired by Burt Hutcherson, an early Opry musician who raised the strings on his Martin and played a "slide" guitar, Wiggins' mother bought him an Hawaiian steel guitar from a traveling salesman when Wiggins was six. He quickly mastered the instrument and before he was fifteen he joined Paul Howard's Arkansas Cotton Pickers.

McNatt and Tucker had lived in Louisville and performed on WHAS before Eddy hired them; he gave the band 45 percent of his fees to be divided equally among them while he took 55 percent. He named the group "The Tennessee Plowboys." Instead of dressing in the popular western style, Arnold dressed like a country gentleman, with a Stetson hat, plaid or dress shirt, slacks, street shoes and topped it off with a striped ascot.

The National Association of Broadcasters held their annual meeting in Chicago during the summer of 1943. Harry Stone went to Chicago for the meeting and had lunch with music publisher Fred Forster. Forster was friends with Frank Walker, head of RCA Victor's country division, and Walker told Forster and others in the music industry to let him know if they found promising country talent. RCA Victor lagged behind Columbia, who had Gene Autry, Bob Wills and his Texas Playboys, Bill Monroe and Roy Acuff on their label. Decca Records had Ernest Tubb, Red Foley, Floyd Tillman and Jimmy Wakely on their label. RCA Victor was the home of Jimmie Rodgers during his career but had fallen behind in signing country talent.

Eddy Arnold had auditioned for Columbia, Decca, Capitol and Majestic and been turned down by all of them.

Forster owned Forster Music (ASCAP) and Adams, Vee and Abbott (BMI) located at 216 South Wabash Avenue in Chicago; Forster's companies owned the copyright to standards such as "Down By The Old Mill Stream" and "Missouri Waltz." Since Forster and other Chicago publishers controlled the copyrights to a number of country songs, it behooved Stone, whose station carried the Grand Ole Opry, to maintain good relations.

During lunch with Forster, Harry Stone talked to the Chicago publisher about Eddy Arnold and told him Arnold was looking for a recording contract. Forster had heard Arnold on the radio and told Stone that he'd recommend Arnold to his friend, Frank Walker, head of A & R for Victor Records "when you feel the boy is ready." Stone replied, "He's ready right now."

That led Forster to call Walker long-distance in New York and Walker replied that Forster's recommendation was good enough--he'd send Arnold a contract. Walker then wired Arnold a message that he wanted him to become a Victor artist. This was good news for Arnold; he was being signed to a label unseen and unheard.

Dean Upson, head of WSM's Artists Service Bureau, had booked Arnold on a number of dates and advised Arnold on his career. Upson had been a member of the Vagabonds, a popular trio on the Opry comprised of Upson, his brother Paul and Curt Poulton. The Vagabonds were formed in Chicago and appeared on WLS; they were more pop oriented than the traditional country and folk based acts on the Opry. The group formed their own label, Cabin Hill, and also recorded for Gennett, Brunswick and Victor's Bluebird label. Upson had a varied career in radio; his trio was on WGY in Schenectady, New York, then he became program director of WMBD in Peoria, Illinois, then back to WSM before he became program director at WSIX in Nashville. He returned to WSM in June, 1943 as head of the Artists Service Bureau, which booked Opry acts.

Dean Upson was college educated and well-respected and Eddy Arnold trusted him. Arnold sent Upson a copy of his RCA contract to look over; Upson suggested Arnold sign a five-year contract with him as personal manager. Arnold hesitated about the five year commitment and instead signed a one year contract with Upson, with the option to renew for another year. Upson spoke with Forster about changes in the contract and on November 30, 1943, after final approval from Forster, Eddy Arnold signed with RCA Victor.

Arnold also signed a songwriter agreement with Forster's publishing company. Arnold had been trying his hand at writing songs since he branched off on his own. During 1943 he'd written songs with Wally Fowler and J. Graydon Hall which were published by Fowler. Fowler published a songbook with a number of those songs, which Arnold sold at personal appearances. Country artists have always depended on merchandise sold at concerts--anything from songbooks to t-shirts--to provide an income. During the 1940s the major source of merchandising revenue came from songbooks, which generally included sheet music of the songs the artist sang as well as a biography and pictures of the artist. The publisher printed the songbooks and then either sold them to the artist, who re-sold them for a mark-up, or provided them to the artist who received a "commission" for selling them. Eddy Arnold had his picture on the cover of the songbooks from Fowler and his fans bought them as a souvenir as well as to learn the songs.

Fred Forster, who did not have any children, took Arnold under his wing and developed a father-like relationship with the young singer. When Forster first called Arnold he told the singer to expect a contract from Victor and that when it arrived he should send it to Forster's attorney to look over. Arnold did so and Forster's lawyer made some suggestions; the initial royalty rate was half a cent for each record sold.

CHAPTER 10

Eddy Arnold's joy at the received contract was tempered with disappointment. In 1942, James Caesar Petrillo, president of the Musician's Union (the American Federation of Musicians or AFM), called a strike to begin August 1. The decision to strike was announced by Petrillo in May, so most labels stockpiled recordings before the strike; this didn't help Arnold, who didn't have his recording contract before the strike.

The central issue for the strike, announced at the AFM's annual convention, was the creation of a Performance Trust Fund to provide money for musicians out of work. That demand came about because of the rising popularity of recordings, which threatened to put musicians out of work if radio played records instead of hiring musicians to perform live. Additionally, Petrillo wanted more money and better working conditions for musicians--a key demand in most labor strikes. The labor leader held firm for 15 months, despite the pleas from President Roosevelt to not strike. However, there was an exception because musicians were allowed to make transcriptions for V-Disks to be sent to soldiers overseas; the proviso was that those V-Disks could not be sold and had to be destroyed once soldiers finished listening.

From August 1, 1942 until early December, 1944, the strike brought the recording industry to a halt, although Victor attempted to make recordings in Cuba and Mexico. In the fall of 1943 Decca capitulated to the union; however Victor and Columbia continued to hold out until they began to run out of stockpiled recordings and releases by a capello groups proved uncommercial. Finally, Victor and Columbia reached an agreement with the union on November 11 and the strike ended. Victor head Frank Walker wired Arnold to go into a radio station immediately to make some recordings. Victor needed a lot of recordings to catch up, so the studios in New York and Chicago were booked solid. Besides, Eddy Arnold was a new, unknown act; he was not a priority. Dean Upson arranged for Arnold to record at WSM's studio and Victor agreed to pay WSM $5 a song for Arnold's first recording session.

Things were hopping in Chicago during the Summer of 1944. In June, the Republicans held their convention and nominated Thomas Dewey as their presidential candidate. The Democrats held their convention in mid-July and re-nominated Franklin Roosevelt for a fourth term. The Democratic convention was dull except for the decision about a vice-presidential nominee; after Roosevelt's current vice-president, Henry Wallace and his first choice, Supreme Court Justice William O. Douglas, were rejected, he settled on a little-known Senator from Missouri named Harry S. Truman.

During 1944 Eddy and Sally Arnold moved into a house on Branch Avenue off Gallatin Road in Madison, about seven miles from downtown Nashville. Arnold's mother often lived with them; she would stay with Eddy and Sally awhile, then go to St. Louis to stay with her daughter, Patty Burns, then to Jackson, Tennessee to stay with son W. D., who owned the Library Barbershop. In June, 1944 she received a telegram at Eddy's house that her son, John, had died during the D-Day invasion. John was a member of a division of paratroopers and lost his life on the second day of the D-Day invasion (June 7) and was buried in France. By this time Eddy and John had become close with their boyhood fights a thing of the past. The death of his brother caused Eddy Arnold to once again face a family tragedy--and it hurt.

During 1944 Eddy Arnold felt frustrated because of the lack of opportunity for recording. He would hear an a capella record--singers did those to work around the musicians strike--and think "Could I do that?" It was embarrassing to have to answer the question: "Do you have a record out yet?" Eddy Arnold wanted a record out so bad he could taste it; he felt the musicians strike attacked him personally, that life was slipping away and he was losing his biggest opportunity.

After Arnold signed with Forster the publisher sent him songs to consider recording; Arnold liked "Cattle Call." The song, written by Tex Owens, had been recorded by Owens and numerous other singers had sung it; Arnold remembered he first heard it in St. Louis when a cowboy singer did it on the radio. He first learned the song before he joined Pee

Wee King in 1940, but Fred Rose re-wrote the original song, added a bridge and edited the lyrics to make it more commercial. Rose never took credit for this; one story said he did it as a favor for his old friend Fred Forster, but other sources noted that Owens never liked Rose's changes and refused to share songwriting credit on the song.

The "yodel" in the song fit Arnold's voice perfectly and crowds loved it. Soon, Eddy Arnold was using "Cattle Call" as his theme song on the Opry and on his personal appearances.

On December 4, 1944 Eddy Arnold took Plowboy band members Gabe Tucker, Speedy McNatt, Roy Wiggins and Butterball Paige into WSM radio's Studio B with engineer Percy White to record four songs. The songs were "Mother's Prayer," "Mommy, Please Stay Home With Me," "The Cattle Call" and "Each Minute Seems a Million Years." Arnold recorded songs he was comfortable with; he had sung those songs numerous times during his live shows. When the session was done, the master's were sent to New York. This was the first studio recording session by a major label in Nashville.

CHAPTER 11

In January, 1945, Eddy Arnold's first single, "Mommy, Please Stay Home With Me" backed with "Mother's Prayer" was released on the Bluebird label, a budget label of RCA Victor. The first single was a story song about a young boy whose mother went out and partied even though the child pleaded "please stay home with me." A number of women worked during World War II--about 20 million or a third of the 60 million domestic workforce--and this song addressed an underlying concern that women had lost their commitment to motherhood and connection to their children and family because they had jobs outside the home. The mother in the song is a wayward woman, who preferred the bright lights and good times of a party to staying home with her child; the end result was the death of her child after she returned from a night of drinking to find him "in raging pain and nearing death." The child died with the words "please, Mommy, please stay home with me" on his lips.

The final verse concludes with a warning to mothers "don't neglect your duty" and don't "ignore your baby's pleading."

The ongoing problem of the record business during World War II was a shortage of shellac. Because of wartime rationing and shortages, it was difficult to obtain shellac to press records. The government imposed controls on the amount of shellac labels could use and how many records could be pressed. Labels such as Victor saved large pressing runs for proven artists such as Perry Como and Vaughn Monroe. For a brand new act like Eddy Arnold, the initial run was all that was pressed. The end result was that, after 85,000 copies of "Mommy, Please Stay Home With Me" were sold, there were no more Eddy Arnold records pressed, even though there was a demand for more.

Arnold's second record, "Each Minute Seems a Million Years" backed with "Cattle Call" was released in June, 1945, and sold enough to chart, with the "A" side rising to number five. "Each Minute Seems a Million Years" has a brisk tempo carried by the fiddle and Roy Wiggins' distinctive steel guitar while the lyrics tell of a longing for a love who has gone. "Cattle Call" begins with Arnold strumming his guitar, then his distinctive yodel. The bridge sections, one of which begins with "He rides in the sun" and the other that begins "He's brown as a berry" where the song moves to the four chord were Fred Rose's contributions.

On July 9, 1945 Arnold went back into the WSM radio studio for a recording session and recorded "Did You See My Daddy Over There," "Many Tears Ago," "I Walk Alone" and "You Must Walk the Line." The first release, again on Bluebird, from this session was "Did You See My Daddy Over There," backed with "I Walk Alone." "Did You See My Daddy Over There" is a World War II story song that tells of a boy stopping soldiers who have come back from the War and asking about his Dad. "I Walk Alone" is a song of faithfulness with the singer telling his love that even when they're apart, he's still true.

This recording session took four hours in Eddy Arnold's very busy life. Each Saturday night Arnold appeared on the Grand Ole Opry on the Purina segment and during the week he toured, performing wherever he could. Many of those shows were in tents with other Opry performers while other performances were in school houses, town halls, or wherever else he could obtain a booking.

Eddy Arnold was building relationships with the RCA Victor label personnel. Victor sold records through its warehouse distribution system; those warehouses stocked RCA products--like phonographs, as well as records--and shipped them to stores. Arnold came to know the managers of each of those warehouses and when he had a new record released he called each of them and talked about the record. They were more inclined to stock a record from an artist who extended this personal touch. On his personal appearances, Arnold stopped by the warehouses and met the managers and employees, then went to record stores and signed autographs and visited with store employees. The result was that Eddy Arnold, with his instinctive feel for the business of music, laid the groundwork for his records to sell. In many ways he was his own best salesman, and the result was that his records were consistently available for consumers to purchase. As a result, all of his records sold well on the discount Bluebird label and caught the attention of Victor executives in New York.

CHAPTER 12

By the end of 1945, Eddy Arnold had a lot going for him. He was on the Grand Ole Opry every Saturday night, which was beamed to thousands across the country. He hosted his own 15-minute segment of the Opry, which allowed him to show his considerable skills as a Master of Ceremonies. Next, he'd had records that sold well enough for the top brass at Victor to take notice. Finally, he had a manager, Tom Parker, who was a genius at promoting acts and guided his career outside the Opry power structure.

Eddy Arnold had gotten to know Tom Parker in Fall, 1944, when Parker served as the advance man for the tent show organized by the black-faced comedy team of Jam-up and Honey. Those tent shows, organized by Opry members, took country acts to audiences who could not travel due to war time restrictions on gas and tires. A number of Opry acts organized tent shows--it was a good way to earn money--and the JamUp and Honey show featured Minnie Pearl as well as singer Eddy Arnold.

The job of an advance man was to let people know a show was coming to town and make sure a crowd showed up to buy tickets. Tom Parker was a genius in this area, perhaps one of the best advance men that show business has ever known. He was good at going into a town, notifying the newspapers, getting posters printed and distributed, and creating excitement for the coming show. He always did it with little or no money for promotion.

People who knew Colonel Tom Parker (the title is honorary and came first from Louisiana Governor Jimmie Davis, a former country music singer, and, later, from Tennessee Governor Frank Clement after Parker became Arnold's manager) often said something to the effect, "Well, you know, Parker was an old carny." This explanation--he was a "carny"--meant he had a connection to the traveling carnivals and circuses before World War II. It was a world filled with magic--the appeal of an exotic group of traveling performers who played all over the country and brought joy and excitement to audiences.

In the carnival world, Parker learned the ropes of advancing shows. In addition to coverage from newspapers and posters, Parker learned how to pay off politicians and town officials and, as radio in the rural south became more popular, he dealt with radio disc jockeys to attract a crowd for the circus.

To be a good advance man and promoter you had to be a fast talker and Parker mastered that art; he also developed the ambition to be the biggest promoter in America. He settled in Tampa, Florida, because that is where most of the traveling circuses and carnivals spent the winter, and around 1935 married Marie Mott, a divorcee with a ten-year old son.

Parker was a man for hire by any show that needed an advance man or PR person; this was how he became acquainted with Gene Austin, the crooner who had a huge hit in the mid-1920s with "My Blue Heaven." In 1939, when Parker and Austin met, the singer was playing small gigs in the South; Parker convinced Austin to hire him as his booking agent and soon Austin was playing numerous dates in small towns with good sized crowds.

Parker elected to stay in Tampa when Austin wanted to move to Nashville in the early 1940s. Parker was hired to head the Tampa Humane Society and raise funds and soon had the Humane Society financially self-supporting; additionally, he convinced merchants to donate pet food and received press coverage when lovable puppies and kittens were adopted by cute girls and boys.

Parker had worked with country music acts who came to Tampa for concerts at the National Guard armory since 1941; he worked for J. L. Frank, Roy Acuff, Bill Monroe and others, promoting concerts. Acuff was so impressed with Parker's success in promoting concerts that he reportedly invited him to work at the Grand Ole Opry in Nashville, but Parker declined and remained in Tampa.

That's where Parker was in the Fall of 1945 when the Jam-Up and Honey tent show, featuring singer Eddy Arnold, toured Florida and other Southern states. Arnold was impressed by Parker's effectiveness at organizing, promoting and advancing shows and, since he decided not to renew his contract with Dean Upson, he entered a handshake agreement with Tom Parker for management.

Every performer longs to find someone who totally believes in his talent, who is competent in handling the demanding day-to-day aspects of live performances--booking the hall, promoting the concert, making sure an audience shows up--so the performer can just appear and perform his show. An artist needs someone who will dedicate their life to promoting the artist and his or her career, someone whose thoughts and activities are constantly focused on making the singer a star. Eddy Arnold found that person in Tom Parker.

Parker had an old Studebaker with a trailer hooked behind with "Eddy Arnold The Tennessee Plowboy" in foot high letters on the back and sides that was used for traveling. Assisting Parker were his brother in law, Bitsy Mott, and Bevo Bevis, who had first worked for Parker at the Tampa animal shelter. This team spent their time promoting the concerts and career of Eddy Arnold.

Eddy Arnold couldn't have asked for a better manager. There is an apocryphal story that Parker once purchased a hot plate and some chickens so the chickens would "dance" while Arnold performed, thus classifying the act as an agricultural event and avoiding the $25 entertainment tax whenever they played. The story has been passed around for years--but it is not true. However, Parker was shrewd and made sure things went well for his act. Once, in Houston, the manager of a venue told Parker that songbooks and other merchandise couldn't be sold during the show without paying a commission to the venue manager. Parker replied that they didn't pay commissions, so the venue manager forbid any merchandise to be sold. When the vender asked about intermission, Parker replied there would be none-- and the venue manager panicked because he realized he would be unable to sell the hamburgers and hotdogs he had cooked. Finally, the venue manager said, "You can sell your songbooks" and Parker smiled serenely.

In Chattanooga, Arnold performed for a promoter who was notorious for not paying the act. Parker and Arnold huddled together before the show and Parker told Arnold not to perform until Parker waved his hand. Parker then went to the promoter and said, "You know, my acts are kinda funny. They won't play until I wave my hand. And I won't wave my hand until I'm paid." The promoter then paid, Parker stepped out and waved to Arnold and the show went on.

Tom Parker was audacious enough to demand top dollar for his act when other country acts were underpaid (Arnold received $500 a week for his Purina radio show, "The Checkerboard Jamboree," when other artists were working for next to nothing), and never let up in his efforts to put Eddy Arnold in the public spotlight.

Parker was so dedicated to his artist that one day Arnold told him he should take some time off or get a hobby. Parker looked Arnold in the eye and replied, "You're my hobby." That was a big reason for the success of Eddy Arnold at the beginning of 1945 when his first record was released. Tom Parker did everything humanly possible as a manager, booking agent and promoter to get him in front of the public and make him a star. No artist could ask for more than Tom Parker gave Eddy Arnold.

Arnold traveled with a four piece band and during his show, like all country shows at the time, the audience expected some comedy. Those skits, generally recycled old vaudeville and minstrel show routines, were done in Eddy Arnold's shows by mandolin player Rollin Sullivan and bass player Lloyd George. Sullivan picked up the nickname "Oscar" from Bill Westbrooks during his Jackson, Tennessee days but George did not have a nickname until one day when Eddy Arnold was at a hotel counter checking the group into their rooms. A woman at the counter yelled to someone on the stairs with laundry, "Lonzo!" Arnold cracked up; he loved the name and decided that George and Sullivan should be "Lonzo and Oscar."

CHAPTER 13

Eddy Arnold's first two sessions for Victor were held at the WSM Radio Studios. They were both done for Bluebird, the discount label that sold records for 35 cents each; the top or "Black" Victor label sold for 50 cents each. That label was limited to pop acts and top sellers. However, with Arnold's records selling well, Victor executives decided his records should be released on the "Black" label.

Sometime in early fall, 1945, Eddy Arnold received a phone call from Steve Sholes, who was in charge of country and blues recordings (then called "hillbilly" and "race" records) for Victor. Sholes, a big, heavy man with a high-pitched voice, said to Arnold, "We think we can make you a star. How about recording in Chicago?" Arnold agreed immediately and a session was set for November 21, 1945 at the Victor Studio in Chicago.

Sholes, whose father worked for Victor in Camden, New Jersey, started work with the firm in 1929, after he graduated from high school. During college, at Rutgers University, Sholes worked for the firm part-time and after his college graduation in 1935 went to work full time, first in the factory storeroom of the radio department and then in the sales department.

Sholes had played saxophone and clarinet in local bands during the Big Band era and this musical background served him well when he decided to move to the record department from the radio department in 1936, taking a $25 a week cut in pay in order to listen to test pressings of recording sessions and assure quality control. In July, 1943 Sholes joined the Armed Services, where he worked in New York with the V-Disk program. Since Victor was one of the major manufacturers of V-Disks, Sholes kept in close contact with the label. Sholes also produced sessions for the V-Discs and gained valuable studio experience as a producer.

When he re-joined Victor after his discharge from the Army in July, 1945 he was put in charge of hillbilly and race music--not a high honor for a New York record man at the time. The power and prestige at a label was in the pop music division; for most executives, being placed in charge of hillbilly and race music was an insult and demotion. It was the bottom rung for most A&R men; however, a few A&R men developed a respect for the music and performers in those fields and brought an integrity to the sessions. Steve Sholes was a rare man; he developed a love and respect for the people in country music as well as the music itself. His first success in this field was Eddy Arnold.

Eddy Arnold and Sholes met for the first time in Chicago the night before their session. Arnold always came to his sessions well prepared, with his band fully rehearsed so they could complete four songs in a three hour session. Sholes sent Arnold songs to consider recording and Arnold found other songs. It was a mutual give and take between producer and artist with Sholes wanting Arnold to feel comfortable with the songs and Arnold needing outside input into songs and the sessions.

With his current band of Dempsey Watts on bass, Roy Wiggins on steel guitar, Rollin Sullivan on electric mandolin, "Butterball" Paige on guitar and Speedy McNatt on violin, Arnold recorded four songs, "(I'll Have to) Live and Learn," "Be Sure There's No Mistake," "I Couldn't Believe It Was True," and "I Talk to Myself About You." This was the beginning of the Eddy Arnold-Steve Sholes team, which grew close personally and professionally.

As 1945 drew to a close Eddy Arnold was better known for his radio appearances than his recording sales, although his sales were strong and promising. Steve Sholes knew he had an artist who was not only talented with an appealing pop-type voice, but also serious, ambitious, and willing to work hard on his career in a determined, business-like manner.

On the personal side, 1945 provided two major milestones in the lives of Eddy and Sally Arnold. They bought their first home, a four-bedroom house in Madison, and their daughter Jo Ann was born on December 17. Not only was Eddy Arnold a rising star in country music, he was a proud papa and successful family man as well.

CHAPTER 14

On April 12, 1945 Eddy Arnold was driving to a personal appearance in Paducah, Kentucky, when he heard on the radio that President Franklin Roosevelt had died. The news stunned him; for the past twelve years--ever since he was a fourteen year-old school boy living on a farm in Chester Country, Tennessee--Franklin Roosevelt had been President of the United States. Since that time Eddy Arnold had lived in Jackson, St. Louis, Nashville and Louisville, had left the farm and began singing on the radio. He'd gone from a farm boy singing in the fields with a dream to sing on the radio to a young man earning his living singing country music. In short, he had gone from being a "nobody" to being on the cusp of becoming a "star" in country music. Like most other Americans, the news of Roosevelt's death was devastating; he could hardly remember anyone else being President of the United States. Still, the show must go on, so Eddy Arnold performed that night in Paducah.

Less than a month later, on May 7, 1945 the Allies captured Berlin and declared Victory in Europe; then turned their attention to the Pacific. In August the United States dropped two atomic bombs on Japan, effectively ending the War in that part of the world. On that August day, when the news of the bombs came over the radio, Eddy Arnold was in Charleston, West Virginia. The end of the War meant no more gas coupons or gas rationing; Eddy Arnold pulled into a service station and asked the attendant to fill 'er up--and paid with cash instead of coupons.

The War lasted four years and servicemen were anxious to get back home; the home folks were anxious to have them back. The War had effectively ended the unemployment problems of the country. In 1940 the unemployment rate was 14 percent; in 1943 it was 1.9 percent. During the War 16.3 million Americans served in the military, a stark contrast to 1939 when there were only 335,000 in the Armed Services. By mid-1945 about 18 percent of the work force, or about 12.1 million, were in the Armed Services.

There were immense changes in the country that occurred during the four years the United States was actively engaged in World War II. In 1940 over a fifth of Americans still lived on farms and less than a third of those farms had electricity while only ten percent had flush toilets. Over half of all households didn't have a refrigerator, about 30 percent didn't have inside running water (in rural areas it was 60 percent for whites and over 95 percent for blacks) and 58 percent of households lacked central heating. Most Americans (56 percent) rented their housing.

The shift away from farms and small towns and towards big cities and working in factories changed the working life of most Americans. Until the 1930s the typical workweek for men in manufacturing was about 50 hours; by the end of the War a 40-hour workweek was established and workers worked five days instead of six. There were less farm workers (between 1940 and 1944 the number of farm workers dropped by 16 percent) but food production was up by 20 percent, primarily because of the increased number of tractors and other mechanical devices on farms.

Approximately 27 million Americans moved during World War II, about 40 percent to serve in the military and the rest primarily to obtain work in manufacturing plants or for defense related work. Since the population of the United States in 1940 was 132 million, this meant that about 20 percent of the population shifted during the War.

During the twenty-five year period 1920-1945 the country became linked by radio. In 1920 there were almost no radio sets in the United States; by 1929 there were 12 million sets. That number continued to increase throughout the 1930s and World War II until by the end of the War about 90 percent of American households had a radio set.

In 1940 approximately 25 percent of Americans had a high school diploma and about five percent had a college degree. The average worker earned less than $1,000 a year; only 7.8 million Americans made enough money to pay taxes. By the end of 1945 the number that paid taxes had increased to nearly 50 million out of a population that had grown to 140 million .

At the beginning of the War most Americans were poor; after the draft was instituted in the summer of 1940 about 20 percent of the young man were declared unfit because of malnutrition or other problems caused by poor living conditions. For many young American men life in the Armed Services was the first time they had regular meals, good housing and a secure job. For some Southern conscripts, it was the first time they'd ever worn shoes or clothes that were new or didn't have holes in them. The country was poor as well; some of the first draftees trained with wooden guns.

During the War the United States was transformed into a powerful, productive, wealthy nation. Prior to the War, unemployment stood at 14 percent and many of the nation's factories performed at limited capacity. During World War II factories were transformed to produce almost 300,000 war planes, over 100,000 tanks, 2.5 million trucks, almost 95,000 ships and 44 billion rounds of small arms ammunition.

The changes in America were immense and almost beyond comprehension but a single example will indicate those changes. At the end of 1941, when World War II began, the United States Army owned 200,000 horses for its cavalry. In August, 1945, the War effectively ended with an atomic bomb dropped by a long range bomber.

During the War years, 1941-1945, things changed a great deal in Nashville and in the country music community; some of those changes laid the groundwork for Nashville becoming the "Capital of Country Music," the city synonymous with country music.

The South, more than any other region, benefitted most from World War II. Most of the new training camps for the

Army were in the South because of cheap, plentiful land and because the mild climate made year-round training possible. Approximately half of those serving in the Armed Forces during the War--about six million young men--were exposed to the South for the first time in their life. While those outside the South came into the region for the first time during the War, many of the residents of the South left the region for work in defense or defense-related jobs in the north and west. California gained over a million residents during the War while northern cities also had population growth, much of it from Southerners moving north. Those who came into the South often heard country music for the first time; those leaving the South carried their taste for country music with them. This led to the spread of country music throughout the nation during the War.

The United States had been defined by regions before the War; people tended to define themselves as Southerners or Westerners. During the War the patriotism at home and the efforts of the Armed Services caused Americans to see themselves as Americans and blurred some of the differences in ethnic, racial or regional backgrounds. Outside this country foreigners did not see a Yank or a Southerner or a Westerner, they saw an American. Americans began to see themselves in this same light.

CHAPTER 15

On Saturday night, December 8, 1945, exactly four years after the United States officially entered World War II, the Grand Ole Opry was broadcast live from the Ryman Auditorium on Fifth Avenue in Nashville. At noon that Saturday there was a one hour matinee featuring Opry acts; that night the radio listings again listed the times for the performers: at 6 was Wally Fowler; at 6:15 Pee Wee King and Lew Childre performed; at 6:45 it was Paul Howard and Minnie Pearl; at 7 Ernest Tubb entertained; at 7:30 it was the Golden West Cowboys; at 7:45 it was Ol' Times and Lew Childre; at 8 it was Eddy Arnold; at 8:15 Uncle Dave Macon performed; and throughout the rest of the evening during the 15-minute segments that structured Opry performances were Clyde Moody, the Duke of Paducah, Bill Monroe, Curly Fox and Texas Ruby, and, closing the show, the Fruit Jar Drinkers.

By this time Nashville had been the place for several recording sessions by a major label; the WSM Radio Studios had first recorded Eddy Arnold for RCA Victor on December 4, 1944. There were other recording facilities, basically connected with radio stations. There were major publishing companies, led by Acuff-Rose (whose founder, Fred Rose, enticed his son, Wesley from his first marriage to leave his job as an accountant for Standard Oil in Chicago and move to Nashville as general manager of the publishing company), and recording label executives were increasingly coming to Nashville to look for talent.

Billboard, the major music industry trade magazine, began a chart on country (then called "Folk") recordings; it showed the "Most Played Juke Box" recordings were "It's Been So Long, Darling" by Ernest Tubb, "Sioux City Sue" by Dick Thomas, "You Two-Timed Me One Time Too Often," by Tex Ritter," "With Tears in My Eyes" by Wesley Tuttle, "Silver Dew on the Blue Grass Tonight" by Bob Wills and the Texas Playboys, "Shame on You" by Red Foley, "Honestly" by Dick Thomas and "You Will Have to Pay" by Tex Ritter.

The top pop songs on December 8, 1945 were "It's Been a Long, Long Time" by Bing Crosby, "Chickery Chick" by Sammy Kaye, "It's Been a Long, Long Time" by Harry James, "I'll Buy That Dream" by Dick Haymes and Helen Forrest, "I Can't Begin to Tell You" by Bing Crosby and Carmen Cava, "Waitin' for the Train to Come In" by Peggy Lee and "It Might as Well Have Been Spring" by Dick Haymes, Paul Weston and Margaret Whiting. Network radio was king and the top radio programs featured Bob Hope, Fibber McGee and Molly, Lux Radio Theatre, Walter Winchell, Edgar Bergen, Jack Benny, Mr. D.A., Fred Allen, Abbott and Costello, Screen Guild, Take It or Leave It, Kraft Music Hall, Eddie Cantor, Jack Haley, the Aldrich Family, The Shadow, One Man's Family and the Family Hour.

In terms of country music in general, the biggest songs to come out of the war were "Pistol Packing Mama" by Al Dexter, "There's a Star Spangled Banner Waving Somewhere" by Elton Britt and "You Are My Sunshine" by Jimmie Davis. All of those songs were incredibly popular and put country music on the pop charts. Country songs were recorded by a number of artists, including the premier pop singer, Bing Crosby. It was Crosby's hits with songs such as "Pistol Packin' Mama," "You Are My Sunshine" and "New San Antonio Rose" that served to make country music widely accepted and acceptable in the pop music world. This, in turn, gave country artists a boost.

The major changes in country music in Nashville were connected to the Opry. The War caused the country to be united by radio, and WSM emerged as a major radio station. The Opry was a major performance outlet with a network program; this attracted advertising agencies with New York connections and the money to promote tours. The Opry, through Jim Denny, had organized its booking agency to capitalize on the demand for live country music shows after the War.

Musically, Roy Acuff was the major star on the Opry through the War years, he presented a "mountaineer" image. Acuff's status came from the fact that he hosted the "Prince Albert Show" over the NBC network each Saturday night. This gave him star power. There were other musical stars ascending from the Opry like Ernest Tubb, who joined in 1943 and represented the Texas honky tonk sound with his hit, "I'm Walking the Floor Over You."

At the end of 1942 Ernest Tubb was a hot commodity, in demand on records and for personal appearances. He decided to leave Texas and had to choose between Hollywood (which he initially favored because of the possibility of future movie work) or Nashville, home of the Grand Ole Opry. The pendulum swung in Nashville's direction because of J. L. Frank, whose solid reputation for booking country acts and promoting concerts was firmly established through his work with Gene Autry and Pee Wee King's Golden West Cowboys. Frank called Tubb in December, 1942, when the singer was in Birmingham for an appearance, and invited him to perform on the Opry. Tubb agreed and on January 16, 1943 made his debut at the War Memorial Auditorium in a guest spot that was beamed over the NBC network. A formal invitation to join the Opry was then extended to Tubb, who accepted.

During World War II Tubb recorded "Soldier's Last Letter," a song written by Redd Stewart, Pee Wee King's fiddle player who was serving in the Army. Stewart had sent the song to J. L. Frank, who gave it to Tubb. During the War Tubb recorded "Tomorrow Never Comes," "Careless Darlin,'" "It's Been So Long Darling," and "There's a Little Bit of Everything in Texas."

By 1945 the Opry was expanding from the sound of acoustic string bands to include the various tastes of its listening audience. Even Bill Monroe, who had a traditional string band line-up, was changing his music and sound.

In 1939 Monroe and his group went to Nashville to audition for Judge Hay, Harry Stone and David Stone for the Opry; he became a member of the Opry in the Fall of that year. Meanwhile, Monroe began to hone his sound, which was a basic string band sound, but played in overdrive. Monroe's group played their music fast and, though he did not have a drummer, with a beat. He changed members as he worked on his sound and by the end of 1945 had assembled what many consider the best bluegrass group of all time: Lester Flatt on guitar on vocals, Chubby Wise on fiddle, Cedric Rainwater (real name: Howard Watts) on bass, and Earl Scruggs on banjo. Monroe's music began to be called "bluegrass" after the name of his group, and the addition of Scruggs, with his unique style of three-fingered picking, defined the sound of bluegrass from that point on. By the end of 1945 "bluegrass" music was named, defined and launched into the world.

The hiring of Bill Monroe represented the taste of Judge Hay, but the hiring of Ernest Tubb, Pee Wee King's Golden West Cowboys and Eddy Arnold represented the vision and taste of Jack Stapp and Harry Stone, who saw the need for the Opry to expand beyond its initial "barn dance" sound into something more commercial for a diverse audience. The updated sound also appealed to advertisers who wanted to reach a large market.

Roy Acuff was the biggest star of the Opry and held the coveted network spot each week. Bill Monroe, with his hard driving sound that evolved to become bluegrass, Ernest Tubb, with his Texas honky tonk sound, and Eddy Arnold, with his smooth countrypolitan sound, were important members of the Opry at the end of 1945. All of those men played a key role in the future of country music, although at times it seemed like they were leading the industry in four different directions.

In terms of national acceptance of country music, there was a fifth direction country music was headed that was not represented on the Opry. Western Swing bands led by Bob Wills and Spade Cooley dominated country music record sales at the end of World War II.

In April, 1946 Roy Acuff left the Grand Ole Opry and the "Prince Albert" show. Acuff was frustrated because the Opry required him to return every Saturday night to perform on the show. Saturday nights were the biggest nights for personal appearances and Acuff's popularity kept him in constant demand for appearances at much higher fees than what the Opry paid. Acuff left and went to the West Coast to tour and appear in movies. He was replaced by Red Foley, a smooth-voiced singer who had been with the Opry's major competitor, "The National Barn Dance" on WLS in Chicago.

Red Foley was more popular with Opry audiences than with Opry members when he started the "Prince Albert" segment. Opry regulars coveted the spot vacated by Acuff and many resented it going to an outsider. The WSM brass knew Foley had network experience; furthermore, the Esty advertising executives wanted Foley and their decision trumped hurt feelings. Foley represented the smooth sound of a country crooner who could be popular with city audiences as well as rural customers.

Another important addition to Nashville and country music came in September, 1946 when Acuff-Rose signed songwriter Hank Williams to their publishing company. Fred Rose soon obtained a recording contract for Hank with Sterling, a small independent label. Hank's first recording session occurred on December 11, 1946 when he did "Wealth Won't Save Your Soul," "Calling You," "Never Again" and "When God Comes and Gathers His Jewels" backed by the Willis Brothers, then known as the Oklahoma Wranglers. When the year ended Hank Williams was still living and performing in Montgomery, Alabama. The following year he signed with MGM Records, headed by Frank Walker, who left Victor at the end of the War to start a new label backed by the movie company.

CHAPTER 16

For Eddy Arnold, the year 1946 began with the release of "I Talk To Myself About You" backed with "Live and Learn." Neither of those songs charted in *Billboard*, although sales were impressive. Arnold's sessions were scheduled so he had four records, or eight songs, released each year. His next session in 1946 occurred on March 20 in Chicago. For this session, Arnold brought Lloyd George on bass, Owen Bradley on piano, Speedy McNatt on violin, Rollin Sullivan on electric mandolin, Johnnie Sullivan (Rollin's brother who had been in the Navy during the War) on guitar, and Roy Wiggins on steel guitar. This was Owen Bradley's first recording session as a musician and Arnold added him to give some "bottom" to the session since, at that time, country sessions did not have drums.

During this session, in RCA's Studio "A," the group recorded four hours--from 1:45 until 5:45 in the afternoon--and completed six songs. Those songs were "All Alone in This World Without Love" written by Vic McAlpin, Owen Bradley and Betty Wade; "Can't Win, Can't Place, Can't Show," written by Paul Westmoreland; "What is Life Without Love" written by Vic McAlpin, Owen Bradley and Arnold; "That's How Much I Love You" written by Wally Fowler, Graydon Hall and Arnold; "Why Didn't You Take

That Too" by Shep Sessions and Mel Butler; and "Chained to a Memory" written by Jenny Lou Carson.

That session marked a turning point in Arnold's recording career because it was the first after he signed an agreement with Hill and Range publishing. The publishing company gave Arnold an income; in exchange, he listened to songs they brought him and, when he found an unpublished song, they received the publishing. The advantage was that Hill & Range eased the burden of finding songs; they brought him good material. On this session two songs, "Can't Win, Can't Place, Can't Show" and "Chained To a Memory" were both Hill and Range songs.

The owners of Hill and Range were the Aberbach brothers, Jean and Julian, who first became involved in country music through their work with the Sons of the Pioneers, signed to RCA in 1944. Hill and Range brought the group songs and in 1946 the Aberbachs captured the publishing rights to "Tumbling Tumbleweeds," a western standard. The relationship between Steve Sholes and the Aberbachs probably went back to when Sholes and Julian Aberbach were both in the service and Sholes was one of the key people in charge of the V-Disc program.

Steve Sholes took over production of the Sons of the Pioneers in 1946 and the Aberbachs consistently brought him good songs, aided by the fact that the Aberbachs and Tim Spencer of the Sons of the Pioneers were joint-owners of a publishing company. Another step in the working relationship between Sholes and the Aberbachs came when

Sholes signed Chet Atkins to his first recording contract. Sholes agreed to sign Atkins only after Hill and Range signed him to a publishing deal and agreed to help promote the guitarist.

Eddy Arnold first came to the attention of the Aberbach brothers when his single, "Each Minute Seems Like a Million Years" sold 125,000 records. In June, 1945, Arnold performed on WMPS in Memphis for war bonds; over a million dollars in bonds were sold during a 12 hour period after Arnold's 15-minute radio show. This was further proof of Arnold's appeal and potential. Hill and Range began to bring songs to Arnold as well as to Steve Sholes for the singer but Arnold was still linked to publisher Fred Forster.

Eddy Arnold was loyal to Forster; roughly a third of the early songs recorded by Arnold were published by firms connected to Forster. Fred Rose had connections with Forster so the songs Arnold recorded that were not published by one of Forster's firms were published by Acuff-Rose.

The Aberbachs courted Tom Parker, and through him, struck a business arrangement with Arnold whereby Arnold sendt unpublished songs he recorded to Hill and Range. Arnold did not want to sign an exclusive agreement to record Hill and Range songs because he wanted to be open to any song he felt could be a hit for him, regardless of who published it. Instead, he entered into the same basic agreement he had with Forster except that Hill and Range gave him an annual cash retainer. The publishing company also agreed that Arnold had a right of first refusal for any of their new songs. The agreement worked well because Hill and Range consistently brought Eddy Arnold hit songs. That agreement ended Arnold's publishing agreement with Forster.

The first release from the Chicago session was "Can't Win, Can't Place, Can't Show" backed with "All Alone in This World Without You." "Can't Win, Can't Place, Can't Show" was an up tempo number with the message that life is a long hard race. There is a jazzy fiddle and some jazzy guitar runs with female vocalists in the background. "All Alone in This World" is a medium tempo love song that was Eddy Arnold's second record to chart in *Billboard*. It entered the charts on July 13, 1946 and rose to the number seven position. The difference in this release and Arnold's previous one was that this was on the Victor label, not Bluebird. The reason was record company economics. Bluebird was a budget label, selling for 35 cents for each record; Arnold's records were selling in such numbers that Victor wanted them on the Black label, which sold for 50 cents. If a record sold 100,000 units on Bluebird, it grossed $35,000; if it sold the same amount for Victor, it grossed $50,000--a sizeable difference.

The next song released from this session was the song that launched Eddy Arnold as a country music star. "That's How Much I Love You" is a sprightly number, full of wit and wisdom as the singer tells his sweetheart in clever terms how much he loves her, using phrases like "If you were a horse fly and I an old gray mare, I'd stand and let you bite me and never move a hair."

"That's How Much I Love You" was released in September, entered the *Billboard* charts on October 12 and rose to number two. Its popularity caused a major change in Eddy Arnold's career. From this time forward, no longer was Eddy Arnold just a popular Grand Ole Opry artist, he was a major national recording artist whose appeal and success went beyond the boundaries of the Opry's listening audience.

Eddy Arnold recorded his first session in New York on September 24, 1946 at RCA's Studio Number One, with John Sullivan on guitar, Eddie McMullen on steel guitar, Rollin Sullivan on mandolin, Speedy McNatt on violin, Lloyd George on bass and Harold Spierer on piano. Roy Wiggins had left Arnold and joined Red Foley briefly before returning to Arnold, so the steel guitar sound is a little different, more "Hawaiian."

During the four and a half hour session that began at 1:30 in the afternoon he recorded four songs: "What A Fool I Was" written by Bob Miller; "Easy Rockin' Chair" written by Fred Rose; "To My Sorrow," written by Vic McAlpin; and "It's a Sin" written by Fred Rose and Zeb Turner. Before any songs from this session were released Arnold released "That's How Much I Love You" and then ""What Is Life Without Love?" which was released on a red 78 disc in March, 1947.

"What is Life Without Love?" has philosophical lyrics about the meaning of life and on the first line Arnold slips into a falsetto; this became his first number one record. His second number one was "It's a Sin" backed with "I Couldn't Believe It Was True." This was a double sided hit with "I Couldn't Believe It Was True" rising to number four on the charts.

CHAPTER 17

Throughout 1946 Eddy Arnold made major strides in his career. He toured a great deal, performed with other Opry acts such as Rod Brasfield, was the star of the "Opry House Matinee" on Saturday afternoons, and had a songbook out, published by Adams, Vee and Abbott. Arnold's second songbook, *Eddy Arnold's Radio Favorites*, contained 20 songs, including "Many Tears Ago," "Each Minute Seems a Million Years," "I Walk Alone," "All Alone in This World" and "Be Sure There's No Mistake." There were pictures of Arnold in the songbook as a further enticement for fans to purchase it.

On Saturday nights Eddy Arnold appeared on the Opry in the prime 8-8:15 p.m. segment sponsored by Purina; Arnold also appeared on the 11-11:15 segment of the Opry sponsored by the *Eddy Arnold Songbook*. The other major star who hosted a national segment was Red Foley, who had the "Prince Albert" segment. Despite the Opry's intention to present the image of one big happy family, there was a good deal of grumbling amongst Opry members because those two had the plum spots.

Still, there couldn't be too much overt grumbling at the Opry. First, the show was a great showcase--the major national showcase for country music—which reached a large audience. Next, it was the sponsors who made the final decision on who hosted their portion, and nobody argues with money. If Prince Albert, or Purina, wanted a certain artist, there was nothing another artist could do about it, no matter how much they felt they deserved the spot. It was out of their--and the Opry's--hands.

Eddy Arnold and Red Foley hosting the two major Opry segments said a lot about the future of commercial country music after World War II. First, both were, in many ways, pop type singers, much smoother than the harsher sound of honky tonk or traditional country acts. Next, both men were good emcees, in line with network emcees who introduced acts and made smooth transitions from one song, or one act, to the next. Finally, the advertisers wanted to reach the broadest possible audience and, since they had the power of the purse, demanded to be represented by artists they felt reached that audience most effectively. Although it has been much overlooked, the plain fact is that advertisers directed the future of country music as much as any producer, songwriter, music executive or artist because the advertiser made the decisions on who was featured on major network exposure.

In addition to Purina and Prince Albert, other major advertisers on the Opry included Crazy Water Crystals, R.C. Cola, the *Southern Agriculturalist*, Wallrite, Cherokee Mills, the *Eddy Arnold Songbook*, the *Ernest Tubb Songbook*, Safkil, Weatherhouse, and Michigan Bulb.

In addition to Eddy Arnold and Red Foley on the Opry,

there were Ernest Tubb, Pee Wee King and the Golden West Cowboys, Minnie Pearl, the Duke of Paducah (Whitey Ford), the Oak Ridge Quartet, the Old Hickory Singers, Uncle Dave Macon, Jamup and Honey, Bill Monroe and his Blue Grass Boys, Curly Fox, Texas Ruby and the Fox Hunters (which featured guitarist Grady Martin), the Cackle Sisters, Rod Brasfield, Paul Howard and His Arkansas Cotton Pickers, the Crook Brothers, Oscar Stone and His Possum Hunters, Lew Childre, Paul Womack and His Gully Jumpers, Clyde Moody, Robert Lunn, The Bailes Brothers, Wally Fowler and His Georgia Clodhoppers, the Happy Valley Boys, Ernest Tubb & His Texas Troubadours, Grandpappy Wilkerson & His Fruit Jar Drinkers, Kirk McGee, Lazy Jim Day, Bradley Kincaid, Lonzo and Oscar and, accompanying Red Foley, a young guitarist named Chester Atkins. They were joined by announcers Jud Collins, Ernie Keller, Grant Turner, Louie Buck, and David Cobb.

It was a strong, talented cast of the best group of country music talent assembled by any radio station in the country. It was also a variety show that kept people entertained no matter what their taste in country music with string bands, comedians, honky tonkers and old vaudeville performers all taking a turn on the stage.

By the end of the year Eddy Arnold had joined the top recording artists in country music with his hits "Chained to a Memory" and "That's How Much I Love You." The entry of Arnold as a top recording artist, along with other Opry acts Red Foley, Bill Monroe and Ernest Tubb, indicated the future direction for country music. More and more, it was no longer enough for country performers to be a great live performer on stage, they had to have hit records. The Opry's cast reflected this as they began to demand artists have recording contracts and hit recordings as a criteria for joining the Opry cast in the years after World War II.

Top recording artists in country music outside Nashville were Rosalie Allen, Gene Autry, Bill Boyd, Elton Britt, Bill Carlisle, Spade Cooley, Cowboy Copas, Ted Daffan, the Delmore Brothers, Al Dexter, the Hoosier Hot Shots, Zeke Manners, Tex Ritter, Hank Penny, Texas Jim Robertson, Floyd Tillman, Merle Travis, and Wesley Tuttle.

CHAPTER 18

During 1946 three engineers from WSM, Aaron Shelton, Carl Jenkins and George Reynolds, began Castle Recording Studio at the WSM radio studios in the National Life Building. The following year they moved to the Tulane Hotel on Church Street, a block away from the National Life building. Although most of the early work done was for local commercials, this studio marked the beginning of the Nashville recording industry.

This beginning can be traced to January, 1947, when Francis Craig and his Orchestra, who performed regularly at the Andrew Jackson Hotel in downtown Nashville, across the street from WSM, went into the Castle Recording Studio (WSM's Studio C) and recorded "Near You." The song was done for Bullet Records, founded by Jim Bulleit, who headed the Opry Artists Bureau before World War II. "Near You" was an enormous success, a pop hit that sold three million records. The next year Milton Berle adopted it as the theme song for his TV variety show, "The Texaco Star Theater."

In August, 1947, Paul Cohen came to Nashville and recorded sessions on Ernest Tubb and other country artists for Decca at Castle and this began the move towards New York A&R men using Nashville as a recording center for country acts. The Nashville sessions replaced the old policy of field recordings whereby New York recording executives and engineers traveled from city to city recording artists. It also solved the problem of scheduling country performers in the major label's recording studios in New York, Chicago and Los Angeles. After World War II the recording industry was booming--in 1947, $214.7 million worth of records was sold at retail--and the label's studios were booked for the pop acts based in New York, Chicago and Los Angeles. Country acts were often relegated to other studios. Nashville, because of Castle Studios and the large number of top country acts on the Opry, began to emerge as a place for country artists to record.

CHAPTER 19

In 1947 Eddy Arnold became a superstar. The impetus was "That's How Much I Love You," which launched him as a major record seller; that record sold 750,000 units. Combined with Arnold's appearances on the Grand Ole Opry in a network segment, his "Checkerboard Jamboree" radio show heard daily on the Mutual network, his touring and his business like approach to his career, he came into 1947 as a major country act. More giant hits followed.

On May 18, Arnold entered RCA's Chicago studio and recorded nine songs, including "I'll Hold You In My Heart (Till I Can Hold You In My Arms)" and "Bouquet of Roses." Those two songs were recorded back to back during the 4:30 to 7:45 session after an hour break in the afternoon. "I'll Hold You In My Heart" was released first--in August--and quickly rose to number one on the country charts, remaining there for 46 weeks and crossing over to the Pop charts, where it rose to number 22.

"Bouquet of Roses" was released as the "B" side of "Texarkana Baby." After the "A" side became a hit, the jukebox operators flipped it over and "Bouquet of Roses" became a huge hit.

Until this point, Arnold was unsure of his position with the record company, carrying a fear that he would be dropped from the label. On a trip to New York in August of that year, Steve Sholes told him that Jim Murray, who headed Victor's record division, wanted to meet him. Arnold was apprehensive; his first thoughts were "What's he want to meet me for?" Sholes replied, "He just wants to meet you." Arnold wondered, "Are they going to cancel my contract?"

When Arnold entered Jim Murray's office, the executive stood up and greeted Arnold with a handshake, then offered him a cigar, which Arnold declined. Murray then said, "Every Monday morning I see those sales figures come across my desk. Those are tremendous figures. I wanted to know what you looked like." That was the first time Eddy Arnold heard about the Monday morning sales reports. It let him know that he was an important part of Victor Records.

Under the management of Tom Parker, Eddy Arnold placed a number of advertisements touting his career. In the February 8 issue of *Billboard* an ad for "What is Life Without Love" b/w "Be Sure There's No Mistake" quotes Eddy saying, "Here's my latest record, Folks! I'm kind of proud of this record because I reckon both sides will be hits. They're the kind of songs that always make the real foldin' money in the jukes. But don't take my word for it. Give a listen and see for yourself."

A *Billboard* review of this record states, "A sweet-singing cowboy, Eddie (sic) Arnold pipes it expressively for both of these torch ballads with the strong support of his Tennessee Plowboys keeping the spin thoroughly rhythmic. Particularly tuneful is 'What's Life Without Love?' and it's torch appeal for 'Be Sure There's No Mistake' as he warns his love that she is breaking his lonely heart."

His show now included his band with Roy Wiggins, Rod Brasfield, the Oklahoma Wranglers, Johnnie and Jack and Miss Lillie Belle. Lonzo and Oscar had left by this time; their recording of "I'm My Own Grandpa" was so successful they struck out on their own.

In November, 1947 he began a period of 60 consecutive weeks when he had the number one record in country music. First "I'll Hold You In My Heart" hit number one; when it dropped out of that slot it was replaced by "Anytime," then "Texarkana Baby," "Bouquet of Roses," "Just a Little Lovin'" and "A Heart Full of Love (For a Handful of Kisses)."

In addition to the hit records, the biggest career boost for Eddy Arnold in 1947 was the beginning of a weekly half-hour radio show broadcast over the Mutual Network during the noon hour. "The Checkerboard Jamboree" was sponsored by Ralston Purina and put together by the Brown Brothers. The show began on November 17 and was broadcast live from the Princess Theater in Nashville. There were actually two shows sponsored by Ralston Purina broadcast back-to-back; Eddy Arnold hosted one and Ernest Tubb hosted the other. This gave both performers national network exposure outside the Opry.

CHAPTER 20

Not only was Eddy Arnold's career heating up in 1947, country music in general was popular. In April, *Billboard*'s "American Folk Tunes" column noted that Arnold and his band were booked by the Jolly Joyce Theatrical Agency for a concert in Akron, Ohio at the Armory. The article states, "With the swing stars and name bands finding fertile fields in the concert and classical halls, there is no reason...why the Western singing and instrumental names can't duplicate the feat as well." The article continued, "Pointing out that many of the Western names enjoy a bigger following away from metropolitan centers than the big name bands, Joyce feels that the time has arrived for the Western names to tackle the concert field. With interest in folk music and in folk entertainers at its highest peak, Joyce asserts that a whole vast new field in the concert sphere is ready to receive the Western names."

Out on the road, Eddy Arnold proved to be a major concert draw; in Columbus, Ohio he drew 4,000, in Akron 4,000, at Dayton 1,500, and at the Sleepy Hollow Ranch in Quakertown, Pennsylvania on a Sunday afternoon in August, 11,000 fans came to see him. In Philadelphia, 3,000 fans came to see him and the gate receipts were $5,000.

Eddy Arnold had already performed before large

crowds at Fairs and civic or municipal auditoriums, but there was a trend emerging where major cities outside the south booked country artists and attracted large crowds. Perhaps the biggest concert that year was at Carnegie Hall in New York when Ernest Tubb took an Opry troupe that included Minnie Pearl and Judge George D. Hay to that venue.

The second biggest concert occurred a few weeks later, on October 31, when Eddy Arnold headlined a country concert at Constitution Hall in Washington, D.C. That led to an article in Time magazine about Arnold. In the article, which came out during the last week of 1947, the Time reporter asked Eddy about the "Plowboy" sobriquet and whether it fit; Arnold replied, "Boy, I sure did plow. That's why I wanted to learn to play that guitar, so I wouldn't have to keep plowin' all my life."

Eddy Arnold had vivid memories of the 1943-44 musicians strike when he could not begin his recording career; he vowed not to be caught flat-footed again. During 1947 there were rumblings of another musicians strike, called again by James Petrillo, so during his August session in New York Arnold recorded sixteen songs over two days, including "The Prisoner's Song," "Rockin' Alone," "It Makes No Difference Now," "Will the Circle Be Unbroken," "Molly Darlin,'" "Seven Years With the Wrong Woman," "I'm Thinking Tonight of My Blue Eyes" and "Who At My Door Is Standing" on August 19 and "Texarkana Baby," "Anytime," and "I've Got a Lifetime to Forget" on the 20th. Then, on December 17, Arnold went to New York again for an all day session that produced "A Heart Full of Love (For a Handful of Kisses)," "Just a Little Lovin' (Will Go a Long, Long Way)," "You Know How Talk Gets Around," "There's No Wings on My Angel" and eight others.

The New York sessions in August and December added another player to Arnold's recording work: Charlie Grean. Grean was working for conductor-arranger Russ Case, who worked on pop discs for RCA, when Sholes hired him as his personal assistant. Before the war, Grean had been a copyist for the Glenn Miller band. Grean worked in A&R, procuring songs for RCA acts; he was also a studio bass player. For the next decade, Grean worked as a bassist and arranger on most of Eddy Arnold's sessions.

The move to stockpile proved fortuitous--the recording ban lasted almost the entire year of 1948 before it was resolved in December. The major record labels could not record during most of 1948 so artists who had the foresight to stockpile recordings had a decided edge over the rest of the field. In country music that artist was Eddy Arnold.

CHAPTER 21

In 1948 Eddy Arnold dominated the country music field like no other artist has before or since. During the entire year he held the number one record on the charts every single week except two.

The year began with a cover story on Eddy in *CashBox*, a major trade magazine. It was announced that he had sold 2.7 million records in 1947--more than the entire pop division at Victor, although he didn't know it at the time. He did know it was his first taste of big money and he bought a new four-bedroom house in Madison.

In January, Arnold appeared on a number of network radio shows: the "RCA Victor Show" and "Sunday Down South" on NBC, "We, the People" and the ""Western Theater from Hollywood" on CBS, the "Spike Jones Show," "Hayloft Hoedown," "The Paul Whiteman Club" and the "Breakfast Club" all on ABC, "Luncheon at Sardi's" on the Mutual network, and "Hospitality Times," which was a transcription.

In addition to his appearances on major network radio shows, the major national exposure for Eddy Arnold in 1948 came from "The Checkerboard Jamboree," a daily 15-minute radio show broadcast over the Mutual Network. In addition to Arnold, who was host and emcee, others on the show were the Willis Brothers (also known as The

Oklahoma Wranglers). That group was brought to Nashville from Kansas City, where they had a radio show, by the Brown Brothers. At this point, they became Eddy Arnold's band (along with Roy Wiggins) and toured with him.

Each show began with the yodeling section of Arnold's theme song, "Cattle Call." Owen Bradley, a WSM musician and local big band leader, served as arranger for the show and wrote commercials. Bradley had impressed the Brown Brothers with his musical ability, his knack for organizing musicians, his cheerful enthusiasm towards making music and his unique ability to be a big band guy and, at the same time, respect and work with country musicians.

Arnold's daily show for Purina was broadcast on more than 300 stations Monday through Friday at 12:45. The fifteen minute show gave him national exposure and his connection to the Brown Brothers and the Ralston Purina company also meant a network spot on the Grand Ole Opry every Saturday night at 8 p.m. In addition to giving Arnold daily network exposure, the show allowed him to promote his latest release on Victor.

In February he was on the cover of *Barn Dance* magazine and was quoted saying, "Everybody was always for me. They all thought I was pretty good, I reckon."

He received rave reviews in the media and an appearance in Fort Worth in March generated three articles. An article titled "Eddy Arnold, Former Plow Boy, is Visitor" in the *Fort Worth Press* by Jack Gordon noted that Arnold was wearing "a dark maroon sports shirt, sharply tailored plaid trousers, fancy socks and leisure-type shoes" during his interview in his hotel suite. The writer observed that Arnold was "Blond and handsome, he looked like a movie glamor boy snatched from the University of California campus."

The article noted that Arnold earned $1500 a night on tour, which was top dollar for performers. Plans were underway for Arnold to do a movie, but the Hollywood producers wanted it to be a singing cowboy picture. Arnold's manager, Tom Parker, stated, "They want to make a movie cowboy out of Eddy. We want none of that. There are too many phony cowboys already. Eddy isn't a cowboy. He is a plain country boy." During his show, Arnold sang the pop song "Now is the Hour," which was a hit for Bing Crosby in 1948 and stated, "I'd sing more tunes like that, but my country fans wouldn't accept them."

He told Gita Bumpass of the *Fort Worth Star-Telegram*, "I enjoy hearing people say I should sing popular tunes, too, but I never will. I want to keep the fans I've already made and take my songs to those who've never enjoyed folk music before."

In an article in the Fort Worth Star-Telegram by Ida Belle Hicks, the writer noted, "Arnold, the show's star, is as plain as the songs he sings and as uncomplicated. He knows what he wants but he has no fancy ideas about changing his way of life. Success startled him more than a little, but now that he is tops among the folk song singers he wants to stay there just as he is. Switching style or going on to so-called better things are not for him."

On his show Arnold sang "I Walk Alone," "Anytime," "I'll Hold You In My Heart," "It's a Sin," "Molly Darling," "What Is Life Without Love," "Cattle Call" and "That's How Much I Love You."

A review in the Richmond Times-Dispatch from a concert in March noted, "The crowd was far from satiated when Arnold finally bowed out after a warm and friendly curtain speech and a promise to come back soon. His hold on the audience is nothing less than magnetic. For the first time in many a moon, a Mosque crowd stayed put until the show actually was over. We've seen symphony concert audiences display less courtesy and less inclination to wait for expected encores."

During his personal appearances Arnold hosted a two hour show, although his portion generally lasted about half an hour. During the first hour, the Oklahoma Wranglers performed, then Annie Lou and Danny, then Brother Slim Williams, who performed in blackface and who "adds a touch of spice and variety with his old-time sermon on love, politics and anything else that he happens to think of." The Richmond review concluded that "The Eddy Arnold show is clean, well-paced and just what the hillbilly fans ordered." By this time, Arnold didn't perform in clubs--it was mostly coliseums or armories.

CHAPTER 22

Country music in the late 1940s attracted attention from the national media. In the April, 1948 issue of *Mademoiselle* an article, titled "Country Music Goes to Town," noted that "The decentralization of backwoods ballads was also helped along by the war. Industrial workers from the South carried their ditties cross country into the aircraft plants and shipyards of the Pacific coast. Service men from the hillbilly districts toted guitars and laments of-and-for home from camp to camp. When they weren't sounding off on their own they had the radio in the USO turned up volume-high for 'There's a Star-Spangled Banner Waving Somewhere' [the] unofficial hillbilly theme of the armed forces." The article continued that "Radio, actually, has been the most important factor in the mass production and consumption of country music. The forefathers of our current hillbilly and Western singers had to travel by mule and wagon to get to where the people were...But day in and day out country people have become accustomed to getting their music over the air." The article concluded that "The triple simplicity of rhythm, melody and lyric, the expression of moral and sentimental values all but universally accepted in the United States are in truth making hillbilly music really popular."

During the 1940s it was difficult to purchase country music records because it was hard to find them. Ernest Tubb attempted to rectify this by opening his own regail store. Tubb was the pioneer and also the most successful; his store was located on Broadway, just across the street from the Ryman Auditorium. He arranged to have a "Midnight Jamboree" broadcast over WSM every Saturday night after the Opry finished which featured Opry artists. Tubb sold a number of records through mail order, advertising his store on the Opry and the "Midnight Jamboree."

On May 15 Eddy Arnold celebrated his thirtieth birthday at the Hotel El Rancho in Las Vegas with a dinner party. Among the guests was actor Robert Mitchum. Two days later, on May 17, Arnold opened a record shop in Murfreesboro, Tennessee, about 40 miles from downtown Nashville. In April, the town of Murfreesboro turned out for a parade and a "Welcome Eddy Arnold Day." It was an example of Eddy Arnold looking for investments outside his performing career.

Eddy Arnold was the first country artist to successfully play Las Vegas. In 1948 he appeared at the Hotel El Rancho Vegas and at the end of his engagement, hotel owner Bernard H. Van Der Steen published a congratulatory telegram stating, "My sincere thanks and congratulations to your Tennessee Plowboy, Eddy Arnold. During his entire engagement at the Hotel El Rancho Vegas he sang his beautiful American folk songs to a top capacity house. He has proven a new theory in our entertainment policy that his folk songs are very much accepted by the Las Vegas public as entertainment. His presentation is sincere and humble and through this he made many friends on and off stage. During the past year he has proven our best find and has done top capacity business. My sincere thanks and may Hotel El Rancho Vegas soon have the pleasure of a return engagement."

By the end of May, Eddy Arnold had the top four songs in the nation: "Anytime," "What a Fool I Was," "Texarkana Baby," and "Bouquet of Roses" with "I'll Hold You In My Heart" at number nine.

On July 22 Eddy Arnold played Hope, Arkansas and a review of the show stated, "Everyone from the Colonel's Lady to Rosie O'Grady was at the Court House last night to hear the Eddy Arnold Hillbilly Jamboree. They came in Cadillacs, Buicks, Model T's, trucks and wagons. They sat on benches, in cars, on cars and in trees. Half of the crowd was standing. No one seemed to get tired and from the whistles, cheers, and applause everyone was well satisfied. The only comment of displeasure was; 'it wasn't long enough.'"

The reporter noted that "To meet Eddy and talk with him, it is easy to see why he has been able to gain such popularity and keep it so long. He graciously autographed pictures and books for an hour after the show. Eddy is a very straightforward young man with a pleasing personality. The success he has gained has not changed him from the generous hearted lad he was while still a plowboy in west Tennessee. ...He takes pride in singing the simple songs that anyone can understand and which most people appreciate. Eddy likes to sing. His profession wasn't chosen because it would furnish him a good living, although it is doing that due to his popularity, but because singing means something to him. 'Unless I like a song,' Eddy said, 'I never sing it no matter how many requests there are for it. I like to feel the sentiments in the songs I sing, and when I don't like a song, I can't put a thing into it to make it live.'" The article noted that Arnold is "never away from home more than 10-12 days a month." It was also noted that he came to Arkansas to help the political campaign of Vernon Whitten for Congress. After the concert Arnold was quoted saying, "My being with Mr. Whitten is purely friendship. The political side of it does not interest me except that I'd like to see Vernon elected."

There were mob scenes at some of his personal appearances and a headline in the Bradenton, Florida newspaper stated, "Eddy Arnold Halts Traffic in Bradenton." The article stated that, during an August appearance in the town, Arnold "literally stopped traffic in Bradenton" during the afternoon "while making several personal appearances in the city." The August tour of Florida lasted ten days and was done in a used Studebaker "Land Cruiser." He wore a Stetson hat and the company advertised that "All Well Dressed Men Wear Hats."

CHAPTER 23

Eddy Arnold made his last appearance as a member of the Grand Ole Opry on September 11, 1948. It was difficult for him to say good-bye and, in some ways, he did not want to leave. But there was friction. First, the Opry demanded he pay them 15 percent of all the money he made on personal appearances; they reasoned that people came to see him because of his connection to the Opry so they were entitled to a commission. Tom Parker wanted Arnold to leave because the singer was at the height of his popularity and could get more bookings--and make more money--if he was not required to be back at the Opry every Saturday night.

The advantage of the Opry was the exposure it provided its artists; there were network shows on WSM and the Opry itself reached a large number of people. Without the Opry, most performers would not have national radio exposure, and this was essential for an artist's success. Roy Acuff left the Opry to take advantage of the demand for bookings but soon returned because he could not be successful without it; the demand for bookings quickly decreased without Opry exposure.

Eddy Arnold had a daily network show over the Mutual Network every day, so he still had network exposure; there was also an offer for another network show on CBS.

In the Spring of 1948 the Brown Brothers Agency negotiated with William Paley, head of CBS, for a show, "Hometown Reunion," to be aired on Saturday nights--prime time for a country artist. The show planned to feature the Duke of Paducah, a cast of 30 singers, the Willis Brothers, Annie Lou and Danny, Donna Jean, and Paul Link and the Hometown band and choir. Starring on that show would be Eddy Arnold. "Hometown Reunion" premiered on September 18, the week after Arnold's last appearance on the Opry, so Arnold didn't miss a beat in terms of Saturday night network exposure.

There were other conflicts with WSM during the year. Tom Parker convinced Ralston Purina to sponsor a weekly half hour transcribed show. The Brown Brothers wanted it to run on WSM on Saturday nights but WSM refused so Purina decided to put it on rival station WLAC. When WSM commercial manager Irving Waugh found out, he decided to program a half hour show against it. This led Ralston Purina to agree to run the show on WSM on Fridays if WSM would put on a show before and after it to help build an audience. WSM agreed in order to keep Eddy Arnold off the competition. Thus the "Friday Night Frolics," starring Opry performers, began on WSM in 1948.

There were questions from WSM executives and fans about why he left the Opry and he was challenged by someone who said "The Opry made you!" Eddy replied, "Then why hasn't it made the Fruit Jar Drinkers?" referring to a group who were long time members of the Opry.

After Eddy Arnold left the Opry, the radio show knew they needed a smooth-voiced singer, so they hired George Morgan to replace Arnold. Relations were strained but cordial.

In 1948 Eddy Arnold's recordings dominated the year's top selling records. "Bouquet of Roses," "Anytime," "Just a Little Lovin'," "Texarkana Baby," "My Daddy Is Only a Picture," "I'll Hold You in My Heart," "A Heart Full of Love," "Then I Turned and Walked Slowly Away" and "What a Fool I Was" were all top selling records. In second place was the artist who pushed him out of the number one position twice that year, Jimmy Wakely, with "One Has My Name, The Other Has My Heart" and "I Love You So Much It Hurts." Other top country artists that year were Hank Thompson, Carson Robison, Moon Mullican, and T. Texas Tyler, followed by Tex Williams, Cowboy Copas, Ernest Tubb, Pee Wee King, Sons of the Pioneers, Red Foley, Tex Ritter, Roy Rogers, Floyd Tillman, Bob Wills and Gene Autry, whose recording of "Here Comes Santa Claus" ended up on the country charts. In addition to Arnold's records, other top songs of the year included "I'm My Own Grandpa" by Lonzo and Oscar, "Tennessee Waltz" by Pee Wee King, "Humpty Dumpty Heart" by Hank Thompson, "Life Gets Tee-Jus, Don't It" by Tex Ritter and "Tennessee Saturday Night" by Red Foley.

Eddy Arnold was always a careful man with his money, but knew he couldn't just hide it under a mattress. In his first investment, for a vibrating mattress, he was promised a seat on the Board of Directors, which impressed him; however the investment cost him $35,000. After that he vowed to invest his money in something he knew something about: land. At least you can see land, walk on it and touch it. And since God quit making land but keeps making people, the value of land is bound to rise. In 1948 Arnold bought his first piece of land for an investment. Located on Gallatin Road at the corner of two major streets, the lot looked shaggy with its weeds, but was a prime location. Arnold purchased it for $12,500.

His political convictions were taking shape during the election campaigns of Harry Truman and Thomas E. Dewey. Some may ponder whether a person's liberalism or conservatism is shaped by family and society or genetic. Are people born liberals or conservatives? Eddy Arnold's father was a dyed-in-the wool Democrat who lived most of his life under Republican Presidents. Eddy Arnold's father lived under only three Democratic Presidents: James Buchanan (who was President when Will Arnold was born), Grover Cleveland and Woodrow Wilson.

Will Arnold came of age when no true southerner could be a Republican because that was the party of Abraham Lincoln, who had waged war on the South. As a young man he lived during the corrupt Grant administration and saw the heyday of the Robber Barons and the Gilded Age as well as the idealism of Woodrow Wilson. Eddy Arnold remembered his father was a staunch Democrat but also remembered his father's sister, Aunt Nannie, who regularly came to the Arnold household and argued politics with his father.

Eddy Arnold was born when Woodrow Wilson was President and came of age during Franklin Roosevelt's administration and wanted to be a Democrat like his father. But he just didn't lean that way. Arnold didn't like Roosevelt's runs for a third and fourth term, although he tended to admire the President while in office. His disliked Harry Truman's administration and during the Democratic Convention, when Truman was nominated, he listened to the radio while Hubert Humphrey, then Mayor of Minneapolis, gave a convention speech. "Hearing Hubert Humphrey's speech at the Democratic Convention made me a Republican," said Arnold. Although he was still not registered to vote he somehow knew deep inside that his beliefs fit the Republican party.

CHAPTER 24

Life was going great for Eddy Arnold at the end of 1948, but it was going to get even better. On January 2, 1949, his son, Richard Edward Arnold, Jr. was born and Eddy Arnold was the proud papa of two children. Shortly after he was born, Arnold purchased a policy from the Life and Casualty Insurance Company to assure his son an education. He had also purchased a policy for his daughter; the policies would mature when they were 18 and guaranteed they could attend college, whether Eddy Arnold was still selling records or not. Arnold also purchased a life insurance policy from New York Life--and paid all the policies in full. It was the way he liked to do business, paying cash in full for everything he bought.

In the first issue of *Variety* in 1949 there was an ad placed by Tom Parker that stated, "Eddy Arnold and I regret that we have no available personal appearance dates for the season of 1949." This was certainly true--no other country artist was in as great a demand as Eddy Arnold--but it was also something of a ruse. Parker knew this would get the attention of the music industry and it did; it also prodded some concert promoters to call requesting dates and, if the dates were particularly lucrative, a spot in Arnold's schedule would be found to accommodate the request.

Arnold's personal appearances were quite profitable; an ad in *Billboard* naming cities and the amount grossed from ticket sales included Fort Worth, $8,323; Dallas, $6,245; Oklahoma City, $7,612; Washington D.C. $9,280; Jacksonville, $6,120; Tampa $4,278; Norfolk, $7,330; Roanoke, $2,555; Richmond, $3,923; Raleigh, $2,730; Little Rock, $4,309; Monroe, (LA) $1,881; and Atlanta (one week) $13,000. In every city except Atlanta, the top price for a concert ticket to see Eddy Arnold was one dollar.

Network radio appearances for Arnold in 1949 included "The RCA Victor Show," "The Spike Jones Show" (3 times), "The Paul Whiteman Show," "Don McNeill's Breakfast Club," "We the People," "Command Performances," "Luncheon at Sardi's," and "The Western Hit Review." He was featured on "The March of Time" and continued to host "The Checkerboard Jamboree" each weekday over the Mutual Network. No other country artist received as much national exposure in the late 1940s or early 1950s as Eddy Arnold. Those network appearances allowed Arnold to transcend the world of country music so his record sales reflected those of a top selling pop artist.

In 1949 Eddy Arnold was a heartthrob. An article from Oklahoma City noted, "The voice has put Eddy across. But his looks haven't hurt him in his stage appearance. Six feet tall, with sandy blond hair, Eddy has a face that is good looking without being pretty. Women call him handsome, but he is still rugged enough for the men."

An article in the Houston Post by Betty Betz titled, "Arnold Gets Marriage Bids in Mail," quoted Arnold saying, "Ah gets a dozen marriage proposals in the mail every week from teen-age girls. Could you please tell 'em ah already got a beyootiful wife at home in Tennessee?" The writer couldn't resist a dig at Eddy Arnold or country music, despite the success of both. Eddy Arnold never spoke like that and he wasn't a hayseed; painting him as one reflected a media bias against Southerners and country music. Indeed, Eddy Arnold always went out of his way to set himself apart from standard "hillbilly" stereotypes.

In 1949 Bea Terry's article, "Folk Music and Its Folks" stated that Arnold "does not care to be classified as a hillbilly singer and tells me he is just a country-boy-singer." The article continued, "The popular singer does not wear the regular cowboy apparel, either. On stage he wears slacks, sports shirt and does not wear boots. He wears a white hat but it is not one of those wide brim westerns. Off stage, he wears suits with semi-dress or sport shorts."

The marketing strategy for Arnold was for him to release four records a year, or eight songs. (This was before the era of long playing albums, which had only been introduced to American consumers the year before.) Each achieved maximum sales before the next was released. This contrasted with some top acts, who released a large number of disks each year (sometimes as many as 24). An article in Variety at the end of the year stated, "Arnold himself is the kingpin of the hillbilly artists on disks....it's not unusual for Arnold to reach into the 1,000,000 copy class. He's had more disks that did go over that figure than any singer or band on Victor." Using this marketing strategy, most of Arnold's records sold over a million copies each and by the end of 1949 he had sold over nine million records.

Arnold released his album *To Mother* in time for Mother's Day, 1949. The songs on that album included "That Wonderful Mother of Mine," "M-O-T-H-E-R," "Bring Your Roses To Her Now," "I Wish I Had a Girl Like You, Mother," "I Wouldn't Trade the Silver in My Mother's Hair" and "My Mother's Sweet Voice." "I did it for my mother," remembered Arnold.

In June, 1949 Eddy Arnold went to Hollywood and filmed two movies. On the way out he stopped for a two week engagement in Las Vegas. Negotiations for the films had begun the year before when Hollywood approached Arnold about starring as a singing cowboy in a movie. Discussing his movie career, Arnold stated, "When those movie producers came to me, they wanted me to put on a ten-gallon hat, leather chaps, a pair of six-guns and be a Texas cowboy singing star in the horse operas. But I didn't believe that I knew anything about horse operas, and I finally convinced them of that, thank goodness."

Gene Autry was an early hero for Eddy Arnold and he saw that Autry, who had a cowboy image, recorded songs that were not "western." Autry's repertoire of love songs and Christmas songs kept him in the public spotlight as a recording artist, something he would not have maintained if he had only recorded western numbers.

Once Arnold was on the movie set publicity swirled about his desire to get back home. An article in the *Detroit News* by Harold Hefferman titled "Studio Nips Flight of Lonely Balladeer" stated, "No singer has ever leaped from obscurity to fame with such speed, and Columbia considers it engineered a smart coup in landing him for his first movie. It's admittedly no great shakes as celluloid drama but should serve its central purpose--a showcase for the man his millions of followers know today only through the sound of radio and records. He's come a long way in three short years and the fantastic Hollywood scene isn't helping him lick that feeling of bewilderment...'I just dunno how it all happened,' replied Eddy when we asked him to sum up his success story. 'All I can say is I'm plenty scared right now. I gotta go into a scene with that girl over there and, boy, the butterflies are playin' ping pong with my stomach.'"

Another article stated, "Eddy Arnold...was so homesick for his family in Nashville that he brought his bags, packed, to the studio yesterday to pose for his still pictures for *Feudin' Rhythm*, and left for the airport the moment Bob Coburn, head of the still department, said 'that's all.'" This story had some elements of truth but missed a central point. Yes, Eddy Arnold loved Nashville and wanted to get back to his family and yes he brought his packed bags to the photo session, but at this point Eddy Arnold was a busy man, much in demand and he needed to return to his obligations on radio and personal appearances. In fact, time was so tight that Arnold had begun flying to his personal appearances in a DC3. Ever mindful of the financial advantages of company tie-ins, an ad proclaimed "For dependable air transportation the Eddy Arnold Show uses Capitol Airways, Nashville, TN."

One of those obligations involved work with his sponsors. As host of "The Checkerboard Jamboree" and spokesman for Purina, Eddy Arnold made a number of personal appearances on behalf of the company, promoting its line of farm feed products. In 1949 the company ran a contest for "Mike and Ike," two pigs who competed for weight gain. One was fed Purina Hog Ration, the other received straight grain. A number of feed stores competed and the winner was the Gross Feed Store. The winner, "Mike" received a large autographed picture of Arnold, presented by the singer, who went from store to store, judging the hogs. He also did remote broadcasts of his daily noon show from various stores.

CHAPTER 25

Television was in its infancy but was making its presence felt. TV was introduced to America in 1947 and the following year was the first full year of network programming. On September 15, 1949 Eddy Arnold made his first appearance on network TV when he appeared on Milton Berle's show.

Back home, he appeared at a concert sponsored by the local newspaper on August 21. On this performance, at Nashville's Centennial Park, Eddy Arnold drew an estimated 30,000 for the free concert. In September, Arnold bought a 107 acre farm just south of Nashville in Brentwood. The farm had been a working farm and the former owner threw in two mules and some farm equipment with the purchase. When Arnold left town for personal appearances, his wife lost no time in selling the mules.

Arnold's concert appearances continually drew large crowds and rave reviews. A review from Chicago noted, "Swooners and boppers, beware! Judging by last night's crowd at the Coliseum any vocalist who hopes to keep his public better hurry on down and get himself a ten-gallon hat and some yodelling lessons. The menace to the moaners comes in the form of a young man named Eddy Arnold-- subtitled the "Tennessee Plowboy"--who last night packed the Coliseum with close to 5,000 raving fans. The boy with the talented tonsils received just about the most caterwauling ovation that ever tickled an entrepreneur's ear. One girl actually fainted, and had to be carried out by a constable."

Another article stated Arnold "now gets upwards of $1,000 a night." In truth, he was often getting $1,500 per appearance and a portion of the gate receipts.

At the end of the year, he remained busy. In October he spent a week in Colorado Springs making short promotional films for the Purina Company. On November 9 he was on the cover of *Billboard* and in December he made a guest appearance on the "Perry Como Chesterfield Supper Club" program. During the Christmas season he released his first Christmas record, "C-H-R-I-S-T-M-A-S" b/w "Will Santa Come to Shanty Town."

RCA promoted their new 45 rpm vinyl single, which they had developed, and Eddy Arnold pitched in to help. An ad in *Billboard* at the end of 1949 pictured Eddy Arnold with his family and a record player with the caption stating, "Home is Where the '45' is says Eddy Arnold. 45 rpm is an important part of our family life!" The label continued to release Arnold's records on 78 rpm as well.

It was a good time for country music in general. In an article by Jack Stone in *The American Weekly* titled, "Millions in Music--Hillbillies in Clover" in February, 1949, the writer noted, "Hillbilly songs account for about 15 percent of music biz, an estimated $30 million worth [which] allows hillbilly singers themselves to flaunt hand-tooled leather belts, Fifth Avenue flannel shirts and drive high-priced cars."

The article stated that Arnold's "Bouquet of Roses" "outsold most pop records" and that "200 record companies turn out an average of 100 hillbilly songs a week." Two former country music performers, W. Lee "Pappy" O'Daniel (Texas) and Jimmie Davis (Louisiana) were governors.

Explaining country music's success after World War II, the article stated, "Once confined to the South and Southwest, [country music] has spread all over the country. What skyrocketed hillbilly music? Radio, mainly. The war, too. Northern boys in Southern camps brought back the hillbillies' melodic tales of hard times and good times, of poverty and pathos, of crop woes and personal tragedy, of bright happiness. Southern boys in Northern camps were hillbilly emissaries. Population shifts helped also. The notion that hillbilly singers are Broadway dudes affecting rural identity is false. Those who make the grade come from small towns, learned their homely warbling at their grandma's knee. Imposters have a tough go of it, for the hillbilly loving public can spot a phony a mile off. In popular music the song's the thing. In hillbilly, it's the performer who sells. There was the case of the hillbilly crooner who, in his first experience with a squalling adolescent girl, mistook her adoration for derision and apologized to his listeners: 'I reckon that was pretty bad, but shucks, you don't have to yell at me.'"

In general, the national media (especially from New York) treated country music rather condescendingly, writing in a smarmy, cutesy vein that put down the music as it told of its success in record sales and income generated from personal appearances.

In an article in *Collier's* in 1946 titled "Whoop-and-Holler Opera," writer Doron K. Antrim begins "There's a moanin' and a wailin' throughout the land as the resurgent hillbillies whang away at their doleful tales of love and woe." The writer stated that country music is "the epidemic of corn that is sweeping the country today" and described country musicians as "barefoot fiddlers who couldn't read a note but who could raise a voice on endless tunes, especially with the aid of corn liquor."

In 1948 the *Christian Science Monitor* ran an article titled "Hillbilly Phenomenon." Writer Robert Schermann noted "Cowboy music is paying off in a big way. In the past year its chief exponent, the hillbilly singer, has been the biggest money maker in show business." The writer continued that during country shows audiences "whoop, stomp, jump and generally raise the roof" while the band consists of "an ill-tuned fiddle, a couple of raspy guitars, perhaps a bass fiddle, and a delicate little instrument known as the steel guitar, from which there can be coaxed anything from the croak of a bullfrog to the clang of a cowbell."

An article titled "Corn Of Plenty" in *Newsweek* in 1949, begins, "'The corn is as high as an elephant's eye--and so are the profits." The article continued that "while the rest of the music business remained in its chronic fluttery state, the hillbilly output remained fairly constant. But the demand for it has multiplied fivefold since the war. This week the industry was still moving in concentric circles and nothing was dependable--except hillbilly music." The article gave some grudging respect, stating, "Once a specialty product marketed in the Deep South, it now has a nationwide sales field" before concluding "it would seem that all a singer needs is a hoedown fiddle, a steel guitar, a mandolin, and a new inflection in his voice--and he's set for the bonanza."

WSM and the Grand Ole Opry also received national attention for their success with country music. An article in the October 26, 1949 edition of *Variety* was headlined, "Fort Knox No Longer Has Exclusive On Pot of Gold; WSM, Nashville, Talent Corners a Good Chunk of It." The article stated, "WSM has been going about its job of cornering the hillbilly market. In the process it has made a lot of people rich, has given the recording business a sizeable hypo when most needed, and has established WSM's distinctive role in the broadcasting and musical pattern of the nation." The article went on to state that the Opry was a 125 person unit, that WSM grossed about $600,000 a year with approximately two thirds of that from the Opry; and that WSM programmed six hours of the Opry every Saturday night. The article also noted that R. J. Reynolds, sponsor of the Prince Albert segment of the Opry, had an exclusive agreement that prevented anyone except local sponsors from sponsoring the Opry.

In addition to the Opry, WSM produced "Sunday Down South" featuring Snooky Lanson, Beasley Smith--the WSM Orchestra leader who had composed "That Lucky Old Sun"-

-and a cast of 45. The article pointed out that WSM had 230 employees and 200 were "talent."

Aside from income from radio, the Opry grossed $640,000 a year on barnstorming units (with an average ticket price of 80 cents) and made $275,000 from Opry shows at the Ryman Opry with ticket prices set at 30 and 60 cents. The Opry received international exposure in 1949 when it was chosen by the War Department for a series of performances at European military bases.

It was pointed out that Nashville had more than just country talent on the Opry; there had been broadcasts from the Hermitage Hotel featuring pop singers Dinah Shore, Kitty Kallen, Kay Arme, Jerry Sullivan and James Melton and the Castle Recording Studio, run by three WSM engineers, "is perhaps the busiest auxiliary plant in the U.S.; that's where the boys groove out the profits for Decca, Columbia, Capitol, Victor, London etc."

At the end of 1949 the major labels for country music were Victor, Capitol, King, MGM, Decca and Columbia. In terms of stars, Victor had Eddy Arnold, Pee Wee King, Texas Jim Robertson and the Sons of the Pioneers; Capitol had Hank Thompson, Jimmy Wakely, Tex Williams, and Tex Ritter; King, owned by Syd Nathan in Cincinnati, had Moon Mullican and Cowboy Copas; MGM had Hank Williams and Carson Robison; Decca had Red Foley and Ernest Tubb; 4 Star had T. Texas Tyler; and Columbia had Floyd Tillman, Roy Acuff, Ted Daffan, Gene Autry and Bob Wills and His Texas Playboys.

CHAPTER 26

In January, 1950 Eddy Arnold's movies were released. In *Feudin' Rhythm*, Ace Lucky (Kirby Grant) has a radio program that is ready to go on TV. Eddy Arnold, playing himself, is a singer on "The Ace Lucky Show" on KXIW. He has a son, Bobby, who has been adopted by Mr. and Mrs. Upperworth--but Bobby doesn't know Arnold is his father.

There are two concurrent plots: Bobby is a raging terror who wreaks havoc on the radio show's cast and crew but has immunity because he is Mrs. Upperworth's son. The other plot is Mrs. Upperworth's attempts to transform the show into "her" show featuring drama and high culture when it goes on television; this is justified because she is the financial backer. The final plot is Mrs. Upperworth's attempt to fire Arnold from the cast to get him away from Bobby before Bobby finds out Arnold is his real father.

Eddy Arnold sang "Cattle Call," "You Know How Talk Gets Around," "Nearest Thing to Heaven" and "There's No Wings on My Angel." The movie falls into slapstick as Mrs. Upperworth's set collapses on TV during a failed kidnap attempt and the crew of "The Ace Lucky Show" comes to the rescue. The basic theme is that country music might not be high culture but it's what the friends and neighbors want.

The other movie, Hoedown, featured Jock O'Mahoney as Stoney Rhodes, a handsome but none-too-bright cowboy movie actor, who is dropped by his studio while in Smokey Falls, Tennessee. Broke and without a friend, the actor learns the tour was financed with $10,000 put up by his mother, who mortgaged her home in an attempt to save Stoney's career. A pretty young reporter, sent to write a sob story on the actor's quick rise and fall, runs out of gas on the way to the interview and stops for help at a farm belonging to Eddy Arnold (playing himself). It just so happens the singer is preparing for a hoedown. Eddy's cousin, Carolina Cotton, falls for Stoney and Eddy, under the mistaken impression that it is Stoney's own voice he heard singing the songs in his movies, wires an agent to come and sign him as a new Western singer. While driving to the farm, the agent, Sam (Fred Sears) is held up by bank robbers. On the day of the hoedown it is discovered that Stoney can't sing a note. (He'd tried to tell them that his movie songs had been dubbed but in the general hubbub he wasn't heard.) The identity of the bank robbers is discovered when they try to steal the $2,000 paid by the audience to see the benefit. A wild battle follows with Stoney against the outlaws and getting much the worst of it until Carolina kisses him and declares her love for him. Thus inspired, he overwhelms the heavies, recovering $100,000 they had taken from a nearby bank. As a result of his heroism, Stoney receives eight movie offers along with a big reward. Further, he realizes he is in love with Carolina Cotton. While all this is going on, Eddy

Arnold and Vera, the reporter, have quietly fallen for each other, so the picture ends with a romantic scene.

In the movie Arnold sang "Just a Little Lovin'," "I'm Throwin' Rice," and "Bouquet of Roses."

Despite Arnold's and Tom Parker's attempts to have Eddy Arnold not appear in a cowboy movie, both were, essentially "B" westerns. Eddy Arnold wore his Stetson hat, but it wasn't a cowboy hat; it was almost a cross between a fedora and a Western styled hat. He wore a sports coat and slacks and didn't have a horse but the rest of the cast dressed as cowboys, rode horses, shot guns and, despite some cars in the movie, staged some shoot-em-up chase scenes with cowboys and horses.

Eddy Arnold did not have a chance to see the movies before they were released and first saw them in a small movie theatre near his home in Madison. He didn't particularly like what he saw and remained embarrassed by the pictures. They were "cheapies," as he put it, made to capitalize on his fame, and the acting was rather wooden while the story-lines were far-fetched and hokum. Still, they gave him more exposure and his popularity was so great that the movies were profitable.

On January 26 Arnold went to Durham, North Carolina for the grand opening of the Liggett and Myers Tobacco Company manufacturing plant; Liggett and Myers' Chesterfield brand sponsored a major radio show hosted by Perry Como on NBC. At the dedication were Perry Como, Arthur Godfrey and Bob Hope; all appeared on the radio program broadcast from the event. This was a major network appearance for Arnold, as was his appearance as a guest on Arthur Godfrey's television show that same month. He also appeared on Perry Como's radio and TV shows in April.

He continued to tour and during May was on a Texas tour with Jamup and Honey, Professor Gabe Tucker, Annie Lou and the Oklahoma Wranglers, and Little Roy Wiggins. In August he performed a free concert in Nashville at Centennial Park before 15,000 people in the pouring rain. The songs he sang included "Take Me In Your Arms and Hold Me," "Enclosed, One Broken Heart," "Why Should I Cry," "I'm Throwing Rice," "Cattle Call," "Cuddle-Buggin' Baby," "Anytime" and a medley of some of his other hits.

CHAPTER 27

In terms of making money, the period 1947-1953 were banner years for Eddy Arnold. In 1948 he earned $250,000 in record sale royalties alone. By January, 1950 it was announced that the *Eddy Arnold Song Book*, which sold for 50 cents, had sold about 85,000 a year since its release. Arnold also merchandised a guitar-shaped pin for fifty cents; it was estimated that he received an average of 5,000 fan letters each week. At a time when the average income in the United States was around $3,000 a year, Eddy Arnold reportedly made over $250,000 during 1950. During this time the highest tax rate was 90 percent of income.

The business side was good, although there were a few setbacks. In August, he closed his record shop and gave $5,000 worth of records to the Tennessee Industrial School to distribute to Davidson County orphanages; this liquidated his stock and eased his losses with a tax break.

He was beginning to see tangible rewards for his success: during 1950 he purchased another farm in Brentwood, just south of Nashville, and in July he moved into a new home. There were personal set-backs as well. On Sunday, September 24, his mother died in St. Louis. She was 76 and had spent her final years living with her children; she stayed with Eddy in Nashville, then W.D. in Jackson, Tennessee, then her daughter Mrs. Patty Burns in St. Louis. In July, while visiting Patty, she suffered a heart attack.

She left a large family; in addition to her children with Will Arnold (Eddy, W. D. and Patty), there were two sons from her first marriage--R. C. Engel and Ernest Engel--and the children from Will Arnold's first family. The funeral was held in Henderson where she was buried in the Methodist cemetery.

The life of an entertainer is one of continuing obligations and demands. No matter what happens in their personal life, a performer is expected to take the stage with a smile, entertain his fans and meet the obligations of fame. Shortly after the loss of his mother, Eddy Arnold was back on the road as well as hosting his radio show and appearing on television.

The day before his mother died, "The Eddy Arnold Show," a half-hour show on NBC, debuted. It was sponsored by Purina and ran on Saturday nights. The show was actually "The Checkerboard Jamboree," extended by 15-minutes, but at this point Eddy Arnold was so popular that it was decided the show would be renamed for its host instead of its sponsor.

Eddy Arnold faced another kind of tragedy in 1950; he was losing his hair. He covered that up by wearing a Stetson hat, but he couldn't wear a hat all of the time so sometime during the early part of the year he acquired a toupee. Eddy Arnold wore a hair piece for the rest of his life. He always purchased a well made, expensive one and many of his fans were not aware that he had a toupee. After all, he was still a young man; he was 31 years old when he started wearing hair pieces.

Eddy Arnold had moved into the ranks of the top selling artists of all time and was recognized for this achievement. In August, 1950 it was announced that Eddy Arnold had sold 12 million records for RCA Victor in five years; by the end of the year that figured had increased to 14 million. By the end of 1950 Eddy Arnold was heard on over 1,500 radio stations each week. Among his shows was "Robin Hood's Eddy Arnold Show," sponsored by a flour company. He was on 300 stations on the Mutual Network sponsored by Purina and received $500 a week for that show. During 1950 he appeared as a guest on six network shows (radio and TV) sponsored by Chesterfield, including those hosted by Perry Como and Arthur Godfrey. He appeared on Milton Berle's TV show, "The Texaco Theater Starring Milton Berle" and "The Big Show" hosted by Talulah Bankhead, which was the last "big" production for network radio. During the Christmas season he released his second Christmas single, "White Christmas" b/w "Santa Claus is Coming to Town."

There were changes in the Nashville music community. Harry Stone, who lost some key struggles in the corridors of power at WSM, resigned in October, 1950 (the reason given was "health"). Arnold came to the rescue of his old friend; he put him on his payroll during this difficult time and paid his moving expenses when Stone relocated to Phoenix, Arizona to run a television station there.

Eddy Arnold's success had a downside as well. In November, 1949, his former manager, Dean Upson, filed a lawsuit alleging that Arnold had violated their contract and Arnold owed him ten percent of the money made since 1945. The case was finally settled in 1954; Upson received $782.94 and his attorneys received $350.96.

In January, 1951, Eddy Arnold went to Houston for a 12-day appearance that earned him $15,000. He bought a western outfit for those appearances at the Houston Fat Stock Show, which was the only event where he wore cowboy garb when he performed. Then it was two weeks on "The $64 Dollar Question," three appearances on Perry Como's network show as well as recording his own radio program for the Mutual Network on Saturday afternoons. He did promotional announcements for the Treasury Department that were heard on almost 1,500 radio stations. His current single, "Love Bug Itch," was moving up the charts.

In addition to his regular concerts, Eddy Arnold opened at the Hotel Sahara in Las Vegas on May 5, 1951.

In July, Eddy Arnold moved his office from the Third National Building in downtown Nashville to a small office building he purchased on Franklin Road in Brentwood, a sub-division just outside Nashville in Williamson County near his home. Arnold kept his office in Brentwood for the rest of his career.

With his career in high gear, Arnold had hit records in 1951 with "There's Been a Change in Me," "May the Good Lord Bless and Keep You," "Kentucky Waltz," "I Wanna

Play House With You," "Something Old, Something New," "Somebody's Been Beating My Time," and "Heart Strings." All were top ten records. In 1952 he continued his string of hits with "Bundle of Southern Sunshine," "Call Her Your Sweetheart," "Easy on the Eyes," "A Full Time Job," "Older and Bolder," and "I'd Trade All of My Tomorrows (For Just One Yesterday)."

In July, Eddy Arnold hosted "The Chesterfield Show" on the CBS TV network as a summer replacement for Perry Como. Filmed in New York, the show was fifteen minutes and aired at 7:45 p.m. (Eastern) on Monday, Wednesday and Friday. The show ran through the summer, ending at the end of August. The success of this show led to important media exposure: his picture on the cover of *TV Guide* on August 8 and an article on him on August 23.

A concert review from Texarkana noted that after singing "Call Her Sweetheart" and "You're So Easy on the Eyes" he performed "Texarkana Baby," "which sent a flock of high school girls in the audience clear out of this world. The sighs coming from the high school crowd were reminiscent of Frank Sinatra's early days." Arnold then sang "Cattle Call," which "went over big with the crowds." The article concluded that "As Arnold started to leave the stage set up in the arena, the fans went wild--they wouldn't let him go. So the country boy from Tennessee came back to do a medley of old time folk favorites, 'Molly Darlin,'' 'I'm Sending You a Big Bouquet of Roses,' and 'I'll Hold You In My Heart.' After concluding the show with 'There's Been a

Change in Me,' Arnold left the arena to a resounding round of applause and cheers."

The article also noted that Arnold "visited polio patients at St. Michael's Hospital" where he sang "Smoky the Bear" and "The Horse in Striped Pajamas."

CHAPTER 28

In July, 1952, Eddy Arnold announced he would not renew his contract with Hill and Range. The publishing company had brought him great songs--such as "Bouquet of Roses"--but they wanted him to record a number of other songs he didn't want to record and he was tired of the pressure. Plus, the money they paid him wasn't as important as it once was and he realized he wasn't really a songwriter; he was a singer and wanted to concentrate on that.

Although Eddy Arnold had an active interest in current events, an avid newspaper reader who read *Time* cover to cover each week, he had never been excited about a Presidential race until 1952 when World War II hero Dwight Eisenhower ran. On November 3, 1952, along with Roy Acuff, he sang at a giant "Jamboree for Eisenhower" rally at the Ryman Auditorium. He also placed a $200 bet with Ernest Tubb, a die-hard Roosevelt Democrat, that Eisenhower would beat Adlai Stevenson. Right after the election Ernest Tubb wrote out a check for $200 to Eddy Arnold to settle the bet. Arnold put it in his top middle desk drawer and never cashed it.

He became an active citizen as well as a recording artist and performed in charity shows: he headed the American Cancer Society drive, and did a series of shows for victims of a tornado in Fayetteville, Tennessee.

In a 1952 interview, Arnold described his recordings as "kind of on the fence. They're not pop, but they're not quite as hillbilly as some of the others. I do a lot of ballads and novelties. A lot of my songs go into the popular field later on--'Anytime' went pop last year, but my record of it sold 650,000 copies in 1948."

In 1952 he had his own network television show, "The Eddy Arnold Show," as a summer replacement for Dinah Shore's show. The 15-minute show appeared on the CBS network on Tuesdays and Thursdays in prime time from Chicago's Studebaker Theater.

Country music on TV was gaining attention and an article in the *Oakland Tribune* stated, "The boys with the string ties, guitars and cornball jokes are madder than all get-out over the way TV has been giving them the high-toned brushoff. They point to the fact that local TV outlets in many cities have Western, hillbilly or country-type programs which net higher popularity ratings than many of the so-called slick type or big time shows. Western melody-makers in this neck of the woods are getting particularly cantankerous over their lot in the video scene. Cliffie Stone, a pudgy sagebrush maestro who conducts the 'Hometown Jamboree' here every Saturday night, is drafting a petition this week to present to the Academy of Television Arts and Sciences."

Stone complained that television executives "continue to look down on us...And when they do give one of us a tumble, they want to change our style, which would make it no longer a Western show. It's the informal atmosphere that gives the proper rollicking pitch to a hillbilly soiree. But a legitimate TV producer shrinks back in abject fear when a Western star explains that 'he don't need no writer feller or director.' There's an ironic but true axiom that a Western melange loses its charm with the fans if the corn is distilled out of it."

In July, 1953 an article appeared in the *San Francisco Chronicle* by noted journalist Ralph J. Gleason. The article discussed country music, and stated, "The Western field, which has shot to such popularity since the war, is a strange mixture of simple singers, pseudo cowboys who never rode a horse, and Arkansas fiddlers from Arizona. It's rife with jealousy; most of the stars being quite touchy about whether they are 'folk singers' or 'Western singers' and they themselves refer to other artists whom they dislike as 'hill billies.' But one and all, they hold Eddy Arnold in awe." Gleason went on to state, "For one thing, Arnold is pretty generally credited with having a major part in the boom of Western Music. He has a good, homely, unpretentious voice and it manages to sound as authentically folksy as a sunbonnet and a corn-cob pipe. On the other hand, he tries to make his songs more than just simple laments, but he never departs far enough from his formula of just plain singing to lose the quality of sincerity that has made him the best selling artist in the folk and Western field for several years."

Gleason continued, "Eddy Arnold attributes one

reason for the sudden popularity of what he calls 'country music' to the big shift in population during the war when people from the country moved to the city in droves to work in war plants and stayed. It wasn't that city people hadn't liked the music before, Eddy believes, it was 'just that they hadn't been exposed to it. There's a feeling and a rhythm to country songs that grows on you,' according to the Tennessee Plowboy. 'And once it grows it stays. That explains my appearance on so many shows that have a wide audience--like the Perry Como and Milton Berle TV shows. For another thing, I find records like my 'Love Bug Itch' and 'I Wanna Play House With You' being played more and more on big city stations. We country music people have moved into town--that's for sure.'"

On September 4, 1953 Eddy Arnold and Tom Parker met in Arnold's attorney's office and dissolved their manager/artist relationship. Arnold had sent Parker a telegram informing him the relationship was terminated and Arnold always stated, "We were two different personalities." An article in the *Pickin' and Singin'* News stated it was an "obvious clash of personalities between the unassuming, easy-going Arnold and the aggressive, energetic Parker." There were conflicts over business arrangements Parker had set-up. Those arrangements came to Arnold's attention in May, 1953 during his second set of appearances at the Sahara Hotel in Las Vegas. Arnold answered a phone call intended for Parker; the caller left a message that let Arnold know that Parker was working with Hank Snow.

Arnold found Parker in the hotel's coffee shop; Parker quickly gathered some papers and put them under the table when he saw Arnold. Eddy Arnold confronted him with the news that he knew that Parker was working with Hank Snow when he was supposed to be serving exclusively as Eddy Arnold's manager. Parker had received 25 percent of Arnold's income for his exclusive agreement; when Arnold found Parker doing other business on the side, he resolved to end their partnership.

After an initial period of awkwardness, Arnold and Parker resumed their friendship and occasionally did business together with Parker booking and promoting some of Arnold's dates through Jamboree Attractions, which Parker formed with Hank Snow. Arnold's radio and TV bookings were done through the William Morris Agency; after the split with Parker, William Morris handled all of Arnold's bookings and Arnold announced he would manage himself.

The split with Tom Parker marked the end of the first period of Eddy Arnold's career and it was an important milestone. The same month that Arnold split from Parker, he recorded a song that pointed to a new direction he wanted to go. On September 21 he went into the studio and recorded "I Really Don't Want to Know." The song had been brought to him during a Las Vegas performance by Julian Aberbach of Hill and Range. Aberbach played the demo acetate sung by songwriter Don Robertson, accompanying himself on piano, in Arnold's hotel room. Arnold listened and said "That's the prettiest song I've ever heard. I'd sing that song if it hair-lipped grandma."

Eddy Arnold's recording of "I Really Don't Want to Know" marked a new direction musically for him, although his first efforts were tentative, not wanting to lose his fan base. He found a song where he could try the type of sound he'd been thinking about. He recorded it with only two acoustic guitars and a male group backing him.

His live shows were also changing, a harbinger of things to come. Sometime in the mid-1950s in either Beaumont or Galveston, Texas he told his band to take a short break during the show and performed some songs by himself with his acoustic guitar. Roy Wiggins was first insulted and then perplexed. "We could do any of his songs exactly like the record," he remembered. "So I didn't see why he didn't want us to play." Wiggins also remembered that the acoustic set came after they had been touring with Tex Ritter and Ritter had a section in his show when he dismissed his band and sat on a stool to do a rollicking version of "Rye Whiskey."

The acoustic set proved to be a popular part of Eddy Arnold's show and allowed him to perform extra songs and do bits and pieces of songs without having to do an entire song. It also allowed him to develop an intimacy with the audience. The audience loved it and he began to incorporate this acoustic set as a regular part of his show; in time it would become, for many fans, their favorite part of his live performances.

CHAPTER 29

In January, 1955 *Billboard* devoted a special issue to Eddy Arnold. It was, in many ways, the apex of his career up to this point.

The "special" had a number of articles about Eddy Arnold and his career. There was a discussion of his recordings written by Chick Crumpacker, RCA Victor's promotion man for Country and Western and an article by Ben Park, the producer, director and writer for the TV show "Eddy Arnold Time." The half-hour show, shot on film at the Kling Studios in Chicago, featured Arnold singing a few songs, then a small story acted out, then a few more songs. Co-stars included Betty Johnson and the Jordanaires. The show was heavy on music; there were 10-11 songs on each show.

The show's executive producer was Joe Csida and the musical director was Charlie Grean, who played bass and helped produce Arnold's records. The show was financed by Eddy Arnold, who was unable to find a sponsor for the show and ended up losing a good deal of money on it. Arnold, Csida, Grean and Ed Burton had gone into business together the previous year with Csida, who was a former editor for *Billboard*, serving as Arnold's manager after the split with Tom Parker. In addition, Csida, Grean and Burton owned two publishing companies Trinity (BMI) and Towne Music (ASCAP).

The special commemorated Eddy Arnold's Tenth Anniversary with RCA and an album, *An American Institution*, was released in conjunction with the special. RCA president Frank Folsom, in his article, noted that Arnold had sold 30 million records in his first ten years with the company. In the article Folsom stated, "This boy from the country has done more to bridge the gap from 'way-out-yonder' to Broadway than most people realize."

The previous year Arnold had another string of top ten records, including "I Really Don't Want to Know," "My Everything," "This is the Thanks I Get (For Loving You)," and "Hep Cat Baby." In 1955 he had hits with "I've Been Thinking," "In Time," "Two Kinds of Love" "Cattle Call," "The Kentuckian Song," "That Do Make It Nice," "Just Call Me Lonesome," "The Richest Man In the World," and "I Walked Alone Last Night." Arnold's remake of "Cattle Call" and "The Kentuckian Song" were recorded with orchestra leader Hugo Winterhalter and featured Arnold with a large, lush section of strings behind him.

Winterhalter had come to Arnold's home in Nashville to discuss working with the singer. The session that resulted brought criticism from many in the country music community, including a disc jockey in Knoxville who opined that he did like the song "with all them bugles in it." Some country fans felt Arnold had sold out by recording with such a "pop" backing, but the recording sold extremely well and Arnold felt the commercial success justified the new sound. By this point Eddy Arnold was determined to pursue his "new" sound. He put steel guitar player Roy Wiggins on a salary and then helped him set up a real estate business, with Arnold providing the financial backing. Guitarist Hank Garland had already left Arnold and become a top session player. Eddy Arnold also ended his daily radio show sponsored by Purina that had been on the air since 1947. However, after 1955, Eddy Arnold hit a dry spell in country music with only a few hits ("Trouble in Mind," "You Don't Know Me" and "Tennessee Stud") until 1962.

The lull in the career of Eddy Arnold corresponded to the lull in the country music industry during this same period. Country music had been extremely successful during the decade after World War II and Nashville established itself as a major player in country music to the point where most of the major recording labels had offices in Nashville by 1955. A major reason those labels established offices in Nashville was the commercial success of country music from Nashville, especially the success of Eddy Arnold. Not only did Eddy Arnold have great success selling records--thus bringing millions of dollars into RCA's coffers--he also demonstrated how successful country music could be for a major label.

Eddy Arnold was committed to his career and worked hard promoting his records so distributors could sell them as well as giving a lot of time and attention to his recordings. While many artists did not learn a song until they were in the studio, Arnold always rehearsed his songs thoroughly before coming into the studio. He acquired a reel to reel tape recorder and set up a room in his home where he recorded himself doing prospective songs, working on the tempo and range, before he decided what to record. In the *Billboard* special, Arnold's producer, Steve Sholes, discussed Eddy Arnold's method of recording and stated, "When the recording dates have been definitely set, Eddy accepts no bookings or heavy outside work for a two-week period prior to the sessions. He actually goes into training with plenty of sleep and all the other contributing factors to insure his health and strength for the forthcoming session." Arnold usually recorded in the morning or afternoon when he was freshest so he could give his best performance.

He was also diligent in his concert appearances. A simple story will illustrate this. Once, when Arnold was appearing in Fort Worth, he received a telephone call from Western swing legend Bob Wills. Wills wanted Arnold to go out drinking with him but Arnold, who knew Wills's penchant for alcohol and tendency to go on a binge that could last several days, declined. "I had a show to do the next day," he remembered. "And I wanted to get plenty of rest for it and be in good condition."

That story not only illustrates Eddy Arnold's commitment to the fans who paid good money to see and hear him in concert, but it also showed why many critics and writers avoided writing about him. Simply put, it is more interesting if an artist gets drunk, shoots up the town, misses the concert or staggers through it, then careens self-destructively towards the next event. It's a great story for writers and makes interesting reading, but for the folks who've paid money to see the performer in concert, it's a waste of time, effort and money. Eddy Arnold always made sure that people who paid to see him got their money's worth.

Joe Csida, in his *Billboard* article in the Eddy Arnold "special," stated that Arnold "is not quick to come to conclusions or make decisions. He thinks and studies and watches and analyzes every situation of any importance for a long time before he decides what his feeling or attitude or action will be. When he finally makes up his mind, his judgment is generally very firm, and he cannot easily be shaken in it." Ben Park, in his article, described Eddy Arnold as "relaxed, easy, warm and honest." Both of those writers captured essential elements of Eddy Arnold.

Eddy Arnold was the quintessential "Southern Gentleman" in public. He was gracious, charming, considerate and hospitable. At the same time, in private he was determined, dogged, dedicated and opinionated. He knew what was right for him--and he did it. Publicly, he strove to please and was genuinely interested in other people, both professionally and personally; privately, he would not be pushed around. He did not make decisions quickly but rather mulled them over--often for a long time--before he came to a conclusion. He was practical and pragmatic yet also a romantic and dreamer.

Eddy Arnold always wanted to be successful commercially; in his own words, "I wanted to sell a lot of records!" This led many to assume that money was more important to him than his music. Money was certainly important to him--he was always careful with his money, saved and invested it--and watched every penny as many who grew up poor in the Great Depression were prone to do. But he valued his music and demanded excellence both from himself and those around him. He worked hard at his recordings and performances with the result that both were top quality items.

In terms of Eddy Arnold and the Nashville country music community, he was often viewed by others as "set apart" from country music. True, he started in country music and was a country boy at heart but he always wanted to better himself, to be successful not just as an artist but as a man and he went to great lengths to educate himself through travel, reading, and listening to others. Some in the country music community whispered criticism that he had put down his guitar and used his hands in expressive gestures while singing. He never matched the stereotype of the hard drinking, hell raising country singer and did all he could to distance himself from that stereotype. "Drinking was never my favorite sport," he said, and that kept him attending to business when others succumbed to the bottle.

While other country singers might hang out in bars, Eddy Arnold joined a country club; while others might dress in flashy rhinestone suits and buy chrome covered Cadillacs, Eddy Arnold wore slacks and a sports coat and drove a Buick. While others might record "honky tonk" music aimed at the barroom jukebox, Eddy Arnold recorded ballads for people to listen to in their living rooms.

Because of his desire to broaden the boundaries of country music, Eddy Arnold changed his singing style. In his early recordings the songs were generally up tempo or medium tempo and Arnold sang in a full-throated tenor. From the mid-1950s onward he lowered the key to his songs (he re-recorded some of his earlier hits two keys lower than the original recordings) and slowed the tempo on numbers he previously recorded while searching for romantic ballads he could "croon." His musical heroes were Bing Crosby and Gene Autry and he loved and admired them as much for their singing style--easy-going, relaxed and warm--as for the fact that they were successful in the musical world as well as outside of it. Like Crosby and Autry, Eddy Arnold wanted to be a major recording artist, but he also wanted to set a standard for success and achievement outside the music business.

In succeeding, Eddy Arnold changed the perceptions of those outside country music as well as the country music community itself. In doing so, he changed the very definition of country music during his career.

Many have attempted to define country music in terms of lyrics (simple, everyday stories), musically (from folk roots, primarily from British folk songs), singing style (untrained, from the back of the throat), musical instruments (the steel guitar, fiddle), recordings (dominated by the acoustic rhythm guitar and sparse instrumentation) or quaint phrases (three chords and the truth). In actuality the core definition of country music must center on it being the music for the working class, blue-collar and originally Southern audience.

The term "white trash" had been applied liberally by those who disliked country music or who were outside the South; in fact, some people simply applied the term "white trash" to anyone who liked country music. The term was used much more selectively by those who liked country music, were from the South, or those who worked in the country music community. Even among the working class there was a pecking order and, while some may describe anyone who they felt was below them economically or socially as "white trash," the term generally fit the stereotypically uncultured, illiterate, uncouth, coarse individual that people loved to caricature when they looked at people who loved country music. Unfortunately, just enough of those kind of folks existed--including a few country music artists--to allow a total dismissal of that stereotype.

Eddy Arnold was not "white trash" by anyone's definition and always distanced himself from anything that smacked of that stereotype or image. Because he had dignity, self-respect and a sense of honor, he raised the level of country music to the music of the middle class. In doing so, he represented a major trend in the United States in the decade after World War II.

CHAPTER **30**

The life story and music of Eddy Arnold reflected the shift in the United States from an agrarian to an urban nation during the post-World War II period. America recovered from the Great Depression--both mentally and fiscally--to become a powerful nation domestically and internationally. Country music moved from being a regional music, confined mostly to the South (with the exception of the singing cowboys in the movies) to become a national music, moving from a musical form on the fringes of American society to part of mainstream American popular music. Eddy Arnold played a major role in country music's rise to respectability in terms of image, status and commercial success.

The year 1945 was the last year of World War II and a pivotal one for country music. At this point, American country music was dominated by Western Swing--particularly Bob Wills and Spade Cooley--and by West Coast country music. Until World War II, Chicago had the top country music show on radio, "The National Barn Dance." Of the top songs in 1945 only one, "It's Been So Long, Darling" by Ernest Tubb, was by a Nashville act. In 1946 it was a virtual repeat of 1945 with Western Swing still dominating country music. The top country music recording acts, Bob Wills & His Texas Playboys, Tex Ritter, Al Dexter, and Merle Travis were all West Coast acts. While Nashville was important for its radio broadcasts from the Grand Ole Opry on WSM, it was not a recording center, nor were its acts well known for their success on records. All that was beginning to change and a key person in that change was Eddy Arnold.

Nashville had all the musical elements that guided the future of country music by the end of 1945. On the Opry was Bill Monroe with the Blue Grass Boys; by the end of 1945 his group included Lester Flatt and Earl Scruggs, and their sound, led by Scrugg's three-finger style on the banjo, defined bluegrass in the coming years. Ernest Tubb and his Texas "honky tonk" sound showed another direction country music took, especially during the late 1940s and early 1950s as this hard driving, barroom jukebox sound virtually defined the sound of "hard" or "traditional" country for the coming years. Hank Williams and Webb Pierce later represented that "traditional" country music, which stayed close to its rural roots.

The star of the Grand Ole Opry was Roy Acuff, whose mountaineer image fit the Opry's image of country music from folk roots in the southern area of the United States and whose full throated vocal sound was a prime example of the country music singing style. Uncle Dave Macon, with his vivid showmanship and vaudeville background, also connected country music to its folk and live performance roots but his sound and style were already part of the past, although a past that was treasured and revisited time and again.

Also on the Grand Ole Opry was Pee Wee King and his Golden West Cowboys, whose tight organization headed by manager J. L. Frank, pioneered business practices in country music artist management and bookings and whose outfits--they dressed in snappy western clothes--defined the look of country music after the mountaineer image was shunned and discarded (except by Acuff) after World War II.

Then there was Eddy Arnold, whose smooth vocal style--reminiscent of a country Bing Crosby--led country music to a more commercial sound and whose image pulled country music away from the rural, hayseed image towards a more urban, urbane, sophisticated look. Of all the acts on the Opry at the end of 1945, it was Eddy Arnold who had the greatest impact on commercial country music and the establishment of Nashville as the center for the country music industry in the following years. It was Eddy Arnold, more than any other single act during this period, who led country music into the mainstream of American popular music.

Country music had proven itself to be commercially successful before World War II. Fiddlin' John Carson, who recorded the first commercially successful country record in Atlanta in 1923, Vernon Dalhart, whose 1924 recording of "The Prisoner's Song" b/w "Wreck of the Old '97" became country music's first million seller, Jimmie Rodgers and the Carter Family, who recordings in Bristol, Tennessee in 1927 provided country music with it's "Big Bang" and the Singing Cowboys—Gene Autry, Roy Rogers and Tex Ritter—proved that country music could be profitable as a business. Major corporations recorded and released country music and this, in turn, led to broad exposure of the music and access to the electronic media and distribution networks that brought the recordings to consumers.

However, some country music proved itself to be more commercial than others. Bluegrass, although it is a vibrant, important music, has never been particularly commercial and therefore the field has been dominated by small, independent labels who record and release the music. The same fate has befallen western music since World War II. Other than a few acts such as Gene Autry and the Sons of the Pioneers (who always transcended the genre and recorded songs that were not just western, this kind of music is primarily recorded and released on small, independent labels. Even Western Swing, though reissued on major labels because it was originally recorded there, doesn't really have a place in contemporary country music. It was popular in its day, but somehow its day passed.

What grew was commercial country music and the leader of commercial country music was Eddy Arnold. This is significant because a much larger picture emerges when the commercial success of Eddy Arnold is examined in light of its impact on the decision of RCA Victor to set up a corporate office and recording studio in Nashville in 1955, which led to the hiring of Chet Atkins and the unfolding of his career as a producer and executive.

The sales success of Arnold, as well as his exposure on network radio and TV, led to a change in the public perception of country music after World War II. First, it was acknowledged that country music had a commercial appeal, which helped assure its becoming part of mainstream American music. Next, Eddy Arnold helped change the image of country music. Before World War II the music was called "hillbilly," a degrading term that signified backwoods bumpkins. Prior to World War II, there were two distinct images for country—the singing cowboy and the musical mountaineer. However, another image gradually evolved, that of a sophisticated singer who had a country background but assimilated the ways of the city. A singer who did not sing with a twang, who sang with violins instead of fiddles and who dressed in tasteful sports coats and slacks—and later, tuxedos—not cowboy hats, rhinestones or dungarees. That was that Eddy Arnold did for country music: He moved it uptown and into the middle class.

As the country's population shifted from rural areas to urban areas, especially during World War II, Eddy Arnold shifted country music, both musically and visually, from the rural, country image to one of the suburban gentleman who kept his down-home roots and rural values but acquired city sophistication along the way.

That is the story of the generation who grew up in rural America during the Great Depression and then got off the farm during World War II. They were proud of their heritage, but they wanted something more; they wanted respect, wanted to be part of mainstream America and wanted to join the American middle class. In short, they wanted to be more worldly and less provincial. This is the story of Eddy Arnold's life as well as his music. He was moving up in the world, a country boy who was not a hick, someone who came from the farm but was not a rube, someone who sang country music but was not a hillbilly, and someone who had been in the hay fields but was not a hayseed.

Eddy Arnold was fortunate to come along at the time *Billboard* established its first country music charts in 1944, but his early success during the 1945-1955 period occurred before the Recording Industry Association of America (RIAA) established its Gold and Platinum Record Awards and the National Academy of Recording Arts and Sciences (NARAS) established the Grammy Awards, both in 1958. Although the phenomenal decade after World War II was, in many ways, the "Eddy Arnold Decade" in country music, the fact often goes unnoticed today because the awards from organizations that boosted popular music (the Grammys, the Country Music Association Awards) in the late 1950s and early 1960s were not in place during that period.

The story of country music from before World War II until the present time mirrors, in many ways, the story of the United States itself. Although the country had been changing from a rural, agricultural-based nation into an urban, industrial-based nation before World War II, the war sped up the process and brought it to fruition. During the War, the population shifted from rural areas to cities, where defense plants were established and workers were hired. It was not unusual for people from the South, still recovering from the Great Depression, to move to a major city during the war for jobs in defense or defense-related plants. In the services, Southerners were mixed with people from other parts of the country, so country music reached a wide variety of people. American music also became international music during World War II, primarily through the V-Disks sent out to servicemen and Armed Forces Radio, Country Music left the South for good and became a national music because Southern servicemen exposed others to country music in the armed forces and because Southerners moved out of the South in large number and fanned out across the country in search of defense-related jobs.

The city exerted a strong pull on rural Americans throughout the twentieth century. It was the place of bright lights because the cities were wired for electricity before rural areas and therefore people were not chained to the cycles of the seasons and daylight. In the city was action, excitement and entertainment around the clock and the city person was viewed as cosmopolitan—cultured, sophisticated, and worldly wise. The rural person was often viewed as a country bumpkin, a rube, a hayseed; all the uncool things nobody wanted to be. In the city were jobs, and for someone raised in the country doing farm work, it seemed like the jobs involved no work at all; it was easy money. This led rural people to move to cities in large numbers throughout the twentieth century, particularly after the 1940s. Rural people reacted to their move to the city in two ways. First, they wanted to keep some of their rural roots, so they planted gardens, read stories of idealized country life illustrated by Norman Rockwell with his idealized view of rural and small town life, and listened to country music. But rural people who moved to the city also wanted to get rid of the hayseed ways and acquire a level of sophistication, so they bought suits and ties, attended social functions and attempted to join the middle class. The middle class was defined not only in terms of income but also in values: the Protestant work ethic, independence, material possessions and, increasingly, a ranch house in the suburbs.

Eddy Arnold was uniquely qualified to bridge the gap for those moving from the country to the city after World War II. He had rural roots; he grew up on a farm in Chester County, Tennessee and knew hard work and hardship. His father died when he was eleven and his family became sharecroppers on the farm they once owned; he grew up in the South during the Depression, an area particularly hard hit. He cut his teeth on country music after he left the farm, performing on radio stations in Jackson, Tennessee, St. Louis and Louisville before he moved to Nashville to join Pee Wee King in 1941.

Eddy Arnold also represented the acquired culture and sophistication of the city-dweller. A performer acquires worldly ways through travel and the experience of meeting a wide variety of people. That was certainly not unique to Eddy Arnold, but he made the most of it. Next, his voice was smooth and pop-ish--like Bing Crosby's or Frank Sinatra's, rather than the harsh country sound of someone like Roy Acuff, Hank Williams or Webb Pierce.

Eddy Arnold openly embraced the middle class values espoused after World War II, values that stressed getting along socially and joining in. He regularly visited radio stations, schmoozed with the movers and shakers, became comfortable socializing with strangers, and took care of business in a responsible, respectable way. He did not show an artistic temperament--moody, self-absorbed--or dress outlandishly; he preferred to wear conservative, non-flashy outfits. Unlike some country stars, he did not cover himself in rhinestones or build guitar-shaped swimming pools. His look was tasteful and understated; here was a man the upwardly mobile middle-class could feel comfortable with. Eddy Arnold accepted his audience; he did not challenge them. His audience responded by embracing him and buying his music; after all, Eddy Arnold's audience was too busy building careers and raising families after World War II to be challenged musically. It was a time of shoulder to the grindstone hard work, raising a family and getting ahead. Eddy Arnold and his music provided a soundtrack for that life.

In many ways, the story of country music is the story of a fight for respect. For a number of years the music and the performers of country music were subjected to stereotypical images of poor white trash. Those who loved the music were often embarrassed by their own tastes. They were both proud and ashamed--proud of their rural past and proud of their taste and connection with country music, but ashamed that the music was linked with so many negative cornpone images. The most important thing that Eddy Arnold did for country music was give it respect. He carried country music into the world, and he didn't embarrass himself or the music.

In short, Eddy Arnold made people proud they were country music fans. In a more general sense, he moved country music uptown, gave it self-respect and dignity. Eddy Arnold proved you did not have to be a hillbilly to sing country music. Because of his commercial success--as well as the commercial success of country music in general--Eddy Arnold helped move country music into the mainstream of American popular music. This led to country music becoming an accepted part of the corporate culture in the American entertainment industry by improving what corporate America looks at closest: the bottom line. By improving that bottom line, country music improved itself and became a major player in the world of music.

Country music is a music that is loyal to the market; it is not loyal to a sound. When Eddy Arnold changed the sound of country music he moved it towards a more commercial sound that consumers found appealing. When this sound proved commercially successful, other country artists followed and the music itself became progressive.

CHAPTER 31

All hell broke loose in 1956. That's when America discovered Elvis Presley. The singer sold 10 million records and became the cultural symbol of teen-age rebellion, the generation gap, the sex revolution, juvenile delinquency, and a new individualism that swept young people into new attitudes and lifestyles.

Actually, it all started earlier than that. Musically, rhythm and blues thrived on small labels in the decade after World War II, the problem of juvenile delinquency was a national concern throughout most of the 1950s and the previous year Bill Haley and the Comets had a number one song with "Rock Around the Clock," which was featured in a movie about juvenile delinquents, *Blackboard Jungle*. It is somewhat unfair to single out Elvis Presley as being responsible for the huge shift in the cultural life of America from the mid-1950s onward, but he was the central figure in the rock'n'roll movement that energized the young generation during the fifties and threatened their parents.

Elvis had his first success in the South in late 1954 on Sun Records in Memphis and, like a steamroller, the momentum kept building throughout 1955. In November, Elvis came to Nashville to the Country and Western Disk Jockey Convention and agreed to a contract with RCA Victor.

The man who signed him was Steve Sholes, Eddy Arnold's producer. The key to the deal was the Aberbach brothers, who owned Hill and Range publishing (Eddy Arnold's former publishing company) who signed a co-venture publishing agreement and agreed to promote the singer. The catalyst was Eddy Arnold's former manager, Tom Parker.

Parker had done it all before with Eddy Arnold; he took a country boy who appealed to the pop world and made him a superstar. Parker had worked with RCA Victor, with Steve Sholes, the Aberbach brothers and the William Morris Agency when he managed Eddy Arnold; that team was the same one that Parker worked with for Elvis. Parker also did for Elvis what he had first done for Eddy Arnold: gave him his total, undivided loyalty, commitment and attention and worked tirelessly on his career.

On January 5, 1956, Elvis Presley came to the RCA Victor studio in Nashville on McGavock Street and recorded "Heartbreak Hotel," which became a number one record on the Country, R&B and pop charts in *Billboard*. That year he sold ten million records for RCA.

While the success of Elvis was the catalyst for the creation of the entire industry of rock'n'roll, it seemed to the Nashville country community that it almost killed country music. Young singers, who might have gone into country music, were enticed to record rock'n'roll songs because young audiences wanted to see and hear young rock'n'roll singers. The demand for country music—and country performers—nearly vanished overnight.

Substantive changes in the country music community in Nashville during 1956 altered the city and the industry permanently. Rock'n'roll was only part of it, albeit a major part. First, there were changes with radio.

Before 1940 most music heard on radio was performed live. That included the big network shows featuring the big bands and elaborate productions as well as the fifteen-minute broadcasts in the early morning when a country music group sang songs and advertised a product because a sponsor paid for the time. Radio listeners heard a variety of music and a variety of shows: Big Band, country music, soap operas, westerns, mysteries, comedies and dramas.

The reasons for live programs were fairly simple. The first twenty years of radio were characterized by that medium's experimentation and discovery that live shows worked well. Sponsors liked the human touch—being linked to performers who promoted their products. But there was another reason why live programs dominated radio: The record industry and the musicians union fought against the broadcast of records on the air.

The record companies fought radio airplay because they believed it hurt sales; they reasoned that listeners would not buy a record if they could hear it free. The musicians union fought the playing of records on radio because it jeopardized musicians' livelihood; if records were played, then musicians would not be hired by radio stations and therefore would be out of work.

Early country music on the radio was mostly live performances on fifteen-or thirty-minute shows. Early morning shows and shows during the noon hour were popular because, the reasoning went, that was when farmers listened and farmers were believed to be the main audience for country music. If there was a show in the evening it was probably on a Saturday night and if it was a big show—lots of performers lasting an hour or more—then it was called a "Barn Dance." Live country music, especially through the barn dances, was the primary outlet for country music on radio until around 1955.

In 1940, the Supreme Court let stand a lower court ruling that when someone purchased a recording, all property rights belonged to the buyer. That meant that when a disc jockey purchased a record, he was allowed to play it on the air. That curbed the efforts of record companies, who had marked their labels "not for radio airplay" and hired a bevy of lawyers to enforce the ban on radio airplay. This opened the door for deejays to play country records on the radio.

CHAPTER 32

In 1946, the year after the war, eight million records were sold; country music accounted for 13.2 percent of sales, topped only by popular with 50 percent and classical with 18.9 percent. The 550,000 jukeboxes, which before the war accounted for most of the sales of country records, now accounted for only about ten percent of the total. Part of the reason for increased country record sales to consumers was the exposure country music was receiving on local radio shows through disk jockeys playing records on the radio.

World War II brought Americans together over the radio to hear news of the world. People employed in the defense-based economy were making money they could not spend because of the rationing of goods, the limited availability of consumer items, and the heavy encouragement of savings by the government through war bond drives to finance the war. That meant there was pent-up savings and pent-up demand when the war ended in 1945; the result was that in 1946-1947 a large number of radio sets were sold. By the end of that two-year period, 93 percent of American households owned a radio. But 1947 was also the beginning of the television revolution; just when radio was at the height of its popularity, TV made its first inroads to replace it as the dominant mass medium in the United States.

There were changes at the network level for country music on radio after the war. NBC cancelled the "National Barn Dance" on WLS in Chicago after Red Foley left to join WSM and the "Grand Ole Opry." Foley was replaced by Rex Allen, who left for Hollywood in 1949; then WLS's "National Barn Dance" moved to the ABC radio network but was canceled there after about a year.

By 1945, the "Boone County Jamboree" in Cincinnati had been renamed the "Midwestern Hayride" and, in 1948, it began to be featured on TV. "The Dixie Jamboree" on WBT in Charlotte appeared on the regional CBS network during World War II; it evolved into the "Carolina Hayride" and, from 1946, was broadcast over CBS on Saturday nights. The "Louisiana Hayride" was formed in 1948 on KWKH in Shreveport, Louisiana; the show and others appeared on CBS as "Saturday Night, Country Style" on a rotating basis.

The number of radio stations exploded after World War II. In 1946 the FCC licensed 500 new stations; in 1948 there were an additional 400. Disc jockeys became increasingly important because there was just not enough live talent to go around; also, playing records was easier and cheaper than hiring live talent. Records carried a wide variety of music, including country and rhythm and blues, which consumers wanted but could not get on network or big city radio stations. Small stations playing records by disc jockeys proliferated. The trend ran parallel to the trend of small, independent record labels recording country and rhythm and blues music. The major labels were locked into the pop sound that evolved from the Big Band era, with vocalists replacing band leaders as the stars, but still featuring a smooth, pop sound. The rough and raucous sounds of hillbilly and race music found their outlet on jukeboxes prior to World War II, especially after Prohibition died in 1933 and bars became legal again.

In terms of technology, 1948 was a great leap forward; ABC went all tape, using the technology that Americans and Russians discovered in Berlin which had been developed by the Germans. Prior to that, recordings were done direct to disk; the German's Magnetophon, the forerunner to analog tape, revolutionized the recording industry. In June, 1948, Columbia Records premiered the 33 1/3 rpm record; in December, RCA brought forth the 45 rpm. The two new formats on vinyl eventually replaced the old 78s. Radio was still the dominant mass medium in the United States; by the end of 1948, 94.3 percent of American families owned a set.

There was virtually no music recorded in 1948 because of a strike called by James Caesar Petrillo, head of the American Federation of Musicians union. The strike stopped new recordings from January until December, 1948. By the end of that period, most of the Big Bands had dissolved, effectively ending the Big Band era, although a few regrouped after 1948 and some even survived into the 1960s.

The 1948 strike was Petrillo's last hurrah. The country resented him calling a strike during World War II, even after President Roosevelt requested that he not do so. Further, some alleged he was a member of the Mafia and Congress accused him of being a racketeer. Finally, the Taft-Hartley Act, passed over President Harry Truman's veto in June, 1947, limited the power of unions.

In the summer of 1947, Universal released *Something in the Wind*, a film where Deanna Durbin played a disc jockey working for a small radio station. As a promotion for the movie the firm created the National Association of Disc Jockeys, paying for eighty of the country's top disc jockeys to come to Chicago as part of the movie's premier. Once in Chicago, the deejays elected Barry Gray of New York to be president and formed an organization that served as an example for country music broadcasters, who began their organization six years later.

On November 22, 1952, WSM invited about one hundred disc jockeys to come to Nashville for a convention and birthday celebration in honor of the Opry's twenty-seventh anniversary. About eighty showed up. The next year WSM President Jack DeWitt, Executive Assistant Irving Waugh, Artists Service Bureau Chief Jim Denny, Program Director Jack Stapp, and Publicity Director Bill McDaniel pulled out all stops and organized a major convention that attracted five hundred attendees—four hundred of them disc jockeys.

The second convention began on November 21, 1953. Major labels were present and RCA Victor, Columbia, Decca, Capitol, and Mercury hosted events. *Billboard* gave out awards for top country talent, which became a forerunner for future country music awards and BMI presented its first country music songwriter awards. The event eventually shifted to October and led to the development of the Country Music Association, the CMA Awards and a weeklong celebration for the business of country music. One of the first organizations to emerge from the event was the Country and Western Disc Jockeys Association.

The Opry saw this as a good business move. First, having all the country music business people in town helped the Opry Artists Service Bureau, headed by Jim Denny, make personal contacts with bookers of country talent. At that time, country disc jockeys were the major promoters of country music shows and the Opey's booking agency made money from commissions.

The success of BMI stemmed in large part from the enormous amount of country music songs that it licensed. (ASCAP, the major rival to BMI, rarely allowed country songwriters and publishers to join their organization.) The future success of BMI and the future success of country music was linked; if more stations played country music, then BMI collected more money for country music songwriters and publishers. No one from ASCAP was present during the early years of the Nashville event, giving BMI an edge in the country music market.

The Country and Western Disc Jockeys Association marked the beginning of a booster organization for country music. Although there was a close connection to the Opry— the Opry's birthday was the reason for inviting everyone to Nashville—the organization operated independently of the Opry. Five years later the organization evolved into the Country Music Association, but from 1953 to 1958 the Grand Ole Opry Birthday Celebration, known informally as the "Disc Jockey Convention," became the major convention for people involved in country music. All the top disc jockeys, talent bookers and other business people, as well as country artists, came to the event. It was a gathering of the tribes for country music and became a significant reason that Nashville served as a focal point for the country music business.

The success of the Grand Ole Opry and its booking agency helped profits grow for the National Life and Accident Insurance Company, which owned WSM and the Opry. The Opry helped insurance salesmen sell policies because, when they announced they were from "the Grand Ole Opry insurance company," doors opened for them.

CHAPTER 33

The recording industry in Nashville developed during the decade after World War II. After the war the economy was booming and local businesses needed advertisements for radio and the early recording studios provided them. There were also transcriptions to be made of the Opry and other shows and shipped across the country in an early version of syndicated programming. Publishing companies needed to demo songs and audition artists. The major labels came to provide an increasing amount of business for economic reasons: (1) it was cheaper to record the musicians in Nashville than bring them to New York; (2) the musicians union charged a lesser rate in Nashville; (3) there was a large group of talented, versatile musicians at WSM available for recording sessions.

The "Nashville Sound" developed initially during this period because a handful of musicians played on the majority of sessions. They developed a way to do sessions by ear (without written arrangements) with head arrangements (done on the spot, instead of worked out by an arranger before hand) very quickly (they could record an average of at least one master recording per hour). Since labels had to make a profit, and since individual country recordings did not usually sell in huge numbers, it was good business to cut as many costs as possible during the production so the release could recoup its money as quickly as possible.

The jukebox was a major purchaser of country records from the 1930s until the early 1980s so a major marketing strategy for labels was getting country records on jukeboxes. Publishers made the majority of their money from radio airplay through BMI and ASCAP, so Nashville publishers earned increasing income by the increased presence of country music on radio in the decade after World War II. Many of the country music publishers were based in Nashville, so the money came directly to them.

BMI was well aware of the importance of country music to their own growth as well as the amount of dollars dispersed to Nashville-based publishers. In 1955 BMI named Frances Williams (nee Preston) to run their office from her home, sign songwriters and take care of publishers. In 1955 business was great and getting better for country music in Nashville.

A problem evolved from the Opry's domination of the country music industry in Nashville: some executives connected with the Opry established their own businesses on the side and were reaping financial benefits from the Opry connection. There was bickering amongst individuals, envy and jealousy--mostly over outside income and personal power that transcended the corporation. This all led to the most important memo in the history of country music.

In that memo, dated August 2, 1955, WSM president Jack DeWitt confronted his staff about their outside activities and told them "It will be necessary to review all of these businesses, and in some cases require that they be terminated in the interest of harmony within our organization." DeWitt was concerned about the ethical questions of WSM employees having outside business interests in conflict with WSM's business; there was also the danger of WSM losing their broadcast license from this activity. The Board of Directors of National Life agreed with DeWitt. The major problem was Jim Denny, who had grown too rich and powerful to be ignored and who refused to divest himself of Cedarwood, a music publishing company and one of his outside interests. Roy Acuff began the final series of events when he complained to DeWitt about Denny giving him lesser bookings due to the power struggle between Acuff and Denny. Each had competing publishing companies and Denny pushed Opry artists to record songs from his firm. Acuff eventually won that battle, but Denny may have won a bigger victory.

The ultimatum from DeWitt caused several history-making decisions. First, the WSM engineers closed down Castle Recording Studios; the engineers wanted to be involved in the new medium of television. This meant that Owen Bradley's recording studio had a lot of new business. Bradley's studio was the first to be located in the area that became known as Music Row. The reasons were financial. Property values were low there and the area had been zoned for "commercial" so Bradley took advantage of this situation. Bradley purchased an old home and a Quonset Hut, which was erected behind the house. Bradley emerged with a major recording studio, which attracted business from record labels and the studio attracted publishers and songwriters. The old center for the music business had been downtown Nashville on Seventh Avenue near the headquarters of WSM and National Life as well as two streets over on Fifth where the Ryman was located. The new center for business was in the area which became known as "Music Row" where Bradley had his studio.

CHAPTER 34

The years 1957-1962 may be considered the "wilderness years" for Eddy Arnold. But, like Winston Churchill's "wilderness years," they were deceptively busy and laid the groundwork for a successful future. Eddy Arnold had always been a man with an enormous amount of energy, always busy, working hard on his career. During this period he tended to devote most of his energies to his businesses and outside investments, away from the spotlight.

In the decade after his first record was released, Eddy Arnold had an amazing batting average with chart records: 66 out of 68 of his releases landed in the top ten on the country music charts in *Billboard*. Both of those that missed the top ten made it to number 12; one was a Christmas song, "Christmas Can't Be Far Away" in 1954 and the other was "Don't Forget" in 1955. During 1955 Arnold had ten songs on the country charts--nine of them in the top ten and two of them number ones. The year 1956 began with a top ten song, "Trouble in Mind," then the next, "Casey Jones (The Brave Engineer)" only made it to 15. The following number, one of Arnold's most memorable ballads, "You Don't Know Me" made it to number ten. That meant he had only three chart singles in 1956.

In 1957 Eddy Arnold had one chart record, a remake of "Gonna Find Me a Bluebird" and he had no chart records at all in 1958. In 1959 there were two chart records, including "Tennessee Stud" which landed at number five, but in 1960 he once again failed to reach the charts with any of his releases. In 1961 he had three songs on the charts--but none of them came close to being in the top ten.

In 1962 Eddy Arnold bounced back with four songs on the charts--all top tens ("Tears Broke Out on Me," "A Little Heartache," "After Loving You" and "Does He Mean That Much to You?") but in 1963 none of his three chart releases reached the top ten.

Eddy Arnold's personal appearances dropped significantly; he no longer went on tour. This was partly because the demand for country artists dropped precipitously after rock'n'roll hit. In 1956 Fort Worth reporter Bud Shrake wrote an article that summed up this problem. He stated: "The old whining hillbilly artist, who sang as if his boots were stuffed with ants and his nose with straw, is a dead item on the modern music market...a new style of music has taken over. It's hard to say what to call it, except that it's rock-and-roll by hillbilly musicians...Popular music, hillbilly and rock-and-roll have gotten all mixed up."

The drop in demand for personal appearances coincided nicely with Arnold's desire to stay home and spend time with his children. For someone who grew up without a father, he knew the importance of having a Dad around. On December 21, 1957 his daughter Jo Ann turned eleven and on January 2, 1960 his son turned eleven--the same time in Eddy Arnold's life his Dad died--and he wanted to be around to share those years.

Eddy Arnold spent time thinking about his life and career and wondered if he should hang it up as a country artist. He had made some good investments and was set for life, so there was no pressure to perform in order to buy the groceries. Sometimes he felt the music industry had passed him by; the pop-style that he loved so much just didn't seem to appeal to teen-agers and the older audience was too busy making a living to buy many records or see concerts. Radio and TV weren't very receptive to country music. Besides, he'd had ten years at the top and few performers last that long; it was hard to imagine he could ever be as successful as he had been after he passed his 40th birthday in 1958.

As much as he knew he didn't have to sing, he couldn't shake the desire to sing. He loved singing and performing; it was as much a part of him as breathing. There was something deep inside him that would not let it go, could not let it go, and so he kept recording. No matter how successful an artist is, the real reason they sing is that drive to perform. Eddy Arnold never lost that drive. No man ever forgets his first love, and singing was Eddy Arnold's first love.

He stayed before the American public through radio and television appearances. In early 1955, as RCA mounted a special promotion to celebrate Arnold's tenth anniversary with the label, NBC did a "Special" on Eddy Arnold. His half-hour show "Eddy Arnold Time" was syndicated in

1955-1956, but the show only lasted 13 episodes. In 1956 "The Eddy Arnold Show," a half hour television show on ABC began on Thursday evenings during prime time; that same year "The Eddy Arnold Show" began on the CBS radio network; this show was broadcast over 1,000 stations in the United States and Canada.

CHAPTER 35

During the mid-50s Eddy Arnold became more involved in the Nashville community, both in business and socially. In 1957 he starred in a play "School Daze" at the Ryman put on by the PTA. In 1959 he was Master of Ceremonies at a Boy Scout Banquet (his son was in the Boy Scouts). He also appeared at a Fourth of July parade in Atlanta sponsored by WSB and was involved in the Day Care Center for Emotionally Disturbed Children and the Fannie Battle Day Care Center, which provided day care for indigent working women.

In many ways his life was that of a successful local businessman: going to his office each day, home for dinner on most nights with his family, attending school and community events where his children were involved and socializing with a small group of friends and business associates.

The 1950s were the Eisenhower years and Eddy Arnold felt comfortable in those years and admired President Eisenhower a great deal. In 1939 Eisenhower--at the age of 48--defined happiness in a letter, stating "only a man that is happy in his work can be happy in his home and with his friends. Happiness in work means that its performer must know it to be worthwhile, suited to his temperament, and, finally, suited to his age, experience and capacity for performance of a high order." That description could have been written for Eddy Arnold.

Biographer Stephen Ambrose described Eisenhower's affect on the nation as "so comforting, so grandfatherly, so calm, so sure of himself, so skillful in managing the economy, so experienced in insuring America's defenses, so expert in his control of the intelligence community, so knowledgeable about the world's affairs, so nonpartisan and objective in his above-the-battle posture, so insistent on holding to the middle of the road, that he inspired a trust that was as broad and deep as that of any President since George Washington."

Clearly, Eddy Arnold agreed with the biographer's assessment of President Eisenhower. Like Eisenhower, he liked "business as usual," stuck close to a routine, and spoke and acted in moderation with a disdain for extremes. On most issues he held a moderate, middle-of-the-road stance and always sought to be flexible in his professional decisions.

Even Arnold's off-hours mirrored the President's tastes. For relaxation Eddy Arnold joined a country club, played golf, and spent time at Claude Cook's plantation in Hazelhurst, Georgia, hunting quail--all favorite activities of Eisenhower.

Always interested in politics and well-informed on national and local events, Eddy Arnold became more involved in politics through his personal friendship with Tennessee Governor Frank Clement. The two became close and Clement often invited Arnold to come over to the Governor's mansion to chat. Clement was a country music fan and liked Eddy Arnold; to a large extent, the country music community was treated well at the top levels of State government because of Clement.

In 1962 Frank Clement ran for Governor of Tennessee for a second term. At that time, the Governor was not allowed to succeed himself, so after Clement served as Governor 1953-1958, he had to sit out four years before he could run again. During the 1962 campaign Eddy Arnold (as well as a number of other country music acts) appeared with the candidate around the state and sang a few tunes, then gave his endorsement. The man who was generally Governor during the years that Clement wasn't, Buford Ellington, was also friends with Arnold and during 1962 Arnold sang at his birthday party.

Tennessee was a Democratic state at this point; there was hardly any Republican opposition. Eddy Arnold was a Republican; during the 1960 Presidential campaign he appeared with Richard Nixon in his campaign, sang a few songs and gave an endorsement. Arnold had been a Republican as long as he had voted, but since there was virtually no Republican party in the South during the 1950s and most of the 60s, Arnold befriended Democratic office holders. Besides, the conservative South was more Republican in spirit and policies than the liberal Democrats of the North. The strength of the Democratic Party in the South up through the 1960s reflected history: the Republican Party was the party of Abraham Lincoln and since the Civil War that was not a party that Southerners wanted to belong to.

On the national level, Arnold met Senate Majority Leader Lyndon Johnson in 1958 at the dedication of a television station in Temple, Texas. Arnold went as a favor for Harry Stone, who worked for the station. In October, 1959 Arnold went to the LBJ Ranch in Texas for a party for Mexican President Adolfo Lopez Mateos. Then, in July, 1961, Arnold was invited to the LBJ Ranch to entertain at a party Vice President Lyndon Johnson gave for Pakistan President Ayub Khan. That performance did not go as well as it should have; Arnold took out his guitar to play after President Khan was introduced--a victim of poor timing by Johnson--and had to sing while politicians swarmed around the Pakistani President. As soon as he finished his songs, Arnold packed his guitar and left the ranch.

Eddy Arnold also continued promotional efforts for his career. In September, 1961 he went to Chicago for the Music Operators of America convention and on October 3 went to RCA's record pressing plant in Indianapolis to honor the one billionth record pressed by the plant (it was one of Arnold's own records!)

Mostly, however, Eddy Arnold concentrated on his business ventures. He was part-owner of the minor league Nashville Vols baseball team and served as Vice President. In that role he managed to go to the World Series, attend sports banquets, training camps and baseball games.

In addition to the baseball team, Eddy Arnold was an investor in Standard Record Pressing Co. Inc., on the Board of Directors for an insurance company, and had real estate developments that included a car dealership (Frank Davis Buick), a Texaco filling station, and an ice cream drive-in in Madison. Arnold's primary interest was in real estate; he purchased land in Brentwood and began to develop it, building houses and selling them. He bought other parcels and simply held on to them, waiting for the value to increase before he sold them. Beginning in 1962 his income increased because President John Kennedy lowered the top tax rate on annual income from 90 percent to 50 percent. Increasingly, pictures showed Arnold in a suit and tie, rather than a sports coat and open-necked shirt.

In 1958 Eddy Arnold appeared on NBC's 30th Anniversary Show and during the heyday of "The Ozark Jubilee" TV show from Springfield, Missouri, he served as a guest host. Before ABC dropped the program in 1960, because host Red Foley's tax problems had landed him on the front pages, the producers asked Arnold if he wanted to take over the show; he declined. At this point the Brown Brothers had re-located to Springfield where they set up an advertising agency to work with the Springfield TV shows. Charlie Brown dropped out of the Agency to run for Congress (he was elected).

After "The Ozark Jubilee" went off the air it was difficult to find country music on television. In 1962, at a TV appearance in Detroit for the United Foundation campaign, Eddy Arnold addressed that problem, stating, "It's because most of the producers of variety shows like Ed Sullivan have never been west of the Hudson River. They think country stuff is corn. Maybe some of it is, but people love it...What those TV guys forget is that a lot of our so-called country artists are really versatile performers."

In the interview Arnold said, "I call myself a country-pop singer, and I think that's just what I am. There's some country music that I won't even sing. It has bad lyrics, bad melody. But some of it is beautiful."

He still performed occasionally and in a performance at a nightclub in Houston in early 1963 a reviewer noted that "the crowd was with him all the way." The review continued, "From the lone woman who kept calling out for 'Molly Darlin'' to the majority who spontaneously started clapping rhythmically to 'Up Above My Head,' his final number...He dipped in a folksong bag and came up with such numbers as 'John Henry' and 'Getalong Home, Cindy,' passing them out with an easy, off-hand manner. And as the evening progressed with a lilting 'After Loving You' and a lowdown 'Lovebug Itch' and an almost sophisticated 'You Don't Know Me,' he emerged in the mood of a country boy who knows the ways of the city but never has turned his back on his heritage. He toyed around a bit with the yodeling in 'Cattle Call,' sang about why he's the 'richest man in the world' with a humpbacked mule and a pond of trout, trotted out 'Molly Darlin'' and some of the others he's identified with. Maybe it was the atmosphere of the receptive audience, but Arnold, backed by the Don Cannon band, worked in an amiable, intimate manner which was most appealing."

Another review of the same show stated, "Well, it's just hard to beat Eddy Arnold, and he may easily have the most winning show in town at the Continental-Houston Hotel. Eddy is doing an early performance in a room open to the public and a late show for French Quarter members, who packed the place last night. Eddy has that old charm and grace, and he comes on singing 'The Wreck of the Old 97' and goes off singing many of his lonesome and/or happy cowboy numbers. Eddy makes you feel goooood. Whether he's singing the blues or peppy tunes. He's a happy man and his songs have a happy, pleasing lilt...this is an evening nobody should miss."

CHAPTER 36

The years 1957-1963 were also "wilderness years" for country music; frantic activity in Nashville was, in many ways, a fight for survival. Opry attendance declined and in 1957 dropped under 200,000 annually for the first time. It was also the subject of some bad press: Ernest Tubb walked into the National Life building's lobby and shot a .357 magnum, intending to shoot Jim Denny. Tubb shot at the wrong man; fortunately, nobody was hit but Tubb was arrested and charged with public drunkenness.

In 1957 there were shifts in the WSM executive line-up with Irving Waugh named general manager of the TV station while Robert Evans Cooper was named head of the radio station, in charge of the Opry, while Dee Kilpatrick remained as the Opry's manager. Also in 1957 the "Friday Night Frolics" were moved to the Ryman Auditorium from the WSM studios and renamed the "Friday Night Opry."

The Opry had lost its unchallenged hold on Nashville's country music industry. During the decade after World War II (1946-1956) the Opry dominated the Nashville country music industry, but during the following decade a number of major record labels, independent and corporate publishing companies and local booking agencies emerged to dominate the industry. Although the Opry remained important, it could no longer make or break an artist by admitting or denying them membership in the Opry. Increasingly, it was a recording contract with a major label that determined an artists viability. With the advent of television, people listened less to live radio programs on Saturday night. They continued to listen to radio but they wanted to hear records by top artists on their local station.

For the country music industry in Nashville, the most important thing that happened was the formation of the Country Music Association in 1958. This organization became the Chamber of Commerce for country music, serving as a booster organization for the entire industry, although Nashville, home of the CMA, benefited directly as well.

At the end of 1957 some country music executives met at a music industry convention in Miami, Florida. There were internal problems within the disc jockey organization and its future was in doubt. At the same time, several country music executives wanted it to have a broader appeal--not just disc jockeys--and wanted more control and say-so. They envisioned a booster organization to help the industry, which was in horrible condition throughout 1957 because of the popularity of rock"n'roll.

Several key executives took the lead: Connie B. Gay, a Washington, D.C. based radio station owner and concert promoter, Wesley Rose of Acuff-Rose, Opry manager Dee Kilpatrick, booking agent Hubert Long, and Jack Stapp, owner of Tree Publishing. The Country Music Association was formed and set up in a two-room office in downtown Nashville towards in the end of 1958 with a desk and typewriter borrowed from Hubert Long. Long also allowed the address machine at his booking agency to be used for CMA business. For mailings and memos, Wesley Rose donated Acuff-Rose's services.

In November, 1958 the young organization held its first Board meeting at the Noel Hotel and elected Connie B. Gay president and Wesley Rose Chairman of the Board. In December, the organization hired Jo Walker as office manager. Early in 1959 they hired Harry Stone to be Executive Director. After Stone was hired he was surprised to find there was no money, only 233 members and that his job would essentially consist of fund-raising. Stone didn't work out and within a year he was gone. Walker continued to serve as office manager until 1961 when she was given the title "Executive Director."

The CMA established the Country Music Hall of Fame and elected its first members--Jimmie Rodgers, Fred Rose and Hank Williams--in 1961. Since there was no building to house the Hall of Fame the plaques were displayed at the Tennessee State Museum. The organization continued to struggle because of lack of money but those involved were determined and dedicated. Frances Williams with BMI (she became Frances Preston in 1962 when she married), also became heavily involved in the CMA. She had worked as a receptionist at WSM from 1948 until she was hired by BMI to recruit writers and publishers in 1955. Williams worked out of her home until 1958 when she established the first BMI office in the L & C Tower in downtown Nashville.

Since the roots for the CMA were in the disc jockey organization--and a number of the CMA's founders came out of the broadcasting industry--they were aware that the essential problem facing them was getting country music exposed on radio. That had become increasingly difficult after Elvis Presley and rock'n'roll hit in 1956. They also knew the way to get radio interested was to get advertisers committed to buying time because station owners followed the money.

In 1963 the Country Music Association held its first major sales presentation for advertising executives in New York; the following year they held one in Detroit. The idea was to convince ad agencies that country music on radio was a viable buy, a good advertising medium. The advertisers were often less than enthusiastic; at one presentation the CMA gave away a Tennessee Walking Horse in order to keep the advertising executives there throughout the entire presentation. (You had to be present to win.)

The programs worked and the essential role of the CMA--marketing country music to the broadcast media--was established.

The CMA was helped in their efforts to promote country music, and, ultimately, establish Nashville as the capital of country music, by the major record labels. In 1957 Steve Sholes was named head of RCA's pop division and moved to Los Angeles. Chet Atkins, who had been the RCA representative in Nashville since 1955, assumed more duties and began producing their top act, Eddy Arnold. In 1957 RCA Victor built a studio (now known as "Historic RCA Studio B") on 17th Avenue South and established the first permanent office in Nashville by a major label.

The first country music business in that area was Bradley's Recording Studio on 16th Avenue South, which consisted of a Quonset Hut purchased from Army surplus. The Bradley brothers--Owen and Harold--established a TV studio and set up the recording studio in the basement of the adjoining house. Since TV was becoming increasingly important, the Bradleys decided to set up a studio whereby they filmed singers performing a song with the idea of providing film clips for TV programming. The idea was that TV would become radio with pictures but it didn't fly at the time, although twenty-five years later the music video industry thrived with this same, basic concept.

In 1958 Paul Cohen left Decca Records and Owen Bradley replaced him as head of the country music division. Unlike Cohen, who was based in New York, Bradley remained based in Nashville.

In 1962 Columbia Records purchased Owen Bradley's studio on 16th Avenue; by that point, it had become the major recording facility in Nashville, hosting Columbia and Decca recording artists, and this committed the CBS organization to Nashville with a spot on Music Row. Bill Denny, son of booking pioneer Jim Denny, was put in charge of the studio while Don Law, head of country music for the label, remained based in New York, although he often traveled to Nashville.

By 1958 a number of major players were in place: Owen Bradley at Decca, Chet Atkins at RCA, and Frances Preston at BMI. All of these would play a major role in country music and the CMA in the coming years.

Country music was helped along by a major trend in the nation after World War II as people increasingly moved to the suburbs. The move came from two directions: people in the city moved out while those in rural areas moved in. This shift in housing was aided by the government, which built roads out of the city for these suburbs, financed car transportation through road building and low gas taxes at the expense of public transportation, and backed low interest loans for home buyers through the Federal Home Administration and Veterans Home Administration.

The Federal government also helped the country music industry in another way. In 1956 President Eisenhower signed into law a bill creating the Interstate Highway System. The idea came out of Eisenhower's concern for the nation's defense and saw the Interstate system as a way to transport troops and weapons quickly and efficiently across the country. The money for the Interstate highway system originally came from the Defense Department but the Interstate system did more than just help the Armed Forces, it changed America by linking long distances with dual lane roads. This helped the creation of the suburbs and gave a boost to the tourism industry because people increasingly drove long distances on vacations. The Interstate travelers needed places to eat and sleep and this gave rise to the motel and fast food industries, which developed chains situated along interstates.

The country music industry benefitted directly from the Interstates because performers could travel longer distances faster and thus personal appearances increased. They could travel on the wide Interstates with large buses, custom fitted for sleeping and traveling, making it possible for country artists to stay on the road for longer periods of time in relative comfort. Prior to Interstate highways, country performers traveled two-lane roads in cars with performers arriving at their appearances tired from having to sleep sitting up. There was a limited amount of space available for equipment--a trailer and trunk could only hold so much--but the large buses had more storage space available for stage costumes and bigger and better equipment.

In its November 14, 1960 issue, *Time* magazine published an article, "Hoedown on a Harpischord" about country music that stated "Its demise has often seemed near, but it is now going stronger than ever, and Nashville has even nosed out Hollywood as the nation's second biggest (after New York) record-producing center." It noted that "One out of every five popular hits of the past year was written and recorded in Nashville" and, discussing the "Nashville Sound," observed, "As nearly as anybody can define it, the Sound is the byproduct of musical illiteracy."

The term "Nashville Sound" as a synonym for country music was popularized by this article. From this point forward the media regularly used the term "Nashville Sound" in discussing country music and this term held a built-in promotion for Nashville as the center of country music. Coupled with the efforts of the Country Music Association, Nashville and country music increasingly became inseparable in the minds of the followers of country music.

CHAPTER 37

For many Americans, the era known as "the Sixties" began on November 22, 1963 in Dallas, Texas when President John F. Kennedy was assassinated. On that Friday, Eddy Arnold was in his home in south Nashville when he heard the news. Just six months earlier, in May, President Kennedy had visited Nashville and crowds lined the streets, cheering him.

It had been a difficult year for country music, a entire year marked by death. In March there were three separate major tragedies: on the fifth, country stars Patsy Cline, Hawkshaw Hawkins and Cowboy Copas, along with Cline's manager Randy Hughes, were killed in a plane crash. A few days later, on the eighth, Jack Anglin, of the group Johnny and Jack, was killed in an automobile accident while on his way to the funeral of the plane crash victims. Then, on the twenty-ninth, Texas Ruby (Ruby Fox), wife and duet partner of Grand Ole Opry fiddler Curly Fox, died when fire swept their mobile home. In August, pioneer country music executive Jim Denny died.

The early 60s also saw the deaths of country stars Johnny Horton (1960) and Jim Reeves, who was killed in a plane crash at the end of July, 1964. The plane went down just outside of Nashville in Brentwood, near Eddy Arnold's home, and a number of country stars, including Arnold, joined in the search. Finally, the wreckage was found and Arnold identified the body.

On February 9, 1964 a new era in American music began when the Beatles appeared on "The Ed Sullivan Show," launching "Beatlemania" throughout the nation. The youngest Baby Boomers (those born in 1946) were turning 18 and had to register with the Selective Service for the Draft. The Draft had not reached a confrontational crisis at this point; the Cuban Missile Crisis in October, 1962 and President Kennedy's speech at the Berlin Wall in June, 1963 made the threat of Communism even more palpable and real. There wasn't much news about the tiny Southeast Asian country of Vietnam but those who did follow the news of that region knew there was trouble brewing; on November 2, just three weeks before Kennedy's death, South Vietnamese Premier Ngo Dinh Diem and his brother Nhu were murdered by military leaders.

When the Beatles appeared in America they brought a message of individualism and questioning authority that was embraced by American Baby Boomers. During the next decade the conflict between young people coming of age and the older World War II generation escalated until there was a major chasm between generations. For the World War II generation, who fought in Europe and Japan for four years to make the world safe for democracy, it was beyond comprehension that young men would say no to military service in Vietnam. To the young men called, it was beyond comprehension that their country asked them to fight in a war they considered lacking in clear and reasonable objectives. Those conflicting views between generations split the United States for years.

Two weeks before the Beatles appeared on the Ed Sullivan Show, Eddy Arnold appeared on that same show. About the same week Arnold appeared on Ed Sullivan, singer songwriter Roger Miller went into a Nashville studio and recorded an album of wacky songs that included "Dang Me" and "Chug-a-Lug" which turned country music on its head. Roger Miller was heard on the same radio stations that played the Beatles, Motown and the Beach Boys in 1964.

Eddy Arnold had not exactly set the musical world on fire in 1963; none of his three charted singles, "Yesterday's Memories," "A Million Years or So" or "Jealous Hearted Me" made it into the top ten. Still, he signed a new five year contract with RCA Victor on September 21 which was announced by Ben Rosner, Manager of A & R for the label.

The new contract was negotiated by Eddy Arnold's new manager, Jerry Purcell, after the label considered dropping him from their roster. Eddy Arnold's career had stalled, he performed a limited amount of engagements, and his record sales had dropped, although he was still a profitable artist. Purcell went to Steve Sholes and requested a "second chance" for Arnold; Sholes agreed to re-sign the singer.

Eddy Arnold appeared on the ABC-TV show "Hootenanny" on October 12, 1963, broadcast from the

U. S. Naval Academy, and appeared on "The Ed Sullivan Show" on November 10. It was also announced at the end of 1963 that the all time top three sellers of recorded music in the history of the music business were Bing Crosby, Perry Como and Eddy Arnold.

There were, however, changes in the wind, and the first hint of those changes occurred on February 1, 1964 when Arnold's single, "Molly," recorded with The Needmore Creek Singers, entered the *Billboard* country charts and came to rest at number 5. Then, in November, 1964, "I Thank My Lucky Stars" entered the chart and reached number eight. Those two releases signaled some important events taking place in Eddy Arnold's life which led him to emerge with a "new" career.

Joe Csida, who had been Arnold's manager since 1954, took a job with a record label and had to relinquish his management company; he handed Arnold over to Gerald Purcell, manager of RCA Victor act Al Hirt. Purcell began working with Arnold in 1963 and on June 6, 1964 there was an announcement in the trade press that Arnold had signed a management contract with Gerald Purcell and Associates. In truth, there was no contract, just a handshake agreement, but Eddy Arnold's handshake was always a solid commitment.

Csida initially did not want to give up management of Arnold and told Purcell the singer would probably retire. Purcell had known Arnold from their mutual association with RCA and liked him. He was not interested in Csida's other acts--a singer and disk jockey--but decided to work with Arnold. It marked a major change in the business side of Eddy Arnold's career.

One of the keys to the success of any artist is good management and this was certainly true of Eddy Arnold. Tom Parker did a remarkable job getting Arnold money and exposure from 1945 to 1953 but from 1954 to 1963 Arnold floundered in his career. This was partly the result in shifting musical trends and tastes and partly from Arnold's desire to stay home with his family while his children were young. He also did not have a Tom Parker or Jerry Purcell working on his career.

Arnold always acquired management outside Nashville. Even though Parker moved to Nashville in the late 1940s, he was always an outsider with connections in Los Angeles and New York. Csida was a New Yorker and so was Purcell; all of those managers represented Eddy Arnold's desire to transcend the image of Nashville and country music as a backwards place. Purcell grasped this quickly and wanted Arnold to change his look and pursue new avenues in his performances by moving him "uptown."

The sound of Eddy Arnold had been changing and developing since he recorded "I Really Don't Want to Know" in 1954. During his first decade recording for RCA Victor, Arnold was marketed as a traditional country act with a smooth voice and manner. In the late 1940s and early 1950s the honky tonk sound dominated country music; this was the heyday of Hank Williams, Lefty Frizzell, Webb

Pierce and Faron Young. Arnold's material wasn't much different from those singers (in fact, he recorded some of the same songs they did) but his delivery was different. Arnold was blessed with a smoother voice than the classic honky tonkers. Since he did not have the harsh country vocals of a Hank Williams or Webb Pierce, he developed his vocal abilities by increasingly picking ballads and pop-oriented type songs. Further, Arnold regularly appeared on network shows--on radio and television--and grew comfortable in the larger pop music world.

Arnold recorded with Hugo Winterhalter's orchestra in 1955 and continued to record with string sections supplementing the basic country rhythm section of guitar, bass, piano and drums. He dropped the fiddle and steel guitar sound and adopted the background vocal accompaniment of two male and two female voices (usually the Anita Kerr Singers) who were part of the emerging "Nashville Sound."

The material Arnold recorded was often a grab bag; sometimes producer Chet Atkins found new songs, sometimes Arnold recorded hits from other singers from the country as well as pop fields, or sometimes a publisher sent a song to him that he liked. In the Fall of 1963 he recorded an album of folk songs, trying to capitalize on the "folk boom" by doing songs like "Where Have All the Flowers Gone," "Green, Green," "Cotton Fields" and "Blowin' in the Wind." Arnold never liked the rock songs of the 1955-1959 period; he thought there was a lot of beat but the lyrics were silly and meaningless. He always loved a good lyric, a song that carried a message, although the message of the folk movement in the early 1960s wasn't always in line with Arnold's conservative political beliefs. Still, a lot of the songs had a good melody and the lyrics conveyed a feeling. Unfortunately, Arnold picked the wrong time to get on the folk bandwagon; by the time he recorded this album, called *The Folk Songs of Eddy Arnold*, Bob Dylan had gone electric at Newport, the Beatles had hit America and folk rock was about to explode.

Arnold's folk album was not mere exploitation of a current craze in the music business. Back when he started recording, what became known as "country" music was called "folk" and he recorded his first album of folk songs in 1955. In the ensuing years he recorded a number of other folk songs and always performed folk songs during his live appearances.

The folk music of the early 1960s was a different breed than the folk tunes that Arnold grew up with. First, the folk songs of the early 1960s could more accurately be labeled "acoustic" rather than "folk" because they were often written by contemporary performers and recorded with acoustic instruments. Next, those songs were increasingly political— or the performers were political--and the politics were often left wing protest politics, which ran counter to Arnold's conservatism. Arnold's folk album became a transitional album for him, lost in the shuffle of shifting musical tastes and trends from a number of directions in pop music, country music, and the music of Arnold himself.

In the meantime, Arnold continued to record with string sections, although that sound didn't quite fit with the Bakersfield sound of Buck Owens who, along with Roger Miller, had the hottest new sound on country radio throughout 1964.

CHAPTER 38

During the early 1960s Eddy Arnold kept recording, hoping for hits and continued record sales, and wondered how he could reach an audience that fit him, one he was comfortable with. The left-wing folkie crowd certainly wasn't it, although he knew their old songs. Rock'n'roll was just too far removed from him; he couldn't even relate to that young crowd. It was just as well--his voice didn't fit rock'n'roll anyway and the Baby Boom teenagers couldn't relate to him, either.

The country sound of Buck Owens, with its driving, honky tonk beat, wasn't him, although Arnold's musical roots went back to that sound. He couldn't see himself singing behind a walking bass, searing steel guitar and nik nik news fiddle again. He knew there must be an audience of people like himself: moving into middle age, with tastes for a softer, smoother music, but he just didn't know exactly how to reach them. He knew he liked the Nashville Sound and the new attitude of Nashville, taking country music into the cities and showing people that those in country music could be as intelligent and sophisticated as anyone else. Like many others in the Nashville country music industry, he intensely disliked the image of country singers as hicks, hillbillies and hayseeds that many in big cities--especially New York and

Los Angles--associated with that field. He wanted that image tossed aside and replaced with a wholesome respect for the music as well as the people who made that music. He continued to record songs that could be played on country or pop radio, songs with strings and smooth background vocals that would prove to anyone listening that the guy singing wasn't some twang town, whiney, through the nose redneck singer.

Eddy Arnold's roots were in country music and he felt an allegiance to the music; he promoted country music as a genre whenever he could. More than any other Nashville artist, by 1964 Eddy Arnold had become a spokesman for country music and Nashville.

Arnold obtained a contract promoting Eastern Airlines in 1964 that led to important visibility. The airlines sponsored a 15-minute nightly radio program entitled "The World of Folk Music" and Arnold attended the World's Fair in New York and interviewed visitors for a radio show sponsored by the airlines. He also did a series of radio promotions for the Social Security Administration.

Arnold preferred the look of a businessman when he went out in public. During one of his personal appearances in Charlotte, North Carolina a newspaper writer noted, "The singer was wearing a conservative summer suit, a light blue shirt and a tie with diagonal stripes at a luncheon. No guitar in sight."

Eddy Arnold was clearly fitting in with the image the Nashville country music community was trying to present to the world in the 1960s. It was an image designed to counteract what had been force-fed to the public by the national media in a steady diet during the twenty years since World War II.

Most articles in national publications gave grudging respect to country music, usually acknowledging that it was the music of choice for many in middle America. In the article "Country Music; Nashville Style" by Richard Marek in *McCall's* in 1961 the writer noted that country is "the most popular music in America today" although "The new sound at the Opry is less authentic country music, more akin to the popular styles of today (although not strictly pop songs)."

The observation that country music absorbed the sounds of popular music was a common one that began in the early 1960s, as the "Nashville Sound" was developed and promoted after the first rock'n'roll revolution. The simple fact is that country music has been influenced by popular music from its earliest recordings. When Fiddlin' John Carson recorded "The Little Ole Log Cabin in the Lane" in Atlanta, Georgia in June, 1923 and began what became the country recording industry, he recorded a song written by Will Shakespeare Hays for minstrel shows--the popular music of its day. And Jimmie Rodgers, the "father of Country Music" who first recorded in August, 1927 and, with the Carter Family, was most instrumental in creating the commercial country music industry, was heavily influenced by popular music and never really considered his songs "hillbilly," although he appealed primarily to rural audiences. Bob Wills was a country boy who grew up in the Jazz Age. He had a swing band with traditional country instruments but was always insulted when people confused his music with "hillbilly" music. The earliest Opry shows often began with a string band doing "There'll Be a Hot Time in the Old Town Tonight." The list can go on to performers who became popular after World War II, or even into the twenty-first century, but the point is clear: country music has never been a rural, isolated folk music dominated by British ballads collected in the mountains and passed down by oral tradition. Still, the image persisted.

CHAPTER 39

Eddy Arnold stated late in his life "I never really knew what good management was until Jerry Purcell came along." The New York-based Purcell was a major factor in Arnold's rise as the primary exemplar and spokesman for the Nashville Sound in the mid-1960s.

There were some bumps in the road. Arnold did not always agree with Purcell's decisions, but went along with them. When Joe Csida's job with the record company fell through and he decided to return to management and announced in the music trade magazines he was resuming his relationship with Eddy Arnold, it caused a problem for Arnold. Arnold decided to face it head-on and flew to New York where he met with Purcell and Csida together. "I love you both," he told them. "But I'm going to stay with Jerry." By this time, Arnold had seen some of the fruits of Purcell's efforts and caught his vision of Eddy Arnold as a pop singer. He also felt that Csida would quit managing him again if an offer came to join another record company.

In early 1965 Jerry Purcell wanted Eddy Arnold to try something new: he insisted Arnold buy two fitted tuxes and booked him on a tour where the singer was presented as a smooth, uptown "countrypolitan" singer who did concerts instead of appearances at Fairs and Rodeos. At first Arnold was skeptical and complained about the costs of the new outfits ("I could buy several good suits for this money," he told Purcell). Purcell promised to underwrite the six-city tour in April, 1965 of Cleveland, Cincinnati, Philadelphia, Chicago, Toledo and Dayton; on that tour, Arnold appeared with Roger Miller, who was the opening act and hotter than a firecracker in country as well as pop. He had swept the Grammy Awards in March that year.

The tour was a revelation to Eddy Arnold. Here it all came together--the look, the sound, the feel of what an evening of Eddy Arnold music should be. The crowds were large and enthusiastic and the entire show was a class act. This is where Eddy Arnold knew he belonged. After the tour he flew to New York and met with Jerry Purcell and they talked; Arnold admitted Purcell had been right. Purcell was pleased with the results--but all the bills hadn't been paid. He'd only won half the gamble--convincing Eddy Arnold that this is what he ought to be doing. Arnold asked how much was owed; Purcell replied "$15,000" whereupon Eddy Arnold pulled out his checkbook and wrote out a check for that amount. Now it was time to launch this new career full speed ahead.

The first step was having hit records on the charts. Not just any hit record; the sound had to be right. Although that ground was laid beginning with "I Really Don't Want to Know" in 1954, the ball really stated rolling for this new career several months before the tour. On November 11, 1964 "I Thank My Lucky Stars" entered the charts; this was a smooth, pop sounding song with the message of positive love. That became his second top ten song, reaching number eight. ("Molly" had reached number five.)

Then, on January 13, 1965 Arnold recorded a song that would be his first number one in a decade: "What's He Doing in My World." The session was recorded with a large string section--there were seven violins, a viola and a cello, led by Bill Walker--for the session that included two other songs, "What-Cha Gonna Do?" and "Laura Lee," from the Columbia picture *Major Dundee*. The song entered the charts on March 27, 1965 and lasted 25 weeks, ending at number 60 on the pop charts. This was the beginning of a string of sixteen songs that not only reached the top ten in the country charts, but also landed on the Pop charts as well.

After the success of "What's He Doing in My World" the decision was made to do an album; Eddy Arnold decided on the title, *My World* and he, along with producer Chet Atkins, set about finding songs. Arnold had heard the song "Make the World Go Away" on the radio by a female singer and liked it immediately. Purcell had also heard it performed in Las Vegas. It was written by Hank Cochran, a Nashville songwriter who had written "I Fall to Pieces" by Patsy Cline, "A Little Bitty Tear Let Me Down" for Burl Ives, and numerous others. Arnold had, in fact, recorded songs by Cochran in the past. The song was published by Nashville's Tree Publishing, and Arnold checked to see how the song had done with sales. He discovered it had sold 50,000 units as a single and felt he could do much better. At this point, he was unaware the song had previously been recorded by Ray Price and Jim Reeves. (Ray Price's version of the song had reached the top five of the *Billboard* country chart.)

On June 25, 1965 Eddy Arnold recorded "Make the World Go Away." It was the second song on a four song session produced by Chet Atkins; the first song was "Mary Claire Melvina Rebecca Jane" and the last two songs were "Here Comes My Baby," a song written by Dottie and Bill West, and "You Still Got a Hold on Me" written by Merle Kilgore. At the beginning of the session "Make the World Go Away" was not viewed as a potential single, but as they listened to the playback, "It sounded mighty good," remembered Arnold, and both he and Chet Atkins began to consider the song as a single.

The session had a rhythm section of Floyd Cramer on piano and harpsichord, Grady Martin and Velma Smith on guitars, and a group of five violins, two violas and a cello arranged by Bill Walker. The Anita Kerr Singers (Anita Kerr, Dottie Dillard, Louis Nunley and Gil Wright) provided background vocals.

"Make the World Go Away" entered the country chart in *Billboard* on March 27, 1965, just before his six city tour with a new look and quickly went to number one, remaining on the charts for 25 weeks. On October 16 it entered the Hot 100 chart in *Billboard* and went to number six. This meant that from the end of March, 1965 through the rest of the year, Eddy Arnold had a major hit on American radio.

In October, the *Miami Herald* reviewed Arnold's album *My World* and stated, "This isn't country music, friends, this is a collection of ballads, love songs and mellow swingers by a top notch singer who can put voice and style on the line with Martin, Bennett, Como, Goulet etc. and come out the winner. There's not a yodel in the lot, and only a hint of the Nashville sound."

Another article discussing "What's He Doing In My World" stated the record "represents the Nashville sound at its best. The title tells the whole story of the song... The Tennessee Plowboy is now wearing a tuxedo, doing guest-shots on network TV shows and night club dates. It's a far cry from appearing at country fairs and rodeos, and Eddy loves it. Some of his old died-in-the-wool fans resent his departure from straight country music, but for everyone who does, Eddy has gained a dozen new fans. After 20 years he has been 'discovered' by thousands of youngsters."

CHAPTER 40

In 1964 *Time* published a major article titled "Country Music: The Nashville Sound" that attempted to define the Nashville Sound by stating, "More than the drawling, sow-belly accents and nasal intonations of the singers, it is the background music provided by the sidemen on twangy electric guitars." Despite the cynicism, there was a point to be made in *Time's* observation.

In terms of the actual "sound," it was created by a relatively small group of musicians (known as "The A Team") who performed together day after day in Nashville studios, creating most of the recordings that came out of Nashville. Many of those musicians may have been musically illiterate in the traditional sense, but they were certainly accomplished musicians. They had the ability to learn and play almost anything quickly and well.

The key instrument was the acoustic rhythm guitar, played with a pick and strum, full strum (from the lower register strings down) or an up and down strum (the strings strummed from the lower register downward, then the pick coming back upwards across the high registered strings in a steady rhythm) over open chords. There was also an electric "lead" or "take off" guitar that played an instrumental riff, a variation of the melody during a break in the song, some fills and, occasionally, a rhythm. A piano, drums, bass and a six-string bass guitar were also important elements of the sound. The electric steel guitar and fiddle were involved on some sessions, as well as the harmonica, but increasingly the Nashville Sound kept the steel guitar in the background and replaced the fiddle with violins or background vocals (and sometimes both). Traditional acoustic instruments such as the mandolin, banjo and dobro were not part of the Nashville Sound. Those instruments were absorbed in bluegrass music at this point, which had continued the string band tradition in country music as commercial country music moved towards a more pop-oriented sound.

Bluegrass was loyal to its sound, which did not change and limited its appeal. Country music changed with the times; the "sound" of country music in 1965 was quite different from the sound of country music from Nashville in 1945.

Chet Atkins once reportedly jingled some coins in his pocket when asked to define the Nashville Sound. Atkins was making a point about the economics of country music--by using the same group of musicians on all the recordings and structuring the sessions as "head" sessions, or sessions where the musicians played by ear and not from sheet music, in three hour blocks of time where three or four songs were recorded--country music was economically viable. The structure of the recording process meant country music kept costs down by recording quickly and economically; since a record company only made money when a recording is sold (they received no money from radio airplay or artists personal appearances) country music did not have to sell many records in order to be profitable. So, from an economic standpoint, country music made good business sense to a record label's home office.

The Nashville Sound was more than just a musical production factory and an economic system. In a very real sense, it was an attempt by those within country music to transcend their working class roots, to better themselves, if you will, and get rid of the old stereotypes about country bumpkins and hicks and be accepted into the American middle class. The Nashville Sound embraced background vocals creating a smooth sound that softened the harsh edges of the traditional country vocals. The strings made the music more palatable to the pop audience, or at least to the audience who didn't care for the old, twangy sound of rural country musicians and their string bands. With the Nashville Sound country music discarded the fiddle in exchange for the violin; by doing this, country musicians and executives hoped to cover up their blue collar roots and escape the working class for the suburban middle class.

But it wasn't that easy. The audience for country music remained a working class audience, the artists still came primarily from the working class, and the sound of country music still had those working class elements in the lyrics that expressed the sentiments of the average, everyday working American. Long-time country fans certainly had working class roots. The executives marketing country music often did not have working class roots or, more likely, had escaped their blue collar roots. The newer executives often did not have the Great Depression and a rural background as their defining passage in life. The blue collar audience was still there and they demanded a country music that related to the working class. Buck Owens and the Bakersfield group (Merle Haggard, Bonnie Owens and Tommy Collins) provided this sound for the country audience.

What emerged from this was a conflict between a country music connected to the working class and a country music industry trying to escape (or deny) this blue collar connection. The story of country music became an effort to sign and produce artists who appealed to the traditional audience while, at the same time, signing and producing artists who were more "pop" and who, hopefully, appealed to a broad-based audience or an audience who was not blue collar working class.

Again, the story of country is essentially a struggle for respect. That struggle has been borne by artists, musicians and executives and often the visible results have been a type of country music that was intended to transcend the working class and be palatable to the broad cross section of middle class tastes.

The Nashville Sound was the most visible example of the struggle for respect by those in country music. Ironically, the one area where the Nashville Sound helped was that it closely identified country music with Nashville. Even the Buck Owens sound from Bakersfield, California became known as "Nashville West" as the image of country music increasingly centered on Nashville, Tennessee. This solidified Nashville as the capital of country music.

This dichotomy was especially apparent in the 1960s when national attention focused on "the Nashville Sound" and country music. On one hand was the smooth, pop-oriented music coming from Nashville; on the other hand, Buck Owens and the "Bakersfield sound" was having a major impact on country music. This dichotomy was also evident in the career of Eddy Arnold, who began as a "traditional" country artist but was soon accepted outside the field.

The story of Eddy Arnold is also a struggle for respect. He wanted to sing country music with dignity, wanted to achieve success and respect with middle America. This was part of the reason he pursued success in the business world, outside country music. It was also the reason he was attracted to the Nashville Sound. Finally, here was a way he could attain the respect of the entire music world with his music. In many ways, the uniting of Eddy Arnold with the Nashville Sound was a marriage made in heaven.

CHAPTER 41

January, 1965 marked Eddy Arnold's twentieth year as a recording artist for RCA Victor. In order to promote this anniversary, he scheduled a series of major media appearances. The year began with a TV appearance on the "Bell Telephone Hour" then, in February, he appeared on Danny Kaye's TV show. Back in Tennessee, his good friend Governor Frank Clement declared February "Eddy Arnold Month." In September he appeared on the "Steve Lawrence Show" on CBS and taped an appearance on "The Jimmy Dean Show." Although Eddy Arnold spent the bulk of the 1955-1963 period off the road, he kept a high visibility with the American public through TV appearances. Thus at this key point in his career, he was in demand as a guest on TV shows; in 1965 his TVQ, which measures how recognizable a person is with TV audiences, was 30--a high, respectable figure.

In addition to appearances on other performer's TV shows, Eddy Arnold had his own TV show, "Today--On the Farm." He spent a week in Chicago on WIND as a guest disc jockey, and in June was in Indianapolis to host the "Miss Indianapolis" pageant. He also had two radio shows, "Eddy Arnold Sings" and "Eddy Arnold Time."

Eddy Arnold's hits and tours led to more exposure in the media. In September an article by Wayne Trevathan in the *Sunday Courier and Press* in Evansville, Indiana was headlined "People Don't Forget Eddy." The article began by highlighting the singer's "niceness," stating "The genial entertainer has delighted the nation's country and western music audiences for more than 25 years with his mild manners, mellow baritone voice and back-on-the-farm aura surrounding him. Arnold makes himself comfortable wherever he goes and whatever happens. Although a millionaire, he can gracefully adjust to a bowl of soup at a truck stop or a plush restaurant." In the article Arnold addressed the obligations of fame, saying "They all recognize me. I autograph for everybody. I walk in and they started asking for autographs. I said, 'Well fine,' just let me order some food first. They see me, they recognize my face. And then some will think they've met me somewhere. They think I'm an old friend or an acquaintance."

Arnold discussed his career, saying "Doing an act, if a performer is any kind of a performer, and has ever given any thought to being a performer, he'll have a system. Cause being a performer is a business just like any other; you strive for perfection, and if you don't you are not going to stay in the business. It takes you a long time to become a good entertainer. You don't become a good entertainer overnight. There is nothing easy about it; nothing easy." He continued, "The hardest part is conditioning yourself, learning your songs, disciplining yourself, being a gentleman, keeping your life straight." This was certainly part of the "Eddy Arnold Philosophy" of show business.

On fans coming around he said, "Without it, you'd be out of business. Now, I'd be less than honest with you if I didn't tell you I get tired of it. I only have a normal body system like anybody else and my energy runs out after awhile. Like anybody else, I get tired, sure." He concluded, "I like to work....I'm still young enough that I have enough energy that I still want to work and be productive."

Some of the old magic was back. On June 29 he was mobbed by fans in Anderson, South Carolina. In an interview there he stated, "Country and western music is current. It's modern, it's being written right now...Live audiences always seem to be after something more than just country music. There are a few still playing and singing in the old tradition. but the moderns are the ones with the big appeal now. Many radio stations which played only 'top 40' tunes and rock and roll during the last decade are now operating on a modern country format... This is giving the music a wider exposure than it has ever had before."

Perhaps the biggest surprise--and the harbinger of things to come--for Eddy Arnold occurred on December 11, 1965 when he performed with the Dallas Symphony. When the Symphony called Jerry Purcell, Arnold's manager, with the request for a booking, Purcell relayed the request to Arnold, who said over the phone "What the hell am I going to do with a Symphony?" It was one thing to put on a tux and change your image--but a 92-member Symphony seemed like a world away. Still, Arnold was flattered and intrigued and decided to do it, even though he felt a vague uneasiness about it. Somehow he felt he might be stepping a little too far out of bounds, out of his league with the symphony booking because this would be a difficult audience. Arnold met with his arranger, Bill Walker, who had been travelling with him and conducting a small string section and they decided to take their existing arrangements and "extend them out" to include a larger symphonic section. Then, he structured his Symphony show like his regular show.

On March 29, 1965 RCA Victor held the Grand Opening for its new offices and studio, next door to their old studio. The 95,000 cubic foot studio represented a million dollar investment in Nashville. Arnold, along with Chet Atkins, Owen Bradley, and Al Hirt, were there. Elvis was not there, but his gold Cadillac was parked outside. The future wasn't all bright and rosy and RCA must have wondered if it had made a mistake with its million dollars. In April it was announced that 16 percent of the Nashville staff in Nashville was let go. The problem, it seems, was that many in Nashville thought the success of "folk music" in the pop world would benefit Nashville, so a number of artists (including Eddy Arnold) recorded "folk" albums. But those were two entirely different audiences; for country music "folk" represented a return to the older, simpler times while for most young people "folk" meant a way to protest what they perceived was wrong with America. The country music crowd, in general, thought there was more right with America so the protest songs fell on deaf ears.

Eddy Arnold addressed this issue in an interview and talked about the changes in country music. He stated, "The folk thing, as we knew it a couple of years ago, is going by the wayside. I think the next thing will be modern country western music." He was making a major transition himself during this year. As "Make the World Go Away" was hitting, Arnold's current album was *Folk Song Book*.

A number of writers wrote about Nashville and the boom in country music. In an article titled "Sing a Song of 60 Million: Sound of Music Pays Cold Cash in Nashville" by Arthur Whitman in The *Commercial Appeal Mid-South Magazine* the writer stated "The noise used to be called mountain music, and it was a twangy, nasal thing that went with corn liquor, family feuding and barefoot courting. A few years back, though, Nashville image builders rechristened their musical lingo, added new sounds and lyrics, and came up with the style that's called Country and Western, known simply as C&W in the trade. Since then, the Nashville sound has come rolling down the mountains, spread to the far corners of the continent, and now is beating on distant shores. The are some 200 stations throughout the country that program it. Despite all this burgeoning acceptance, no one has yet defined just what country music is. It has roots in the songs and laments the earliest colonists brought over from 17th century England, but it has since had infusions of new vitality from almost every mode of popular music from high society jazz to lowdown blues to gospel songs. Today, it is as cosmopolitan as Rome."

The article also noted that in Nashville there were a dozen talent agencies, 26 record companies, four record pressing plants, 265 music publishers. Ten major record companies had recording studios, Decca and RCA Victor had both recently expanded their facilities, and it was estimated that over 5,000 people were connected to the country music industry.

By the end of 1965 it was obvious that the "Nashville Sound" was changing country music. In an interview with the *Gary (Indiana) Post Tribune* at the end of 1965 Arnold stated, "The wholesome, melodic appeal of country-western songs is unchanging. But the By-Cracky-My-Aunt-Millie-wanted-me to play this here song bit went out with bib overalls."

Eddy Arnold was certainly leading by example. Another interview with him concluded, "That's how Arnold is, easy-going, impeccably honest and thoroughly appreciative of other people. They are unique qualities to find in a show business personality. But then, Arnold is pretty unique, as his 40 million records testify."

CHAPTER 42

In 1966 the city of Nashville cranked up to firmly establish itself as the capital of country music. Mayor Beverly Briley donated city owned land at the corner of Division and 16th Avenue that had formerly been a park for construction of the Country Music Hall of Fame. A fund raising committee comprised of Andrew Benedict (chair), Ed Shea of the Chamber of Commerce, businessmen Harry Sadler, C.A. Craig II, Fred Harvey Jr, Owen Bradley and Bill Denny set out to raise $350,000 to build the Hall of Fame. This was announced in March, 1966. The Governor at the time was Frank Clement, an avid country music fan, and the business community in Nashville had clearly seen the advantages of trumpeting their connection with country music.

Although a number of influential business people in Nashville saw the advantages of promoting the country music connection and the city, many of the social elite preferred to think of Nashville as "the Athens of the South" and wished country music would just go away. That street ran both ways; if the Nashville social "establishment" looked down their noses at the country music industry it was often because the country music crowd kept their distance from the social set types. Neither felt totally comfortable with the other, although city leaders knew the importance of country music-

-and cultivated the country music business--while some key country music executives made it a point to join mainstream business leaders. (Owen Bradley was elected to the Board of Directors for the Nashville Chamber of Commerce.) In an interview, Chet Atkins stated "People down here now are accepting us because of profits and national image. Those of us who belong to the country club or the boat club have a social life that includes people from other walks of life. But in the main, the music people stick to their own."

Chet Atkins belonged to the Hillwood Country Club, not the old money Belle Meade Country Club; they had turned him away.

Eddy Arnold was the focus of articles on the Nashville Sound and Country Music and had to endure the slurs and indignities of the country hayseed stereotype. In an article on Nashville and country music from a New York publication, it stated. "Riding its crest, like a surfer heading for the sand, is a 48-year-old reconstructed Tennessee farm boy named Eddy Arnold who is becoming as familiar a figure on network television as he once was on the corn circuit of barn dances, plowing contests and country fairs. But as Northerners have reconsidered their distaste for country music, Arnold has moved a little away from the farm in recent years. Pure country music is all right for the home folk, he says, but he needs to capture what he calls 'the masses' with the 'modern country sound,' and even at that he still inserts among his upbeat songs of the sod a few that Northerners can recognize such as show tunes and popular ballads."

The article then quoted Arnold this way: "'Ih'm getttin' what Ih wont,' he said recently in a soft Tennessee voice. 'Ih'm sellin' to the masses, and that's what Ih wont. Some of myh kuntreh boih friends put me down for that. But Ih'm not tryin' t'be a slick pop singer, but neither 'm Ih uh tywangy kuntre boih.'" Anyone who knew Eddy Arnold--or heard him speak--knew he never talked like that. Yes, he had a southern accent, but he spoke well, clearly and enunciated his words. Still, the New York writer wanted to make him sound like some sort of Southern redneck to fit his own perception of country music performers. Arnold did not complain publicly about those articles, believing that, in the long run, the exposure helped him and country music. But privately he fumed. This was not the image he wanted to create, and he worked hard to educate himself beyond his country boy background. It was an insult to be profiled this way, but Arnold, as always, remained a gentleman in public and let this slide.

Eddy Arnold fared much better when writers came to his concerts and reviewed them. In those concert reviews, writers often noted his "smoothness" and uptown sound. From a concert in Hartford, Connecticut, the review stated, "Showing real versatility--and a range from a whisper to a clear call that kept the sound man busy--Arnold went from 'Dear Heart' to 'Lonesome Me' then slipped into 'Hello Dolly' with all the brass anyone could want." A review of his show in Providence, Rhode Island, where Arnold closed the show after performances by Jim Ed Brown, Dottie West and Don Bowman, stated, "Arnold is one of the few, if not the only performer in his field who has the ability to relax an audience and make it concentrate on two things--the music and Eddy Arnold. In a way, it's amazing, for he sings simple songs simply and to simple people. What is not so amazing is the fact that he has the knack to turn a sentimental program into a crying good time."

Eddy Arnold never denied his country roots. In an interview with Stephen E. Rubin of the UPI news service, Arnold stated, "You know, you can't deny your background. I'm a man that likes to be honest in whatever I'm involved in. And that is my background, that is where I came from. No, I don't live in the country now. I live in the suburbs of a city and I enjoy the life and comforts that anybody else manages to have--read books and see shows and wear shoes and all those things. So, now I'm not a country boy, but that was my background and that was where I came from."

In that same interview, he talked about the changes in his music. He said, "I've changed the background, added a string orchestra, which I wanted to do. I wanted to broaden my appeal. I never wanted to desert the country field, and I will not. But I wanted to broaden my base. I wanted my style and my image to be enjoyed and accepted by a broader segment of the people."

When the reporter asked if success had "gone to his head" Arnold answered, "I'm sure some of it has. I'm a proud man. I came from parents that were very poor, but very proud...I have a fear of winding up broke, and that's what's made me somewhat of a conservative. I like to conserve and invest what I earn. ...I guess you're proud of what you've accomplished."

Not all country fans liked the Nashville Sound and the trend towards making country music more pop-oriented. Some fans liked the hard core honky tonk sound and believed country music should stick with those roots and that sound. So there was a backlash amongst country fans over the smooth "Nashville Sound" and particularly Eddy Arnold. From Arnold's vantage point, it was something he had to do; after all, his smoother sound had proven its appeal with huge record sales and large concert audiences.

In an interview, Arnold told *New York Sunday News* writer John Patrick, "This may make the purists mad but I figure for every purist I lose, I gain five other fans who like country music the modern way. Actually, I don't think I have lost too many people because even though I've modernized to reach the pop market, I still keep my songs simple."

Despite the criticisms, Eddy Arnold's moves into the pop world worked, and more and more people saw the fruits of those efforts. In an article in the trade magazine *Record World* by Doug McClelland, the writer stated, "Arnold [has] proved himself without peer in country or pop fields. He is not only an artistic marvel with a voice that actually has improved with the years, but a music phenomenon who has managed to retain the loyalty of his initial following while firmly establishing himself in areas of the globe where moonshine means something to hold hands in while listening to Eddy Arnold recordings."

CHAPTER 43

Ninety sixty-six was a landmark year for Eddy Arnold for three reasons: (1) he made his first trip to England and had his first international hit when "Make the World Go Away" became a hit there; (2) he performed at Carnegie Hall in New York; and (3) he was elected to the Country Music Hall of Fame.

Eddy Arnold made his first trip to England with his manager, Jerry Purcell when the two went over to lay the groundwork for personal appearances and discuss the release of "Make the World Go Away" with RCA's London office. Arnold and Purcell were frustrated that the RCA executive in London insisted on releasing another song that he owned publishing rights to instead of the American hit. Arnold and Purcell were adamant that "Make the World Go Away" be released and finally prevailed. He returned in January, 1966 to promote the record, whose sales had stalled at 6,000 copies. Because of his shows and media appearances the record sold 300,000 copies.

In the small country of England, Arnold was surprised that several select appearances in the media could blanket the entire country. Talking about his trip, Arnold stated, "I came to England…without knowing what the scene was. For instance in the States every city has at least five or six radio stations and at some places I have to do at least fifteen radio interviews. I did a couple of BBC shows, and an interview with Radio London over here--I thought that was because nobody wanted to know about me. When I arrived in Manchester for "Scene at 6:30" I assumed I would be interviewed by at least six radio stations, because of Manchester's population. When I was told that the BBC covered all of Britain and all you had to do was one interview for the whole country I was delighted." He stayed at the Mayfair Hotel in London and charmed everyone around. By March 9, "Make the World Go Away" was number nine in Great Britain, behind "19th Nervous Breakdown" by the Rolling Stones, "These Boots are Made For Walkin'" by Nancy Sinatra, "A Groovy Kind of Love" by the Mindbenders, "My Love" by Petula Clark and "Barbara Ann" by the Beach Boys.

Country music was receiving a good amount of international exposure: Jim Ed Brown, Marion Worth, LeRoy Van Dyke, George Hamilton IV, Bill Carlisle, Ernie Ashworth, Billy Walker, Roy Acuff and Roy Drusky all had international tours, mostly arranged through the USO for military bases. Most of the tours were in Europe to German military bases, although Roy Acuff visited Viet Nam and Korea.

As a follow-up to "Make the World Go Away," Arnold recorded "I Want to Go With You," written by the same writer, Hank Cochran. The session, on October 25, 1965, was produced by Chet Atkins in Nashville and featured the rhythm section of Floyd Cramer on piano, Ray Edenton, Jerry

Kennedy and Wayne Moss on guitars, Henry Strzelecki on bass and Buddy Harman on drums, along with five violins, two violas and one cello, led by Bill Walker. There were also four background singers—Gil Wright, Louis Nunley, Dottie Dillard and Millie Kirkham. Arnold recorded that song on the first of three straight days of recordings to put together a single and album to follow "Make the World Go Away" and the album *My World*, both of which had achieved "Gold" status.

"I Want to Go With You" entered the *Billboard* country chart on February 12, 1966 and rose to number one, going up to 36 on the pop charts in *Billboard*. It was also released in England in time for Arnold's second 1966 appearance in that country and a two week tour. The song has the same big ballad feel as "Make the World Go Away" and sounds remarkably similar, a fact that did not go unnoticed by one British reviewer who compared "I Want to Go With You" to "Make the World Go Away" and said the former "possesses the same kind of basic simplicity of melody and charm that characterized his first big British hit."

On Monday, May 30, Arnold landed in London and that first day recorded a half hour show for the BBC Light Programme. On Thursday, June 2 he appeared on the television show, "Top of the Pops," and performed concerts in England and Scotland. The tour lasted two weeks and gave Arnold a lot of exposure. He also picked up a "Silver Disc" for "Make the World Go Away."

In England Arnold mimed his records on Radio Caroline's Saturday night dance at Wimbledon Palace, appeared at

London's Marquee Club, on the BBC's "Light Programme" and several other TV programs. He also did a number of interviews, including one with the Daily Sketch where the writer noted he "refused to disclose his age, but did admit to being a millionaire." At this point, Eddy Arnold had just turned 48 in a time when young record buyers were advised to not trust anyone over 30. This was probably the reason that one of his bios during this time had his birth date listed as 1928, ten years after he was actually born.

The scruffy, long-haired look was in vogue, a sharp contrast to Eddy Arnold's clean cut conservative image. In an interview later that year Arnold admitted he was "slightly puzzled by his ability to get through to young people in an era which features 'kooky' types," although he had come to the conclusion that "the present set of teen-agers is probably not as different from youngsters of yesteryear as we're inclined to fear." Arnold noted "There's a vast majority of fine young people in our country. Maybe they're a little more sophisticated than they used to be but that seems perfectly normal in view of a world of astronauts and rockets." The writer noted that "the only lament Eddy makes about the young male singers today is that many of the long-haired variety too often look like their locks could do with a good shampooing. 'I'm almost resigned to fellows wearing long hair,' said Arnold, 'but just a little soap and water would add a lot to their appeal, to my way of thinking.'"

CHAPTER 44

A highlight in Eddy Arnold's life came on February 14, 1966 when he and Sally were invited to the White House by President Lyndon Johnson for a State Dinner. It was especially meaningful to Arnold because "I didn't have to sing for my supper."

The dinner was given for Haile Selassie, Emperor of Ethiopia and scheduled for 8 o'clock that evening. A little snafu caused considerable consternation for the Arnolds as they headed to the dinner. Outside their hotel room, the Arnold's pushed the elevator button and waited. And waited and waited and waited. A phone call confirmed that the elevators were out of order--and the Arnolds were on the ninth floor. There was nothing to do but race down nine flights of steps in formal evening wear.

Eddy Arnold--who hated to be late or for others to be late--was in a turmoil. By the time they reached the East entrance of the White House, President and Mrs. Johnson had already received the Emperor in the Oval Room, colors had been presented at the foot of the stairs, and guests were being received in the East Room as the United States Marine Band played. As they waited to be received, Eddy Arnold looked at his wife and said, "It's a long way from Chester County!" That line provided the title for his autobiography, which was published several years later.

Eddy and Sally Arnold were not seated together at the White House dinner. There were only 140 guests and they were seated ten to a table where they dined on roast filet of beef, Duchess potatoes, asparagus and a salad. After dinner entertainment was provided by Metropolitan opera singers Richard Tucker, tenor, and Nedda Casei, mezzo-soprano. Arnold sat with Benny Goodman and Hubert Humphrey, who barely acknowledged Arnold; instead the Vice-President spent the evening talking with Benny Goodman. This became another reason Arnold did not particularly care for Hubert Humphrey.

Eddy Arnold began 1966 by doing a concert with the Phoenix Symphony and clearly enjoyed his new audience, new image and big hits. In February and March he was the spokesman for RCA's sales campaign, "Welcome to the Wild World of Country Music" that sought to capitalize on the renewed interest in country music and the success of the "Nashville Sound." Then, on May 19, 1966 he achieved a pinnacle in his career when he did a concert at Carnegie Hall in New York. Here was country music in the Big Apple, packing a crowd of urban sophisticates with a kind of music that many in the New York media looked down their noses at. He even charmed the critics.

In a review of the Carnegie Hall concert in the *New York Times*, noted critic Robert Shelton wrote, "Whether done in an intimate, personal fashion, or with a sweeping theatrical projection, Mr. Arnold was a sure-footed, expressive interpreter. He showed much of the unpressured crooning and relaxed phrasing that have made him such a long-standing favorite with listeners."

A long review in Time magazine noted, "What was a li'l ole country boy doing in a big fancy place like that?" It quoted Arnold saying "This is the fulfillment of a lifetime dream" and stated he was "all fancied up in a tuxedo and string tie" with "a mellifluous baritone that poured out just as warm and creamy as milk fresh out of the barn cow." According to the review, Eddy Arnold possessed "a broad, half-moon smile and an ultra-relaxed manner that could charm the warts off a hog's back" and noted that the appearance "marked a new era for country music. A few years ago, any country crooner billing himself as 'The Tennessee Plowboy' would have been run out of most Northern cities. But now, in an age of shifting population, country music has penetrated the metropolis in a big way."

"Arnold has never gone in for the spangled Western getups, nasal mewings and twangy guitars that have made country music so tiresome," said the reviewer. "He is more the Country Como, a slightly citified slicker in sports shirt and slacks, singing to arrangements laced with violins and a generally humming chorus." The article then quoted Arnold saying about the "new" country music, "Once we cut out all the by-cracky nonsense and give respect to our music, then people will respect us."

The following night Arnold performed at the Brooklyn Academy of Music and won over those fans as well, performing a song set that included "Wreck of the Old 97," "Make the World Go Away," "Love Bug Itch," "Cotton Fields," "Dear Heart," "Richest Man," "Tennessee Stud" and "Cattle Call."

In March, Roger Miller swept the Grammy Awards for country music, winning six with his hit "King of the Road" leading the way. In fact, the only country Grammy Miller did not win was for "Female Vocalist," and that was won by Jody Miller (no relation) whose hit, "Queen of the House," was an "answer" song to Roger's "King of the Road." The event was held in four cities: Los Angeles, New York, Chicago and Nashville. The Nashville Grammy's were held at the Hillwood Country Club.

Eddy Arnold was there, hosting the event as President of the Nashville office of NARAS. His album, *My World* had been nominated for a Grammy but lost out in the Roger Miller sweep. The previous fall he recorded one of Miller's songs, the ballad "The Last Word in Lonesome Is Me," which was on the "B" side of Miller's hit, "England Swings." This became his follow-up to "I Want to Go With You," entered the *Billboard* country chart on May 14, and rose to number two and number 40 on the pop chart. In July he released "The Tip of My Fingers," which reached number one on the country chart, and then in October released "Somebody Like Me," a peppy, up tempo number after five straight ballads, that reached the number one position on the country chart.

CHAPTER 45

The greatest honor of Eddy Arnold's life came on Friday evening, October 21, 1966 when he was inducted into the Country Music Hall of Fame.

The induction came during the week-long "Disk Jockey Convention" held in Nashville. On October 19 the *Billboard* Country Awards were presented and Arnold received "Favorite Male Vocalist." Arnold caught the flu that week and did not plan to attend the CMA Banquet and Dance that Friday evening. In fact, he cancelled plans earlier that day to attend a football game at Battle Ground Academy where his son played on the football team. Instead, he stayed home in bed and would have remained there except his manager, Jerry Purcell, called and insisted he get out and come down to the Municipal Auditorium and accept an award from *Cashbox* magazine. It was a ruse designed to make sure Eddy Arnold was there to receive his Hall of Fame honor.

When Eddy Arnold's name was announced by Hal Cook, the CMA Board Chairman, the singer, wearing a grey suit and striped tie, came forward and said, "It's a long road. I'm delighted to be here." He cried openly and held hands with Sally in front of the audience of 1,150 as the applause engulfed them. When the applause subsided Arnold said, "Could we go now?" Even this great honor couldn't overcome the flu bug so Arnold skipped the dance afterward and headed back home to bed.

Eddy Arnold was one of four inducted that evening into the Country Music Hall of Fame. The others were Judge George D. Hay, who could not attend, and two who were deceased: Uncle Dave Macon and Jim Denny.

By the end of 1966 Eddy Arnold had marked a lot of milestones. In addition to his trips to England, his appearance at Carnegie Hall and his induction into the Country Music Hall of Fame, he appeared several times on network television shows, had the honor of seeing RCA's one billionth record pressed be his single, "One Grain of Sand," performed a number of personal appearances, played in the Music City Pro-Celebrity Golf Invitational tournament with partner Dizzy Dean and served as the Middle Tennessee Chairman for the Red Cross Fund.

He had emerged as a country and pop superstar, but his image went beyond music. In a number of articles his role as a successful and wealthy businessman was stressed. In one article he said, "I swore to myself...that if I ever managed to make any money, I'd hang on to it."

In another interview he talked about his British trip and stated, "It's funny, you know, during my near 30 years in show business I haven't travelled all that much. That last English trip was my first and I have mainly been restricted to America and Canada. I would dearly love to travel more, see all the things I've always wanted to, meet many new people and show my son the world." He talked about his family, saying of his son,

"Dickie plays electric guitar and sings Beatles songs," adding that "I think I get on better with my boy Dickie than anyone else. He really is the greatest! I want him to come to Britain with me next time I'm over for there's so much for young people over here. All the clubs and the organizations."

He still had his television show on NBC, "Today--On the Farm," and his radio show, "Eddy Arnold Time." He noted that "I answer all my fan mail personally because I decided a long time ago that it helps sell records. If a fan writes in and asks me where he can buy a certain record, I may have to tell him I never recorded that song, but in the letter I include a list of every side I ever cut and I may even tell him which one I think he might like. Now if that fan shows my letter to a few people, I've bought myself a lot of good will and happy customers just for a few minutes of my time and a stamp."

Eddy Arnold defended his desire to make money selling records, telling a British interviewer "Heck, too many people in this line think that money and business are dirty words." It was noted by several interviewers that he was on the board of directors of insurance and air conditioning companies, owned a real estate firm, was a partner in a land development company and had been appointed by the Governor to the Tennessee Industrial Commission.

At this point he performed one week out of each month, had an annual income of over $200,000, was on Boards of three companies, owned a 400-unit apartment house, a realty company, a water utility, record pressing firm, a farm, music publishing company, and automobile agency.

He was increasingly mentioned as a candidate for political office, primarily because Tennessee Governor Frank Clement kept encouraging him to run. At the end of 1966, Clement's second term as Governor was up and Tennessee law stated a governor could not serve two succeeding terms. Buford Ellington, a Clement rival, wanted to run and Clement wanted to head him off. Clement reasoned that if he could get someone he knew and trusted--like Eddy Arnold--into the office, that would divert Bufford Ellington and Clement could easily reclaim the Governor's seat in 1970.

Arnold thought it over but decided against it. First, he disliked the rough and tumble of politics, and especially disliked that "everybody wants something from you." There would be a line of job seekers a mile long, and he'd have to turn most of them down--something he was loathe to do. Also, Clement was a Democrat and Arnold would have to switch parties and run with Clement's Democratic machine, although Arnold liked Clement's politics; it was Southern Conservatism. In July he accompanied Governor Clement to a Lion's Club convention where Clement "blasted draft card burners" to thunderous applause while Arnold served as Master of Ceremonies on "Tennessee Night" and dedicated "Tennessee Stud" to the Governor. Eddy Arnold was a dyed in the wool Republican and would not abandon his party even though, in 1966, the Republicans were at a low point after Barry Goldwater's defeat in the 1964 Presidential election.

Arnold also reasoned that he'd have to give up a lot of income and could not perform after he left office because the dignity of the office would not allow it. His wife Sally hated the idea of her husband being in politics, so he decided to stay out of the scramble for political office, but kept his interest in politics as a contributor and observer.

He also enjoyed home life and told Margaret McManus for the *Milwaukee Journal*, "I enjoy a few comforts and I'm going to enjoy a few more. I'm about to get me a new boat. I'm not what you call frugal, but I'm conservative about money. I'll spend a lot of money on my home but I've also invested a lot of money. I belong to a little syndicate back home and I told those people, right before I came up here, 'Now, that's the last I'm putting in those apartment houses. Now we're going to spend some.'"

CHAPTER 46

Eddy Arnold capped a banner year in 1967 by winning the Country Music Association's "Entertainer of the Year" award. He earned more money from appearing at Fairs than any other entertainer, appeared at the prestigious Coconut Grove nightclub in Los Angeles, starred in several Kraft Music Hall Shows, and had three major hits: "Lonely Again" and "Turn the World Around" each reached number one on the *Billboard* country chart while "Misty Blue" reached number three. A fourth single, "Here Comes Heaven," entered the charts in December, 1967 but did not reach its top position--number two--until the following year. All of those records also reached the Hot 100 Chart in *Billboard*, although none rose past the 50s.

In the world of music, 1967 was the "Summer of Love" for the rock world, the year when *Sergeant Pepper's Lonely Hearts Club Band* by the Beatles was released and the Monterey Pop Festival was held in California. In San Francisco, young people wore flowers in their hair, played music in the parks, and took Timothy Leary's advice to turn on, tune in and drop out. There was a cosmic cloud of smoke hanging in the air in the Haight-Asbury district, known as "Hippie Haven." Musically, it was a time for the Jefferson Airplane and Grateful Dead playing psychedelic long-running musical jams.

Despite the attention that rock music received--and it was indeed the music of the young generation--country music achieved a great deal of success. The liberal crowd never noticed; psychedelic sounds drowned out the Nashville Sound. But outside psychedelic circles, the combination of Eddy Arnold and the Nashville Sound won converts across the country. In Atlanta, columnist Dick Gray, reviewing an appearance of Eddy Arnold with the Atlanta Symphony, noted, "I never was much of an Eddy Arnold fan until I experienced his Atlanta performance. But he sold me---just as he's been selling millions of people around the world for many years."

A number of other critics agreed. Writer Al Freeders, in an article headlined "Country Music Makes It Out of the Backwoods" stated, "Eddy has converted a host of new listeners to uptown country music. To those who claim he has deserted country music, I say he's merely brought it out of the backwoods to show the rest of the world that it's here to stay." In a concert review from Mobile, Alabama, the writer noted, "Far more than a wailer of hillbilly lamentations or a crooner of pop songs, he is first, last and always, a showman. Born to entertain, he has the heart of a Jolson or a George Burns and, happily, a heckuva lot more voice."

In a number of interviews, Eddy Arnold defended the Nashville Sound and his move away from hard core country music. He told *Los Angeles Times* reporter John L. Scott, "I gave the traditional style a lot of thought, and decided to urbanize it into the mainstream of pop music. Pop-country has become a tremendous force in the recording medium. It always was big in rural and small town areas, but in the past few years we've been able to get it going in the big cities, too."

In another interview, Arnold pointed out that it wasn't just the music that was changing, country fans were changing as well. He told writer Rex Polier, "I got news for you, the country people are pretty well educated today. They like all kinds of music, too."

In one review, critic Dick Gray noted, "Mr. Arnold...is as down-to-earth and amiable as if he were one of us poor folks... 'I'm not a singer,' he said. 'I'm a performer...And I know how to sell.'" The notion that country singers were salesmen who "sold" a song was not a new one; Roy Acuff used this same analogy. It brought home an important part of country music: the connection with an audience. Eddy Arnold, who was comfortable in the business world, saw himself as someone who combined the world of business with the world of country music. In February, 1967 Eddy Arnold received the award of "Salesman of the Year" from the Sales and Marketing Executives of Nashville. The award was given for Arnold's "selling Tennessee" to the world through his trips to England, appearance at Carnegie Hall, and numerous network TV appearances.

If the pinnacle of the rock world was the large, outdoor concert, the top of the country music world was state and county fairs while the top of the traditional pop world was the elegant night club. Eddy Arnold hadn't performed much in either night clubs or at fairs until 1967, but that year he found both rewarding and lucrative.

Arnold avoided Fairs until the year before, when he began to perform for them. He explained, "I never played country fairs because the producers never put the stage close to the grandstand. But now they're getting smart and they're putting the stage where you can be close to the audience. I'll go in now, yes sir. If you're not close, you don't have the communication. I want to feel the presence of the audience." There was big money in fairs: in San Antonio, Eddy Arnold took home $40,000 and at the Houston Livestock Show in the Houston Astrodome he drew a crowd of 62,000 for two shows.

On TV Eddy Arnold was seen on the "Kraft Music Hall" with Perry Como, on the "Danny Kaye Show," as a guest host on "Mike Douglas," and as a replacement host for Johnny Carson on "The Tonight Show." He also continued with Symphonies, performing with those in Atlanta, Phoenix and Beaumont, Texas.

In October, Arnold performed at the Coconut Grove club in the Ambassador Hotel in Los Angeles. In the audience were Hollywood notables Pat and Shirley Boone, Judy Carne, Anjanette Comer, Omar Sharif, and Peter Duel. The reviewer noted, "He proved a hit with the celebrity-crowded audience--most of whom were surprised to see Eddy dressed as one of them. Instead of wearing western attire a la Roy Rogers, the singer donned a tuxedo with appropriate appurtenances. Didn't even wear cowboy boots."

Before performing at the Los Angeles club, he told John L. Scott of the *Los Angeles Times*, "For several years I played in small, smoke-filled joints and got to hate 'em. That's probably why I shy away from club dates now, although there are a few areas I'd like to work--Lake Tahoe for example. My personal appearances these days are mostly in the concert and state fair mediums."

He was careful with his bookings and noted, "My managers and I have always agreed that either a booking would be something I'd be proud of or forget it. No matter what the money, you can't buy back your reputation." The Coconut Grove booking proved to be something he was very proud of.

A review of the concert by Bill Libby in *Cornet* magazine stated, "Opening night at the exclusive Coconut Grove in Los Angeles: From mansions in Beverly Hills and Bel-Air, the customers came, by invitation only, in long, shiny cars... celebrities...a mink-coat-and-tuxedo crowd--plus a number of stunning starlets wearing mini-skirted evening dresses with deep, plunging necklines, frantic fans waving autograph books, and the movie-magazine photographers popping flash bulbs. The elite swept through the ornate old Ambassador Hotel lobby to the great, dark, potted-palm-fringed room crowded with more than a thousand persons, including the short fat men and their wives whom no one recognized but who own the movie and TV and record interests, banks and insurance companies. As they ate their seafood cocktails and steaks, drank their Scotch, and waited for the show to begin, they marveled that they were here to hear a hick, a hillbilly, a country crooner. Eddy Arnold has given class to country music. He has backed it with violins and even full symphony orchestras; he has helped to bring it from the sticks to the big cities, and he has made many millions of dollars which, it is well known, he conserves carefully...If he does not always wear a tux, as he did at the Grove, he wears sports shirts and slacks, never star-spangled cowboy suits. If he cuts up country style, he doesn't overdo it. 'I know better,' he says, grinning. 'I don't dig this by-cracky nonsense myself and if I hear it on a country-and-western radio station, I turn it off. I love the music and I've always believed that if you present it with respect, the people will respect it.' ...He had rehearsed four hours just before the precedent-shattering show and he worked for more than an hour, singing more than two dozen songs. He was sweating, weary, and wilted when he took his last bow. Backstage, he shrugged. 'I don't mind working hard. I have found that you have to work hard for anything worthwhile.'"

At the end of the evening, he was exhausted and told the reporter, "I enjoyed the performance--I always enjoy performing--and I enjoyed meeting the prominent people, but the party pooped me out. Oh my, but it was an ordeal." In response to what he thought while he was performing and at the star-studded party later, Arnold replied, "I thought the same thing I thought when I performed for the President at the White House last year. I turned to my wife and I said, "Well, baby, it's a long way from Chester County.'"

Eddy Arnold enjoyed the life of a major star, although he had learned to avoid one temptation. Admitting there were a number of letters at the Ambassador Hotel for him, he stated, "Most of these are from women who want to meet me or spend some time with me. They're wherever I go, as I suppose they are for most entertainers. Here, in Hollywood, they're more persistent. They come up to you in the lobby or knock on your hotel room or come back to the dressing room, rubbing their minks on you, and practically ordering you to come have a drink with them. Oooweee, I'm no prude, but I been there before, when I was younger and more open to temptation, and I ain't about to start going back there."

In 1967 the country music industry in Nashville began giving awards to bring recognition to its performers. This was the first year for the Country Music Association Awards, held at the Municipal Auditorium but not televised. Eddy Arnold was performing at the Coconut Grove when he received a phone call informing him he had been awarded the top honor, "Entertainer of the Year."

In the public eye, Eddy Arnold was always smooth, polite and made people feel at ease. In Camden, New Jersey at a Korvett's store, a reporter noted, "Arnold acted like a politician, posing for pictures, hugging record clerks, bussing customers and autographing records." He made no bones about why he was there: "I'm not here to plant a cornerstone. I'm selling albums. We've got 26 of them here." One of those albums was *The Best of Eddy Arnold.*

RCA had put the package together, declared May "Eddy Arnold Month" and Arnold went out to promote his catalog. This album joined the *My World* album by reaching "Gold" sales (over half a million copies sold).

Finally, he had some advice for other country singers who wanted to enter the world where he lived: "If you don't overdo the cornball humor and the cornball clothes, if you present your music simple, straight, with dignity, and give it quality backing and setting, it will sell. There is a great audience for our music and we have tapped only a part of it so far."

CHAPTER 47

The Sixties came to a head in America in 1968. During that year the Vietcong launched their massive Tet offensive and the United States responded with stepped up fighting and more troops. On March 31 President Lyndon Johnson announced on television that he would not seek reelection after Senator Eugene McCarthy won a surprise victory in the New Hampshire primary. Robert Kennedy soon joined the race while, in the South, George Wallace attracted the attention and support of a number of voters, especially in the country music community. On the Republican side, Richard Nixon, whom many had written off after his defeat for Governor of California in 1962, was gathering strength and support.

A week after Johnson's surprise announcement Martin Luther King was assassinated in Memphis, Tennessee, which led to race riots in a number of cities. In June, Robert Kennedy was assassinated in Los Angeles right after he won the California primary. This led to Vice President Hubert Humphrey's nomination as the Democratic standard bearer, but riots in Chicago during the Democratic Convention seemed to seal his fate as a failed Presidential candidate. For many Americans in the middle class, the country was simply out of control. Anti-war demonstrations increased throughout the country, radical students took over Universities, locking themselves in administration buildings, and black athletes at the Olympics accepted their medals with a Black Power salute. In November, Richard Nixon was elected President while former Alabama Governor George Wallace received almost 14 percent of the vote.

It was painfully obvious there were two different Americas in 1968, and the gap between them was increasingly wide. On one side were young students who objected to the Viet Nam War, wanting to smoke pot and do their thing. On the other side were hard working parents who sacrificed during World War II to make this world a better place for those young people.

The middle class was comprised mostly of those who wanted a safe, secure America, who worked hard for their success and believed in the values of fighting for the flag, hard work, obeying laws, and common, personal decency. They could not understand a world where young men snubbed their noses at American patriotism and the value of hard work to embrace drugs or a culture that valued dropping out more than it did pitching in. Neither side could see the other's point of view, and neither side could really understand the other. If the American Civil War was brother against brother, the Vietnam War was father against son.

The world of middle class values was the world of Eddy Arnold. He became a spokesman for country music and the Nashville Sound, then became a spokesman for the hard working middle class--the "Silent Majority"--and he sang for them. In a world dressed in jeans and tie dyed t-shirts, Eddy Arnold wore a tux; in a world of shaggy hair and beards, Eddy Arnold was clean-cut and neat; in a world of drugs, Eddy Arnold was straight. In a world of liberalism and radical activism, Eddy Arnold, like so many in his generation, was a conservative.

He remained friends and allies with a number of Democratic politicians in Tennessee. Tennessee (and Southern) politicians and voters have generally been conservative, but they were almost always in the Democratic party. As the years rolled by--from the 1960s to the 1990s--the bedrock beliefs of Southern voters and politicians remained fairly constant, but they shifted party affiliation from Democrat to Republican. Eddy Arnold was way ahead of this curve. The 1968 elections confirmed Eddy Arnold's conservative beliefs and his connection to the Republican Party.

The news of the day was filled with riots on campuses against the Viet Nam war, footage from Viet Nam that brought the war into American homes, Civil Rights discord, and angry young men and women. Years later, the 60s, and especially 1968, were viewed through a haze of tumultuous change and confusing forces pulling in all directions. Those who remember those years remember a time of confusion, yet it was also a time of simplicity. This was a time when the liberal agenda held sway, but it was also a time when a conservative backlash made itself felt.

It almost seems like an anomaly to look back to 1968 and see country music become popular in America, or an artist like Eddy Arnold become a major star in both the pop and country fields. Then again, Eddy Arnold spoke for the great majority of Americans who did not deny problems, but wanted them solved civilly; did not deny injustice, but wanted it corrected in an orderly and peaceful way; and did not deny there were things wrong with America but thought there were more things right with the country and wanted to see wounds healed rather than opened wider.

CHAPTER 48

Nineteen sixty-eight was a watershed year for country music as well as the country. The country-pop sound that Eddy Arnold pioneered, and the uptown image for country music he cultivated, became the look and sound of the day. Two of the top country artists that year were Eddy Arnold and Glen Campbell, both of whom had a clean-cut image that served as a marked contrast to the shaggy look of unkempt youth.

In terms of the popularity of country music, Arnold told the *Louisville Courier-Journal,* "Television has had a lot to do with it, but radio is the real factor. In almost every major city now, there is a station that uses nothing but country music, modern country music. I was in Philly the other day, and one of the big stations--I mean a 50,000 watter--is doing it and their revenues and listenership are way up."

In that same article, Eddy Arnold attempted to promote a more cosmopolitan view of country music. He stated, "As of this moment, in every major city in this country--New York, Chicago, Minneapolis, Los Angeles--you have a country music station. I sell more records in New York than I do in Nashville. Maybe it was true ten or 15 years ago that country music had appeal only in the South, but we've taken the hayseed out of it; it's gotten exposed on major TV shows. It's a lot more acceptable than it ever was before."

But there is another side of country music--the hard driving, traditional sound of honky tonk that represents the working class. This group was represented by Merle Haggard, who finished the year as one of the top three artists in country music, and by Buck Owens, who finished in the top ten for radio airplay and country sales. Haggard and Owens were from Bakersfield, which challenged Nashville as a creative force in country music. Still, of the top twenty-five artists in country music during 1965, the great majority (21 out of 25) were "Nashville" artists.

Despite the tremendous growth of country music and the Nashville sound, there were still the snide comments about country music coupled with some backhanded compliments from the media, especially the New York based media. An article in the *New York Daily News* in early 1968 began "There's golden music in them thar hills, folks. And if you don't believe us, just take a look at the record--the record business. Country music, once flufffed off as corny "hillbilly" noise, is now a multi-million dollar enterprise."

An article in *TV Guide* in January, 1968 began "Let's see: there's corn pone, corn fritters, corn meal, cornstarch and corn sirup (sic). Among the uses of corn there is another that emanates from 16th Avenue South--so-called Record Row--in Nashville, Tennessee, and supports a $100,000,000 a year industry with tentacles into every state and to some 400 radio stations broadcasting an unvarying and largely uninterrupted quota of Country and Western Music...Funny thing about Nashville! It stands at the crossroads of several great music traditions that have roots deep in America's memory: Negro blues, Southern mountain balladry, 'Bluegrass' string bands, and work songs. And yet the city has become to many music fanciers the international symbol for a musicality of such numbing mindlessness and banality that some either won't or can't listen to it....The automatic assumption about Country and Western music is that it is the private domain of rural white Southerners and that the better educated and more affluent Northern urbanites are much too sophisticated for it. ...Time was when the banjo, mandolin and dobro guitar were the staple instruments of Country and Western music. Now violins and pianos and harps provide a more elegant background for the same soppy sentiments that always have characterized the more commercial aspects of Country and Western music."

If clothes make the man, as the old saying goes, perhaps they make the music as well. Writers and critics had been surprised for years that Eddy Arnold dressed in conservative outfits. It was a never-ending source of amazement for writers and reporters from the mid-1940s onward (over 20 years!) to discover Eddy Arnold dressed fashionably instead of in rhinestones or duded up like a cowboy. In an article titled "Clothes Show He's No 'Plowboy' Now" writer Lou Ganim noted that during their interview Arnold "was wearing a herringbone jacket and sporting a bright orange turtleneck underneath it--a far cry from the 'frizzles and pintos' of other country singers."

Eddy Arnold knew that sounding more pop-ish was only part of the deal; you had to look the part as well. Never one for cowboy garb (except for his long-ago appearances with Pee Wee King's Golden West Cowboys or at the Houston Fat Stock Show) nor loud, flashy rhinestone outfits, Eddy Arnold had worn semi-dressy slacks and a shirt, often with a sports coat, during his entire solo career. Still, the image of country artists for many in the media was either someone dressed as a cowboy or covered with rhinestones. Arnold always made it a point to let writers know that image of country music did not fit him. In one interview the writer stated, "In terms of stage apparel, Arnold disavowed the rhinestone look. 'I never did dress like that,' he said. 'I usually wore a plain sports shirt and a nice pair of slacks, and I still do at fairs and things.'" At a press conference in Beaver Falls, Pennsylvania it was noted that he had on a "brown sports jacket, flashy green turtle neck." Still, many newspaper writers continued to find it difficult to believe that Eddy Arnold didn't dress to fit an old stereotype. At a show at the Academy of Music in Philadelphia, the reviewer began, "One may have expected him to appear in cowboy garb, but Eddy Arnold, king of the country and Western singers, looked handsome in a tuxedo."

For a number of years, Eddy Arnold had not considered himself just a "country singer" and made that plain to interviewers in 1968. He preferred "singer" but if there was a category or label, he told Ronnie Joyce of the *Pensacola (FL) Journal*, "I'm a country pop singer...I want you to know though, that I'm not taking anything away from the country and western or any other kind of music. They're all important to the entertainment field. Country music has been good to me, and it still is. But, like I say, I don't really consider myself a country singer anymore...I want people to think of me as a more versatile singer. I hate the thought that I've worked so hard these many years and not achieved broad recognition."

He attempted to define himself beyond the limits of country music. He told a writer in Monroe, Louisiana "I sing a combination of country, folk, and popular music, and to me it all goes together." He observed to one reporter, "I've been gradually moving towards being a performer rather than a country and western singer." In several interviews Arnold described himself as "a Heinz 57 singer. A little bit of western, a little bit of pop, a little bit of folk."

Arnold told Monte Zepeda of the *Charlotte Observer*, in an article headlined "I'm Really a Pop Music Artist," that "Since I started in this business I've never thought of myself as a country and western singer. With the type of material I do, I'm really a pop music artist. But I don't play to any particular type of audience. I want my songs to be accepted by everyone." He was described in an Orlando newspaper headline as "The Frank Sinatra of the Pop country field."

He admitted the "new" look and sound of country music wasn't really all that new for him. "I was flirting with a more sophisticated urban style in the late Fifties but it just didn't come off for me," he said, referring to his recording of "I Really Don't Want to Know." "It was sometime in late '65, I think, that I found the song 'What's He Doin' in My World' and it was right for this treatment. Right after that I got 'Make the World Go Away' and made my transition.".

Reporter Zepeda noted that "Arnold is very certain to make sure that no one classifies him as a hillbilly or anything remotely close to it. He pointed out that he always wears suits or evening dress when making appearances. Arnold was also quick to correct any statement that he ever wore or wears even simply styled western-tailored suits, much less the spangled, glittery bright-colored outfits many country and western performers wear."

When he performed with the Hartford Symphony, the reviewer wrote, "From conversations overheard in the lobby during intermission, it would seem that country music buffs from far and near had gathered to acclaim their idol. Arnold's versatility sets him apart from the 'run of the mill' country-western balladeers, and popular ballads, novelty songs and cowboy tunes were included in his repertoire ...Blessed with a pleasing, not particularly unusual voice, the singer uses it in a way which makes his audience cry for more."

Eddy Arnold always saw his music in simple terms--a good lyric, a memorable melody, presented in an easy-going straight forward, relaxed style. The "other" kind of music in 1968 seemed too confused, too complicated, without melodies and with convoluted lyrics. Arnold told a reporter for the *Watertown Daily Times*, "There always will be a place for simple music, you can't forget the feeling in a song.

It is not my intention to be strictly a 'country boy' performer and it is proving out. I stick to commercial songs and giving them a pop treatment."

An article from the Napoleon, Ohio, *Northwest Signal* summed up Eddy Arnold and his importance to country music in 1968. The article stated: "Above all of them, Eddy Arnold has brought sophistication to the Country and Western field. He's helped to build Nashville into a recording mecca where, like New York and Hollywood, the kids go with their dreams and talent. You listen to Eddy Arnold sing something like Roger Miller's 'If That's Not Lovin' Me' and you can sit back and relax. It's a good voice, an untrained voice, but the voice of someone you'd like to know well enough to call friend. There is a youthfulness to the Eddy Arnold sound, something comfortable, something grand. The sound comes at you like the village minister helping you through a time of grief, the family doctor cooling your fever. Eddy's like the Pied Piper. If you hear him and like him, you stick to him. You can't shake him."

CHAPTER 49

In 1968 Eddy Arnold spent a lot of time on the road performing and it paid off handsomely. During a concert at the Corn Palace in South Dakota in the Fall, the show grossed $169,244 and Arnold took home 65 percent or $77,222. During an 18-city tour late that year the shows grossed $550,000 and Arnold carried home $300,000. His concerts became smooth, relaxed affairs and both audiences and reviewers responded enthusiastically.

A review of his Milwaukee show stated, "He's a talent, a pro. Wearing a blue sports jacket, blue shirt and blue tie, he prowled the stage to be sure all the spectators had a good view and shuffled his feet in 'aw, shucks' style whenever applause greeted his efforts. Arnold has the relaxed execution that makes his work appear effortless. The effect is like entertaining a guest in your parlor. There is a lot of the old Nashville sound left in his delivery of ballads, pop and country western, but all the corn is shucked."

A reviewer in Monroe, Louisiana noted, "Many of the tunes were songs that possibly appealed more to the older folks. Not to say the young ones didn't enjoy him, but songs like 'September,' 'Tip of My Fingers,' 'Bouquet of Roses' and others he made famous, are usually more appealing to the 'older set.'"

Another concert review stated, "Don't let the shiny suit and the Ivy League tie fool you. That was a country boy who brought down a sold-out house at the Eastman Theater last night, and he did it with plain old ordinary country charm, easy and relaxed as a Southern summer evening."

He was adjusting to performing in a concert setting. During a concert in Monroe, Louisiana, "spectators seemed to annoy Arnold by snapping cameras in his face, and he asked seriously, that anyone who had a camera and wanted to take pictures, to come forward and take them while he could pose for them. This held the show up for a few minutes, but as Arnold put it, 'Taking pictures during a sentimental love song just don't go good, and besides, other people have to look at your backsides.'"

In a review of his show in Portland, Oregon, reviewer Charlie Hanna stated, "Easy Ed kept up an almost constant flow of past and current record hits while moving easily about the stage as he sang. Arnold's baritone holds a ton of magic, and his imperturbable pace shows that he's in complete control. Still, though a ton of mellow is always mighty nice, a body gets thinking along about the 1,999th pound how just a little ginger might come in nice. Still again, Arnold takes on just about every type and tempo of song any kind of singer has a right to take on. Along the way he does justice to a broad range, the likes of 'Hello, Dolly,' 'The Last Word in Lonesome is Me,' 'Up Above My Head,' and new 'super-country' or 'super folk' such as 'By The Time I Get to Phoenix' and the Jimmy Rogers composition, 'It's

Over.' Arnold's ease and grace are delightful, and he would be the first to admit that 30 years experience has helped a little in putting on the polish."

A review by Samuel Singer of the Academy of Music Show in Philadelphia stated, "Arnold himself chatted with the audience, but not at great length; the songs were the thing. His wisecracks earned chuckles, not belly laughs. They usually had a bizarre twist that made the audience do a mental double take. 'I wasn't born here,' Arnold informed the audience. 'but if it should happen again...' Arnold ...sings in a serviceable baritone that can do tricks. He slips into falsetto with ease, or dips into the bass register for an effect. But it is his straight-forward style that holds the greater part of his manifest appeal to both sexes....Yes, the girls--of all ages--would squeal when they recognized a tune in a medley...Arnold is a homespun fellow and many of his songs are homespun."

Even when the reviewer didn't particularly care for country music or Eddy Arnold there was grudging respect. One review, which caused both ire and humor with Eddy Arnold, was found by his manager, Jerry Purcell, and sent to him along with a few choice comments. The review, written by Bob MacKenzie, in the Oakland (CA) newspaper, stated, "Arnold, for those who don't dig the country scene, is a nice-looking soft-talking gentleman with a plain straight face, friendly gray eyes and a comfortable midriff who sings rural songs in a trickless straight-forward way, owns some 20 million dollars and doesn't bother to get his teeth capped.

He is a plum likeable cuss, and his music is easy to take, even for a non-addict of C & W music. Arnold's tunes are not the hard-core twang-and-moan hillbilly stuff, they are softer and mellower, somewhere between country-western and popular songs. His delivery is sincere and easygoing; his songs are sweet ballads with sentimental lyrics, corny but nice. When he tries a swing tune or a pop ballad with no country flavor, he sounds a little better than the average shower baritone, but not much. But when he gets into a country tune he puts his heart in it and sings it as only a genuine country boy could."

In March, Eddy Arnold made his second Carnegie Hall appearance and once again wowed the New York crowd, including the media. Robert Shelton, in a *New York Times* review, wrote "His singing is smooth, earnest, buoyant and uncomplicated. He is sentimental and direct. For women he seems to be a sort of non-challenging romantic figure, and for their husbands is non-theatening....Mr. Arnold has sophisticated many elements of country music to the point where identification with straight country songs comes only after he dismissed a large orchestra and perched on a stool with his guitar. In ballads or country songs, he is one of the pinions of our pop music, and it looks as if he'll be around a while." A review in another New York paper stated, "Arnold takes the twang out of the music, substituting soft strings and orchestral effects."

During the concert, RCA executives Norman Racusin and Harry Jenkins presented him with a Gold Record to commemorate 50 million records sold. It was noted he was only the fourth artist in the music business to accomplish this feat; the other three were Bing Crosby, Elvis Presley and the Beatles. He was also given an award from the National Association of Record Merchandisers (NARM), which represents retailers, for "Best Selling Male Country Artist" in 1967.

In addition to his active schedule of personal appearances, Eddy Arnold also appeared on a number of TV shows. The most prestigious was an NBC Special on country music, "American Profile: Music From the Land," where Arnold served as narrator. He appeared on six "Kraft Music Hall" shows on NBC during the summer, the "Jackie Gleason Show" on CBS, a "Kraft Music Hall" Christmas Special, as host on "The Hollywood Palace," a guest on "The Red Skelton Show," and as guest host for Johnny Carson on "The Tonight Show."

In May, Arnold filmed a pilot for a proposed TV show, "Mr. Deeds Goes to Town," based on an old Gary Cooper movie. When asked about the taping, Arnold said "Nothing has been finalized on the series and it may or may not be" then added, "I'll level--I'm not overjoyed at the prospect. I suppose I could do it but, gee, it's a lot of work. They promised me a schedule I could live with--a four-day week and one week off a month. If I get it, OK, if not, I'm just as happy on my boat." He got his wish: the pilot wasn't picked up by the networks.

In June he made a quick trip to London to tape "Showtime," a summer variety series and sang "Cotton Fields," "Sitting on Top of the World," "Across the Wide Missouri," "Turn the World Around," "Dear Heart," "Oh, Lonesome Me," "Hello, Dolly" and "For Every Man There's a Woman."

CHAPTER 50

One of the great untold stories in country music is the importance of advertising agencies on the history of country music. In 1939 it was the William Esty Agency that bought advertising time on the Grand Ole Opry for their client, R.J. Reynolds for Prince Albert tobacco and thus launched the Opry as a major player in country music. In the 1945-1956 period it was the Brown Brothers Agency who bought advertising time for their client, Ralston Purina, that played a key role in the national exposure of Eddy Arnold. In 1968 it was the J. Walter Thompson Agency whose client, Kraft Foods, became the sponsor for the Country Music Association Awards Show, giving that show network exposure in prime time.

The first CMA awards show--in October, 1967--was held at the Municipal Auditorium in Nashville; the following July a group of CMA Board members--Hubert Long, Jack Stapp, Frances Preston and Bill Denny--had lunch with Irving Waugh, head of WSM television in Nashville, and sought his help in securing a network slot for the next CMA Awards scheduled in October. That lunch was on a Friday; on Sunday night Waugh and Jack Stapp caught a plane to New York where, on Monday morning, they called on an old friend of Stapp's, Dan Seymour of the Thompson Agency.

Kraft Foods had long been a sponsor of music shows--Kraft's Music Hall Series--and that show had featured Eddy Arnold a number of times. There was a Kraft Music Hall Show scheduled for October entitled "Texas State Fair" to be hosted by Roy Rogers and Dale Evans. Seymour made some phone calls and the show was changed to the Country Music Association Awards Show with Roy Rogers and Dale Evans as the hosts. The New York Agency was reluctant to let country music performers appear and, since the sponsor retained creative control, a number of non-country acts appeared on the show to appease the New York advertising executives. The show was taped and broadcast several weeks later; however, the show was so successful that the Country Music Association obtained creative control by the eighth broadcast and eliminated most of the non-country elements.

The televised awards show did more than just put the Country Music Association's Awards program in prime time, it also put the organization on firm financial footing. In the first year the network paid the CMA $25,000 for the show but as the show proved itself popular, and the CMA obtained more clout, power and control, the show brought millions of dollars into the CMA's coffers, allowing that organization to go full steam ahead in its efforts to promote country music. No longer did the CMA have to worry about funds or try to come up with ideas for fund raisers in order to do their job--the awards telecast took care of those problems.

In Nashville there was a "building boom" to capitalize on the success of country music. The previous year the Country

Music Hall of Fame, located at the head of Music Row on the corner of 16th Avenue South and Division, opened. There were new buildings under construction to house the performing rights organization, ASCAP, publishers Tree, Cedarwood, Hill & Range, and Pamper, talent agencies Moeller and Show Biz, and an announcement about a 14 story building on Music City Boulevard. The Boulevard was planned to be a four-lane road that would follow 16th Avenue South from Demonbreun to a point north of Belmont College--where it would veer west and join Hillsboro Road in the vicinity of Fairfax Ave. The multi-story office building was scheduled to be constructed on the east side of 16th Avenue between South Street and Grand Avenue. The investors in the office building included Eddy Arnold; however, the Boulevard was never built and neither was the office building.

RCA planned a 50 foot extension to their building on 17th Avenue South while WSM announced they had hired Economic Research Associates of Los Angeles to study feasibility for an entertainment complex called "Opryland USA." This was the same firm that aided in the development of Disneyland and Sea World.

Arnold enjoyed family life, especially when he had a chance to get out on the lake in his boat. In July he spent three weeks off the road. He talked about his 30-foot boat with Frank Langley with the *Boston Herald* and stated, "Every man should have one great love other than his family or his work. Mine is that boat. Every time I can put more than two days back-to-back, no matter if I'm in New Orleans or New York, I zip back home and make a beeline for the lake. Out there on that boat it is just me and whoever I bring along. Sometimes I look on it as almost unnatural, the calm, the peace and most of all just being alone."

In answer to a question about "slowing down" he said, "Maybe someday I'll have to, but I'm sort of like Bob Hope and Bing Crosby, I guess. I can't quit. I'd be bored stiff. I have to have the sense of creating something or else my ego is not satisfied." There was a little bit of tragedy as his dog "Nuggles" died in 1968.

As for the demands of fame, he stated, "I love it all and if I didn't I wouldn't still be in the business." He told a reporter for the Fort Smith, Arkansas newspaper, "Show business requires a dedicated pride. If you don't love it, you will not be successful."

In terms of record sales, country music was booming-- and moving into the middle class. The Armed Forces Radio Network announced that 65 percent of all records sold at military post exchanges were country music records. The number of radio stations playing country music was steadily increasing and country music was visible in the national media. When the country records of 1968 were tallied, Glen Campbell emerged as the top selling artist, with Merle Haggard second and Eddy Arnold third. Clearly, there were two directions for country music: the smooth pop-type sound of Campbell and Arnold and the traditional honky tonk sound of Merle Haggard.

At the end of May the Presidential race heated up, two months after President Johnson announced he would not seek re-election. A number of Nashville country artists endorsed third party candidate George Wallace, although Arnold preferred Richard Nixon in the November elections. Arnold never considered endorsing Robert Kennedy but he did feel the tragedy of Kennedy's assassination in a personal way; on the day Kennedy died, Arnold gave a concert in Portland, Oregon and the air was heavy with grief.

As a businessman, Arnold was spokesman and representative for Mary Carter Paints during the year. He was also Chairman of the Board for the newly formed Tennessee Fried Chicken, Inc. Fried Chicken franchises were popular in Nashville; entrepreneurs Jack Massey and John Jay Hooker had both made fortunes with Kentucky Fried Chicken from their Nashville base.

At the end of the year, Arnold told a reporter with the *Charlotte Observer*, "My tastes are simple. Ever since I started singing, I've had the fear of making a lot of money and then ending up without any. I've seen it happen to too many others. So I live in a simple house, nothing elaborate. My car is several years old. I've gotten used to it like an old pair of shoes"

Shortly before Christmas a reporter from *Music City News* asked Eddy Arnold what he wanted most for Christmas. He replied, "I wish someone would turn up my first guitar, the one I started strumming with 20-odd years ago in Tennessee. My mother bought it for me, and it's how it all began."

CHAPTER 51

The last year of the 1960s was a good year for country music on television. During this year "The Johnny Cash Show" and "Hee Haw" both debuted while "The Glen Campbell Show" continued its successful run. Eddy Arnold appeared on the Kraft Music Hall a number of times; by the end of 1969 he had appeared on a total of 11 "Kraft Music Hall" shows, a summer "Kraft Music Hall" series titled "County Fair" and a Kraft Christmas Special.

The popularity of country music on TV inspired Mary Ann Lee of the *Memphis Press-Scimitar* to note, "Once regarded as somewhere beyond the range of the TV screen, the popularity of music with a country twang has been slowly building over the years--a song here, a special there, Eddy Arnold as host of some 'Kraft Music Hall Specials' plus the success of 'The Glen Campbell Show'--and this summer the trend is in full swing."

Financially, it continued to be a good time for Eddy Arnold; a column by Walter Winchell announced that he earned about $300 a minute on stage or about $22,500 for a 75-minute concert. During a 30-city tour that year he grossed approximately $750,000 and a subsequent 19-date tour grossed $574,655 with attendance of 171,253 for a personal take of $342,670

The year before he turned 50 and found himself at the top of both the country and pop worlds as a superstar. He enjoyed his success more the second time around and continued to receive rave reviews. Fred Cicetti of the *Newark Sunday News* wrote, "The man is candid in a trade that thrives on sham. His attitude toward his fortune is especially refreshing. He's not ashamed to reveal his pride in his ability to accumulate comforts and security for himself, his wife, and two children." Cicetti stated, "Eddy Arnold's decades in show business and years in corporate board rooms have made him cautious. Routine questions are pondered. His responses are delivered carefully. Inquiries he would rather not answer are simply not answered; he smiles warmly and stares interminably. The wordless message is clear: 'I don't want to have any embarrassment here. I don't want to refuse you, but the truth is a private thing and I'm not going to give you the baloney. Go on to another question, please.'"

In the *Memphis Statesman*, writer Bruce Ebert stated, "Mr. Arnold said his personal pride caused him to change his style of singing. 'I felt that my kind of thing should appeal to the general public, not just to a specific minority. I realized that if my singing was to earn the respect I wanted it to, I had to smoothen it. I wanted to present a more polished sound. So, I added the violins and the orchestral accompaniment.' He continued that 'I'm happy that I'm now regarded as Eddy Arnold the performer, not just Eddy Arnold the country singer. I once performed strictly in the West and the South. Today, I can perform all over the country, including the colleges. This change in style has afforded me the opportunity to do many things I could not have otherwise done, such as appear on national TV and in cities outside the South.'"

In terms of losing traditional country fans, Arnold stated, "I'm sorry about this; however, for every fan I lose because of that, I find I have gained three. Those down home people are the most avid of all music fans. They stay with you and love you."

As for future ambitions, he admitted that "I wouldn't mind doing a good movie with a good part that I could fit into comfortably. That would offer me a challenge. But that's about the only thing I haven't had a chance to do."

Country music had come a long way in the twenty-five years since the end of World War II and there were explanations offered. "I think the writers deserve a great deal of credit for this," said Arnold, discussing the appeal of country music. "Country songs are now more tasteful than they once were. Time was when every country song was about some catastrophe--mother dying, poverty or something like that. Today, they're written about love...Because people like the simplicity of the country song combined with the smoothness of the ballad, I believe country music will continue to be the accepted thing."

On the popularity of the Nashville Sound, he stated "It seemed like the right time for this kind of thing to happen. Country music got a little more dignified. It got more exposure on TV and radio. I think the whole movement is responsible for it. I know I started to change my background, adding softer guitars, violins, more of a pop music feel to give me wider appeal...Many of the other boys started getting national exposure, national acceptance. Now in every major metropolitan city is a radio station devoting itself entirely to the modern concept of country music. The radio stations got rid of the 'hayseed' disc jockeys, the ones that said, 'Hello, by cracky, my grandma sent me a cake.' They have given country music some dignity, started to respect it. The only way for the public to respect it is for it to respect itself."

In 1969 Eddy Arnold returned to Las Vegas, where he had not appeared since 1954. The terms were appealing: a $1 million long term contract by the soon to be finished International Hotel. The deal meant that Arnold would headline at the International four weeks a year for the next five years. This marked the beginning of an era when he became a top nightclub performer in Las Vegas in addition to being a top concert draw throughout the nation.

In July and August Arnold was at the Las Vegas International, at the end of August he was at the Sahara in Lake Tahoe, and then at the Nugget in Reno at the end of September. He conquered the world of Nevada clubs in short order; still, a reviewer couldn't resist making a few digs at Eddy Arnold and country music in the high rolling world of those clubs.

A review of one of his shows at the Circus Room in the Nugget Casino in Sparks by Rick Pavlik stated, "Arnold is as American as Mom, apple pie, the flag and the Washington Monument. He's the prototype of Mr. Straight and the people love him--at least the country-western, middle America, silent majority hardhat, cow country types do. The audience...was made up primarily of these types, and they loved every minute of the Tennessee Plow Boy's hour on stage. He sings 24 songs, spins some cracker barrel stories about the folks back home, and drawls a few risqué jokes that add spice to the evening's dialogue--not much, but just enough to let you know he's kind of earthy and just a 'real folks' type...Arnold is good. He's a charmer with a good personality and all this folksy charisma certainly helps. But, best of all he's a singer and as good a country-western type as I've ever heard."

Arnold had developed a tried and true method that prepared him for his shows which involved an intense rehearsal before each show. He told Joan Smith, "I always go to rehearsal. If I go, I can get along with the stage hands and sound people. I can get more out of them than anybody else just by looking them in the eye, shaking hands, and saying 'thank you.' I always go meet them; I don't want them to come to me. I go up and say, 'I'm Eddy Arnold, how are you'...I'm a live kind of a person and I like to communicate with an audience. I work a lot with a hand mike...it makes me feel closer to people. I work the whole stage. I perform for every audience as though it were a challenge, and I'm trying to sell 'em something--trying to sell 'em me. I want them to leave liking me...I need it; I love bein' loved."

By 1969 he had developed his method of performing. He came to town and spent the afternoon rehearsing his show with local musicians hired for that evening. He brought along a guitar player, Jim Lance. In Ellsworth, Maine, a reporter watched the rehearsal and reported, that at 3 p.m., "wearing a trimly cut suit and a bright yellow turtleneck" he appeared for the rehearsal."

"On stage he was all amiability and ease," stated the reporter. "He raced through the layout of his show with the light heart and confidence of a professional who knows his work. The skips and double-timed spins, which might have passed for extemporaneous clowning, were actually a fast run-through of every well-practiced movement that accompanies his performance. He seemed to take himself, the band, and the program very casually, like a businessman who is perfectly familiar with his stock in trade. He smiled when he gave the band instructions, and he joked when he told a man at the amplifier where to pitch the volume, but he made his points very clear and he didn't waste a word. Whatever he said and did, it was always with the same good-humored ease. On stage he offers a smooth parody of the classic country boy, but in person he is quiet, sincere and unpretentious. He is perhaps the most courteous individual in the entertainment business."

When asked by the reporter what he thought about while singing, Arnold stated, "Mostly the thought running through my mind is whether the people out there like what I'm doing. Am I getting to them is evermost in my mind. I always wonder if they like me, if they like what I'm singing, if they're pleased. I'm always concerned with their reaction to me. As far as my own feelings go, it's been years since I had stage fright. I did once, but I'm relaxed now."

He admitted that "When I'm not rehearsing or giving a show, I'm usually in my hotel room. I'm very seldom any place where there's anything I really want to see," although he did admit that the previous summer, while appearing at the Illinois State Fair, "I made a visit to Lincoln's house and his tomb. I enjoyed seeing them. The state police gave me an escort there" before adding, "It's not easy for me to sight-see. People recognize me. No, there aren't mob scenes, but I always end up signing autographs. I don't get to see much. If I stop to read a sign, all of a sudden a little lady is tugging at my arm saying 'My daughter will kill me if I don't get your autograph! Then I turn a corner and someone is pulling on my other arm and asking for another autograph and then I spend the whole afternoon saying 'Yes ma'm. Thank you, ma'm. You're welcome, ma'm. All right, ma'm. And I don't see anything.'"

CHAPTER 52

During 1969 Arnold made his New York nightclub debut at the Waldorf-Astoria, where he received $10,000 a week to perform. In a review of his New York nightclub debut, Ray Knight wrote, "Even for a staunch country music non-fan like me, Eddy is a pleasure to hear. He can and does sing 'Hello Dolly' and other citified ditties without the use of his nose. And he has such a good voice that his country songs, also non-nasal, are easy for anybody to take--especially backed by a 22-piece orchestra."

A review of the New York show in the Hackensack (New Jersey) paper by Dan Lewis began "Call me a silo sophisticate or a hoe-down snob if you choose, but the truth of the matter is that I enjoy listening to Eddy Arnold immensely. That's why I could even condition myself to sit through the ya hoos who frequently and incongruously pierced the elegant Empire Room at the prestigious Waldorf-Astoria Hotel Monday night when the old Tennessee plowboy created some sort of history by ascending its stage and singing country-western, hoe-down and clippity-clop music before a black-tie audience.....In the main, the simplicity of his performance added to the beauty of the songs and made for a worthwhile evening. Most of it was also warmly--in fact enthusiastically--received at the Empire Room, although I'm sure curiosity created as much of the interest as anything else. People wanted to know just how well a country-western singer could do."

A review of the Waldorf show by Jerry Parker stated "Arnold was not awed by the big city surroundings. He may be country, but he's no bumpkin. 'I played the Coconut Grove in Los Angeles and I sang at Carnegie Hall twice,' he said. 'and that ain't exactly Flatbush, you know.'" The article stated he "bristled when someone commented on his urbane appearance. 'I'm from the modern school of country boys,' he said. 'Don't you go trying to put boots on me! I'm not a cowboy. The only time you'll see me in a fancy shirt or boots is at a rodeo, when everybody is wearing them.'"

As the sixties came to a close, many viewed the country as a complicated, complex maze. Anti-war protests were rampant on college campuses while President Nixon announced a "Vietnamization" plan for the withdrawal of American troops from that country. Former President Dwight Eisenhower died that March and in July Neil Armstrong walked on the moon. It was the summer of Woodstock and the autumn of the largest anti-war rally in Washington D.C. when 250,000 protest marchers descended on the Capital.

It was the heyday of the counterculture, which had books like *The Making of a Counterculture* by Theodore Roszak and *Do It* by Yippies founder Jerry Rubin. The voices of the counterculture were answered by Vice President Spiro Agnew who called war protesters "anarchists and ideological eunuchs" and the national press "an effete corps of impudent snobs who characterize themselves as intellectuals." He called journalists "nattering nabobs of negativism" and called for "a cry of alarm to penetrate the cacophony of seditious drivel."

Although the world seemed a complex maze for young people in search of themselves while wearing illegal smiles, for Eddy Arnold it was a simple time, a time to stick to the basics of hard work, honesty, respect for others, patriotism, and self-responsibility. Love songs and romance are timeless, so that's what he sang. He believed strongly and deeply that people should be polite, decent, and loyal. Yes, there might be problems, but problems are solved best within the system- -not by trying to tear the system down.

Eddy Arnold stood opposite the sixties counterculture, but he stood right in the middle of conservative American values. In an era often characterized as anti-business and anti-establishment, Eddy Arnold was a marked contrast. An article in the *Memphis Press-Scimitar* by Margaret McKee began, "Talking to Eddy Arnold is like talking to a conglomerate. There's Richard Edward Arnold, successful businessman and potential fried chicken magnate; Eddy Arnold multi-multi-million record seller and showman; Eddy Arnold sought after to be an office seeker; and Eddy Arnold, country boy come way uptown."

Eddy Arnold's ideas and views might have been out of step with the counterculture during its heyday, but they were firmly in step with many Americans who found the counterculture to be an example of how not to fix America's problems. Many of those Americans liked Eddy Arnold's old fashioned values, liked his relaxed performances in the midst of this cultural upheaval, and agreed that romance and love songs were timeless. In many ways, Eddy Arnold was an anchor for a culture adrift, a rock in a sea of change, and his audience responded by clinging to him.

In 1970 Richard Nixon gave a speech where he first used the term "the Silent Majority" to describe most Americans. This seemed to sum up those not in the news who comprised the bulk of the population.

Some newspaper writers realized country music was the musical voice of this "silent majority." In her column, "Prime Time" in the *Cocoa (FL) Today* in January, 1970, Margot Reis-El Bara wrote, "One of the reasons for the nationwide growing popularity of country music may be the songs themselves. In an age that is so fraught with problems and complicated technology, country music simply tells a story. The music is down to earth, putting in the simplest words imaginable the problems of domestic life or the nostalgia for the freedom of a less hectic era. The tunes and verses, with a simple guitar beat, are neither complicated nor unfamiliar."

In her column she stated further, "Country and Western music, generally a regional attraction, has at long last hit nationwide television. The networks have decided to plow this old, but largely neglected field, in the hopes of reaping a rich harvest. In the past there were shows on the fringes of this area--Jimmy Dean had his own program several seasons back, and Eddy Arnold is a frequent guest star on variety shows--but the trend is emerging to tout 'name' Country-Western stars by having them headline their own shows. The Johnny Cash Show was dropped into ABC-TV's summer lineup as a replacement show and did so well in the ratings that it returns to the air this month as a permanent part of the prime time schedule. Likewise, CBS TV's incredible success with 'Hee Haw,' a silage of country corn and music, has caused its return."

Country music was certainly gaining respect. In a column titled, "On the Scene" writer Mike Jahn stated, "Right now country and western ranks second only to rock as the most-widely-heard form of American music. Its geographic boundaries encompasses virtually the whole country. Country stations are heard in most big cities--including New York. In Los Angeles it is almost impossible to watch evening television without turning on a country show. The Apollo 12 astronauts had country music piped up to them on the moon. Network television carries a respectable amount of it....Country music is unpretentious, uncomplicated, easily sung and it makes you feel good."

The changes in the public perception of country music owed a lot to the shows of Eddy Arnold. In a *Jacksonville (FL) Times Union* concert review, Jo Anna More wrote, "As in all his numbers, Arnold's personality and vivid imagination made familiar melodies reborn. Country fans must agree that he is one of the greatest, yet he still sounds at home with the top of the popular music crop. If the audience at the Coliseum came only to see a country music star they must have been pleasantly shocked. No longer can Eddy Arnold be placed in any one category. His music knows no boundaries and his knowledge of the sounds of today is limitless."

At the end of the year, in an interview with LaVelle Alexander, Arnold stated, "You almost have to be reborn once in a while in this business. The best years of my career have come since then....I had to be able to reach more people. I wanted my songs to appeal to middle-America. I knew I would lose some of the country fans. I was willing to take that chance and I've been well rewarded for it."

CHAPTER 53

On August 1, 1971, Eddy and Sally Arnold were on their boat on Old Hickory Lake with their friends, Frances and E.J. Preston. It had been a nice, relaxed day, far away from crowds and telephones. However, when they arrived back at the club where they docked their yacht, there was an emergency phone call: Their son had been in a horrible accident.

Dick Arnold had just graduated from the University of Alabama with a degree in broadcasting and journalism. He came home for the weekend then, with a Sigma Alpha Epsilon fraternity brother, headed back to school to collect some belongings at his apartment. Dick was tired and let his friend drive the little red sports car. In Bessemer, Alabama, a car pulled out and hit them, smashing the sports car. An ambulance rushed Dick to a Birmingham hospital where he was pronounced dead before medics brought him back to life.

A plane was chartered for Eddy and Sally Arnold to take them to Birmingham; they arrived that evening. Eddy Arnold wanted to cancel his personal appearances but was persuaded to fulfill his immediate obligations and did so. From October to the following February, Eddy Arnold did not perform, spending that time at home with Dick.

Dick Arnold stayed in a coma for nine and a half weeks. During that time his parents were with him at the hospital; they played some of Eddy Arnold's records and the TV in the room allowed him to see his father. Finally, after two and a half months he regained consciousness and said his first word, "Sally." The Arnolds took him home to Nashville where he began his long road to recovery.

The accident devastated Eddy Arnold, but he was determined to help his son any and every way possible. For months he lifted Dick out of bed and bathed him. He purchased a metal walkway with rails and helped Dick stand and make his way to the other end. At first it was just a shuffle; gradually, steps returned. The accident had bruised Dick's brain and he had to re-learn a number of things. Throughout the ordeal, Eddy Arnold stood with his son, helping, encouraging him. It was the greatest test of fatherhood a man could face, and Eddy Arnold met the challenge.

When your son has been hurt that badly, things like a recording career, hit records and personal appearances fade in importance. Although Eddy Arnold continued to make selective personal appearances, TV appearances and recordings, he did not have a single record reach the top ten in country music during the entire decade of the 1970s.

He had been slowing down for awhile, tired of the one-nighters and a schedule that had him flying into a city, rehearsing all afternoon, then performing a concert that night--tired. He met the obligations of a performer on the road: the meet and greets backstage, interviews with the media, staying "up" and friendly for everyone, giving everyone a little piece of himself, giving up his privacy to sign autographs, posing for pictures and shaking hands and chatting with whoever showed up took much of his energy.

Eddy Arnold had always preferred a quiet lifestyle off the road. He told one reporter that he lived "a very frugal life, just like anyone in the middle income bracket." In answer to music in his home, he said, "I don't perform at home. We have a piano and we all enjoy music. We put on records or tapes and if we have friends in, and if someone wants to play the piano and sing a song, that's great; but it's never something we plan, always something that happens spontaneously. I guess that's how I live my whole life." Sally admitted she liked to listen to Andy Williams, Perry Como and Bing Crosby.

Eddy Arnold enjoyed entertaining at home. "I love to have my friends in," he told a reporter. "We tell a few corny stories and have a couple of laughs." Arnold especially enjoyed grilling steaks for his guests.

He enjoyed his family and had a good marriage. He said, "I think a marriage, to be successful, must have its bad times and good times. There just have to be differences, but above all a couple has to really know each other well, all of the time." He told a reporter, "We've kept our kids out of the show-business limelight. They don't even listen to my music, and they don't know many of our show-business friends. I did not take them with me when I traveled."

On holidays, "We have a big turkey. My wife, Sally loves to cook the dinner. It's really our family day," said Arnold. Sally noted, "Our children planned our holiday dinner years ago and we always have the same menu for both Christmas and Thanksgiving. We have roast turkey, dressing, giblet gravy, ham, string beans, creamed potatoes, candied sweet potatoes, congealed salad, hot rolls and about four kinds of dessert." She added that "coconut cream pie is Eddy's favorite dessert."

Eddy added, "Our holidays are spent with just the immediate family and a few close friends. I'm a very private person. When I'm home, I'm a husband and a father. I don't like going out to night clubs or big parties. If you invite me to a party where you're going to have 200 or 300 people, I will say 'Thank you very much but I won't be there.' People pull or drag on me if I'm at something like that, especially when everybody's in the music business. Many of my closest friends are not in the music business, and do you know something, I never hear them talk about business when we go out socially."

He still played golf occasionally but admitted, "I really don't play enough golf to consistently break 100…I like golf… But I kinda let my game go a couple of years back when I discovered boating. Now I'm really hooked on boating." He owned a 34-foot Hatteras that could sleep six with a pair of 290-hp Chrysler marine engines.

He waxed enthusiastically about life on the lake. He told one reporter, "Those Tennessee Valley Authority lakes are the greatest in the world. They provide the most pleasant boating you'd ever want to find. I can't tell you how great it is to stay out for days. Why, once three of us took our boats from Old Hickory Lake in Tennessee right on through four other lakes all the way into Barkley Lake in Kentucky. That was about 400 miles. It's really something tricky to maneuver those boats through dams and locks. We were out 12 days."

He also admitted that "next to singing, I like to read sports sections [of newspapers]...They're the first thing I turn to every day."

Early in 1971 Arnold closed his fried chicken operation; he attributed the failure to the high overhead cost the company incurred. He noted, they "were competing with the Kentucky Colonel, but we went about it wrong. First off, we built very elaborate buildings. I figure we spent 60 percent more on each building than the Colonel does. We went bust pretty quick." He noted, "I want you to know we paid all our creditors and abolished the corporation. Nobody except the four original investors ever lost any money, and we lost that in stock. I lost about $150,000. I know I shouldn't complain because I can afford it, and I'm gettin' it back in dribs and drabs as a tax write-off. But, oh, my how I hate to lose money. I was a Depression child. I never will forget bein' hungry and I'm very frugal."

CHAPTER 54

Eddy Arnold returned to Las Vegas at the Sahara early in 1971; during the 1970s he concentrated on appearances in Nevada, generally two week stands three times a year at Harrah's in Lake Tahoe and Reno.

Even though he worked less, he had the same work ethic as always. An article by John F. Steadman in the *Baltimore News American* stated, "The formula is still hard work. If he's at a party with friends, it's not that he's anti-social, but Eddy excuses himself before the hour grows late and makes sure he's going to get a full night of rest. This afternoon, he'll rehearse four hours. ...Later in the day, he'll order a cup of soup from room service and take a nap before the show. [He has] impeccable attention to detail, to his appearance and, of course, the material he sings. The last thing he puts on are his trousers in the dressing room because when it's time to go out and sing for the people he doesn't want his pants to be a maze of wrinkles."

In March, 1972 Arnold appeared at the Circle Star Theater in San Carlos, California with the Mike Curb Congregation. Curb was a music business wunderkind. He was the 27-year old leader of his vocal group who had a pop hit with "Burning Bridges" from the movie *Kelly's Heroes* in 1970 and had been president of MGM Records since

1969. He and Arnold hit it off and at the end of the year Eddy Arnold left RCA after over twenty-five years with that label and signed with MGM.

The decision to leave RCA was difficult; Eddy Arnold was a loyal man who stuck by old friends and associates, but things had changed a great deal at RCA Victor since he'd first signed in 1944. Chet Atkins, who had produced Arnold's 1960s hits, was tired of the corporate routine and wanted to just be a guitar player; in December, 1973 he stepped down as head of the label and Jerry Bradley, son of Owen, took over as label chief. Atkins had produced a large number of acts and could not give Eddy Arnold as much attention as the singer needed so Arnold sought fresh input and began to work with new producers.

Both Arnold and Atkins owed a lot of their success to Steve Sholes. In the summer of 1957 Sholes was named head of RCA's pop division and moved to Los Angeles. This meant that Sholes could no longer serve as Eddy Arnold's producer and that Chet Atkins had additional duties in RCA's country division and took over production chores for Eddy Arnold's recordings. Arnold enjoyed working with Sholes and was reluctant to take on a new producer, but gradually Arnold and Atkins developed a good working relationship, culminating in a series of hits in the sixties. That was changing in 1972 so the idea of going to MGM to work with Mike Curb seemed appealing.

While at MGM he re-recorded a number of his old hits and released nine singles that charted. At the end of 1975 his contract was up and Curb was no longer head of the label, so Arnold returned to RCA.

There were major changes afoot in Nashville during the early 1970s. In 1971 the first Country Music Fan Fair was held, attracting 10,000 fans, and the National Life and Accident Insurance Company broke ground for a theme park they planned to call Opryland.

At the end of May, 1972, Arnold did a one week stand at the Shady Grove Music Fair in Rockville, Maryland. By this time his son Dick was recovering well and told his Dad he wanted a dog--and he wanted it to be a Bulldog. Arnold found a Bull-Mastiff advertised in a newspaper and went out to the owner's home to see it; he arranged to buy it and have it sent to his home. Dick named the dog "Hoss," after the character on "Bonanza," and the two became great friends. Unfortunately, after about seven months the dog wandered out on the highway and was hit by a car. Dick and his father were both devastated; Arnold wanted to buy another dog but Dick wasn't interested. Finally, Eddy bought another Bull-Mastiff from the same parents and Dick named it "Mr. Ed." Arnold fenced in about an acre for the dog to run in. It was a good dog--but it wasn't a "Hoss." Still, it helped Dick continue to recover.

Towards the end of 1972 Arnold talked openly about retiring. "I've talked to my wife, my son and my daughter," he told a reporter. "And I've told them, in a general way, that I'm thinking about it. I don't know when, but I'm not gonna keep singing all my life. A man needs to start thinking about what he'll do when he retires, how he'll keep involved in life. I'm involved in a little real estate, and I have a boat that I just love, and I think I could be happy retired. It's just that the thought keeps coming up in my mind more than it used to…but I don't know yet."

In a reflective mood he told writer Peggy Russell, "I suppose that I'm the type of guy who appeals to the average person, country or non-country. Sort of middle-America, bread-and-butter kind of guy. I would like to think that I was wise enough to see several years ago that there was an added market there for me if I wanted to reach for it. At that point my records were selling to a minority of people, what we call hard-country buyers who like that type of music and that alone. I like that kind of music but I also knew I liked a little more modern song and a little more modern arrangement, and I wanted to do that….That's the way I feel about music, all fields of it, whether it's rock, country, pop or whatever. I just know what I like. I can listen to the Carpenters for hours and I like Kenny Rogers."

When asked if he had any disappointments during his career he answered, "Disappointments. I really don't know…disappointments, come in personal lives. I can't say that I have ever been disappointed in this business. Tired maybe, sometimes disillusioned, a lot of things, but disappointed? I don't think so. It's a great life. I've been very fortunate."

At the end of 1972 he talked about his son to a reporter, stating that Dick "should be back in shape in about another year." He said that he called his son every night he was away and that "People have asked me about 100 times in the past few years what my goal is. Well, I tell 'em my goal is to get my son well and back in the mainstream!"

CHAPTER 55

During the early 1970s, some of country music's pioneers passed from the scene. In 1972 Elton Britt, whose hit "There's a Star Spangled Banner Waving Somewhere" defined country music in World War II died; in 1973 Opry comedian Stringbean and his wife were murdered. In 1974 Tex Ritter and Nelson King--a disc jockey from 1946-1970 died. King was one of the founders of the Country Music Disk Jockeys Association back in 1953.

In 1975 promoter Oscar Davis, comedian Clell Sumney (Cousin Jody), artists George Morgan and Lefty Frizzell, and Audrey Williams, wife of Hank Williams, all passed away. Also in 1975 Ernest Tubb handed over his "Midnight Jamboree" to his son Justin, and the Music Row area received new names for their streets. Formerly known as 16th and 17th Avenues, they became known as Music Square East and West.

In Branson, Missouri a small group known as the Baldknobbers Band opened the Hillbilly Jamboree Theater in 1973. Nobody in Nashville noticed, but this marked the beginning of Branson as a major tourist attraction for live country music shows.

In the Spring of 1974 President Richard Nixon came to Nashville to inaugurate the opening of the new Opry House at the Opryland Theme Park while the last Opry performance at the Ryman was held, marking the end of an era.

By the early 1970s it was difficult to hear the traditional, hard core country music sound. It looked like the countrypolitan sound pioneered by Eddy Arnold had won the day; in 1973 Roy Clark won CMA's Entertainer of the Year, in 1974 Charlie Rich won the honor.

By 1975 country music had reached the limits of the "countrypolitan" sound. That was the year John Denver won the Country Music Association's Entertainer of the Year award, and "Back Home Again" by Denver won "Song of the Year" honors. Charlie Rich, the previous year's "Entertainer of the Year" winner, showed his displeasure by opening the envelope that announced Denver's selection, then setting the card on fire in front of the television audience. The previous year Olivia Newton-John won the CMA's Female Vocalist of the Year Award.

A major national recession occurred in 1975 after the Arab oil embargo, which resulted in a vinyl shortage and a cutting back in the number of older records pressed. For an artist like Eddy Arnold, whose catalog of recordings continued to sell, this hurt.

In 1976 the "Outlaw Movement" brought a new group of young fans to country music. Along the way, the "Outlaw Movement" effectively ended the era of the "Nashville Sound." The outlaw movement represented a rebellion of artists against the Nashville system of producers and session musicians being in control of the music. Leading the outlaw movement were Waylon Jennings and Willie Nelson, two long-time Nashville recording artists who achieved a degree of success in Nashville, but also felt thwarted in their efforts to expand their own artistic visions.

Ironically, Waylon and Willie were both part of the Nashville establishment for a number of years. They knew the system, and knew the rules when they began the revolution of producing their own recordings. The other part of the revolution was drugs. No longer were these artists content to sip martini's for relaxation; no longer was liquor the drug of choice. Liquor is a depressant and renders you incapable of making decisions; marijuana and "speed" are stimulants that put you in action. This change in the method of escape had a profound effect on the way Nashville did business. Along with the drugs and changes in the cultural landscape came an anti-authoritarian attitude. Ever since Viet Nam, people who were given orders demanded to know "why" and, if the answer wasn't satisfactory, chose not to follow the order. This bled over into other parts of society. People in charge had to "earn" respect; there was no more following orders "because I said so." Rank still had its privileges, but it also had obligations. Those in charge could no longer expect their decisions to be carried out by those below; those below had ideas of their own.

The Outlaw Movement ushered in the next phase of the country music business, a phase that returned the musical decisions to the artists. The Nashville Sound was not dead; there were still studio musicians who worked on the bulk of the albums from Nashville, as well as advertising commercials, gospel product (Nashville became the center for Contemporary Christian music and Southern Gospel), and other projects. The idea that country music had to be smooth and pop-oriented to achieve respect and success in the middle class went out the window as well. The Outlaw movement featured a sound with rough edges, more raw with a heavy beat and no aspirations towards middle class respectability. The very term "outlaw" made that plain.

The Outlaw Movement changed country music because it brought in young people and Baby Boomers who had previously shunned country music. No longer was the country music audience representative of the World War II generation; now the Viet Nam generation was in the audience as well. Instead of driving cars with bumper stickers saying "America: Love it or leave it," country fans could be found driving pick-up trucks with bumper stickers that said "Question authority."

With the rise of the "outlaws," country music let its hair grow long and got a new attitude. It was, essentially, the rock'n'roll attitude of rebellion and doing your own thing and it attracted the Vietnam generation like no other movement in country music had done before.

CHAPTER 56

In 1976 Eddy Arnold returned to RCA and his first release, "Cowboy," rose to number 13--his best showing since 1969. He continued to have chart singles throughout the 1970s for RCA, but none hit big.

Although Eddy Arnold was not an "outlaw" in country music by any stretch of the imagination, he applauded their success. He said, "Those guys aren't doing anything except making records with a little heavier beat and singing some pretty good songs....Guys like Willie and Waylon are doing a fine job. Heck, I've known Waylon for years, and those guys aren't doing anything but helping this business. Maybe their lifestyle is something else--letting their hair grow long, skipping a couple of baths and puffing that stuff--but their music is fine."

Eddy Arnold continued his investments as a businessman; in 1977 he invested in a line of food products: seven varieties of beans and also continued to perform in Nevada. During an appearance in Las Vegas in 1977 he proved he had not lost his touch with an audience. A reviewer stated, "Arnold epitomizes the country boy who can reach the most sophisticated cabaret audience by his simple, honest delivery. No gimmicks or stage tricks for this man--he sings 'em straight and there's something about his open-faced look that just makes you a believer."

In 1979, Eddy Arnold announced he was going to "resume" his recording career. The effort paid off; in 1980 he had two top ten records, "Let's Get It While the Gettin's Good" and "That's What I Get For Loving You." With those two songs, Eddy Arnold achieved the distinction of having a chart record in five different decades: the 40s, 50s, 60s, 70s and 80s. He continued to have chart records throughout the 1980s, although he failed to have a big hit single.

In an interview Arnold said he wanted to resume his recording career "because I'm an ambitious person and an egotist, too. There's nothing wrong with ego. I think we all want to feel productive. Actually, I guess I've just decided to outlive the tax man."

The decision to resume his career came about for several reasons. First, his son Dick had made a remarkable recovery from his automobile accident, although he still walked with a limp. In 1978 Dick obtained a job in Nashville and moved out of the Arnold home into his own apartment. Next, he wanted to have a chart record in the 1980s, which meant he would appear on the country charts for six different decades. It was a long time to be an active force in the country music business and Arnold was both proud and amazed at his continued success.

In terms of his longevity and business acumen, he stated, "It's no lark. I advise young people to get a good accountant, a good lawyer, a good manager and listen to them. Then, if you have a show to do, show up on time. I've never missed a show in my life and I've never been late. And I've never shown up any other way but sober."

Since he decided to concentrate on recording again, he needed to look for material and said, "I'm only as good as my songs, and I pick the best I can find from professional writers. I don't fool with amateur songs because they are never good. Lots of people think writing a song is a lark. They think all they have to do is make a few rhymes and they have a song, write to Eddy Arnold or somebody and he's going to make them a millionaire. All of them need to go to a music publisher. They need tutoring as a writer. They have to pay their dues. A writer of songs must have experience...he must have someone say 'This is lousy. Go back and rewrite the third line.' That is what the music publisher does. My producer and I listen to as many as 150 songs for an LP. Sometimes we have to rest and wait awhile because they all begin to sound alike. In some instances, we take as long as three weeks to find a song. We're not in a hurry."

In terms of finding songs, Arnold stated, "It boils down to my tastes. My producer also listens for me, and he listens very well for me. Then we both get together and listen together. It's a long process and sometimes it gets very boring, just sitting and listening. Sometimes...you have to get up and walk away from it and give your ear a rest."

The commitment Eddy Arnold made to his recording career led him to concentrate on his recordings, personal appearances, and generating publicity. The image of Eddy Arnold was pretty well set: he was known as a class act in country music.

Eddy Arnold may have been a country crooner wearing tuxedos, but he was still asked about cowboys. It was a logical question in 1980 when *Urban Cowboy*, a movie about a contemporary cowboy riding mechanical bulls in Houston, appeared starring John Travolta and cowboy mania swept America. Eddy Arnold's most famous song was "Cattle Call" and his single that made the top ten in 1980 was "Cowboy."

Arnold set the record straight whenever the subject was broached. He told one reporter, "I never tried to be a cowboy because I wasn't a cowboy. I came from a rural area, and I knew country life. When you dress like a cowboy, people ask all kinds of questions and make all kinds of remarks. If you don't have on cowboy clothes, you don't have to answer all those questions--'Do you have a horse? Do you ride a horse?'"

He admitted he grew up loving Gene Autry but didn't want to follow in those boot-steps. "I just really wasn't interested in being a cowboy. I liked and admired the cowboys who sang, but I knew I wasn't a cowboy and I knew cowboy songs per se normally didn't become too popular. I always felt like if you were going to be a cowboy, you had to sing cowboy songs rather than love songs and even though we all love 'Tumbling Tumbleweeds'--it's great nostalgia--if you're going to be an artist who sells records, you gotta sing love songs."

CHAPTER 57

By the 1980s Eddy Arnold had defined himself: he was a performer. It was a part of his life that he approached seriously, in a business-like manner.

He told reporter Jim Ruth, in Hershey, Pennsylvania, "Frankly, I wanted to become a performer. I was going along making records, singing and that kind of thing. What I really wanted to develop was the art of performing. I think that's what moved me. There are some people--and I was one of them--who made records but didn't spend a lot of time learnin' to communicate with the audience. There's a great difference between record artists and performers. I just got out there and started to put a lot of thought into it, building an act. I even took some dance lessons although I don't dance, just to loosen me up. I went into training. I don't stay quite as active as probably I should. I used to do a lot of TV but not anymore. The variety shows are gone. That's the biggest reason. I may be square but I always hesitated singin' about triangle love. I always preferred singin' about love between two people. I've noticed you can take any audience, let an old couple come up who've been married a long time, and it'll always put a warm feelin' in the hearts of people."

He told one reporter, "I don't want to sound boastful, but I've given an awful lot of thought to performing. Not just singing now, but performing. I've always thought of it as a business. I know that sounds very straight-laced and square, but I do. And every day when I'm not on the road I go to my office and I answer all my mail. People write and ask me all kinds of questions. And I answer them. I acknowledge all the mail I get. And another thing. I have never walked on stage drinking. Never given a drunken performance. Never missed a show. I don't want to sound like I'm bragging about myself, it's just the way I am about all my little businesses."

He told another reporter, "I'm still basically a country boy and always will be but I became a performer instead of just a singer. It really moved me into a more general audience than what I was reaching before. I would be less than honest with you if I didn't say it was planned. I wanted to move to where I would have a more general audience. I wasn't trying to go uptown and be a slick kind of person but I knew there was a more general type of audience there that I could reach if I just tried a little bit. It worked out that way for me. I just started changing my background a little bit, didn't change the songs very much. I mean I didn't change the kind of songs--very little, very little--but changed the background a little bit and it worked."

He added, "I entertain. That's my style. That's my way of thinking. I just picked the route of pleasing people. If you don't please them, you'll be out of the business. If I'm going to sing for art's sake, I couldn't make a living. You can't put art in the bank. I'm not ashamed of what I do and make no apologies for it."

In the age-old debate of "art" vs. "business" in the music business, Arnold was emphatic. He told Nancy Bigler Kersey of *The Cleveland Plain Dealer* "I'm not stupid. It's all profit and loss. If you want to be an artist get a brush and start painting. I want to make records that please the most people." He told S. Lovejoy of the *Phoenix Gazette*, "Whenever I have to listen to people talk about strings in the background damaging the authenticity of my music, I just say you can't put art in the bank. I had to make saleable records or get out of the business."

Then he gave an example from 1955. "There was a disc jockey from Knoxville," he said. "I mean this was a country jock and I remember him saying, 'I don't like that there record; they got all of them bugles in there.' Well, I guess I was a little concerned at the time. It was 1955 and what we did was a remake of 'Cattle Call' using a big orchestra. Well, sir, that record went on to sell a half-million copies, and I mean to tell you, that was a lot of records back then. Well, when I saw what was happening with the record, I stopped worrying. I just cried all the way to the bank."

His attention to his performances paid off handsomely for him. A concert review by Mel Shields began "In a world of live entertainment where it is becoming the norm to act as if an audience is assumed, where ego seems the key word, where superstars consider it a privilege granted to show goers even to appear, where audiences are insulted for not reacting vociferously, or for being small, or for just being an audience (translate "little people")--in such a world it's nice to have Eddy Arnold still with us. Arnold gives his audience an hour of good, old-fashioned manners. His respect for those paying to see him is almost tangible. He's a millionaire many times over, but the ones who feel rich when he's on stage are those listening...Young entertainers should be required to see him just to learn style. Parents should take their children ('Awww, Mom---who's he?') just to learn that quiet grace is often as effective as sound and sight attack."

A review of his Reno show in the *San Francisco Chronicle* by Gerald Nachmann stated, "Around here they eat up Eddy Arnold like 99-cent breakfasts....he quietly leads you into a land that's less bitter, mean and mawkish than the one inhabited by the Tammy Wynettes and Merle Haggards. Hearts break more gently, and are more repairable, in Eddy Arnold country...He seems at first suspiciously pleasant, even pat, as set in his unthreatening, law-abiding ways as the nasty outlaw singers are in theirs...he's as basic, direct and middle-of-the-road as Gerald Ford. He ropes you in with his warm, understated, understanding style, and darned if you don't find you like it in there. ...Country songs now fill the sentiment void. They deal with complex emotions bluntly stated (the lyrics aren't sophisticated, but the feelings are), with love, romance and lost and found hearts. Eddy Arnold is all gently plucked heartstrings, with a a honey-coated twang."

In a review by Howard Rosenbert in the *Hollywood Reporter* the writer stated, "Eddy Arnold is a classy example of one of today's handful of performers who dare risk a showroom appearance sans the protection of the standard overcharted, overamplifed, prepackaged production. Arnold is a singer, recognizes that's what he does best and what the folks have come to hear and places his major emphasis accordingly. His voice improves with age, has become even smoother and more mellow, washing over the room like cool spring water, not a sharp edge anywhere, even when he finds it necessary to gently rebuke a couple of talkers intent on horning in from the audience. He paces a turn well, shrewdly breaking the musical segments with some of the oldest, corniest, most appallingly tacky, yet bitingly funny jokes ever. With his altar boy twinkle, slow, measured Southern Drawl and wickedly disarming delivery, both he and his stories are just about irresistible."

Eddy Arnold's voice wasn't as strong as it used to be and he couldn't hit the high notes like he used to but, as he noted to an interviewer, "I've been around long enough I feel like I can do whatever I want to do. There is an audience there for it."

Although Eddy Arnold loved performing, he didn't care for being on the road, away from home. In 1980, Arnold told Virginia Lucier "I get lonely when I'm away from home. I turn down many offers just because of the loneliness that comes over me when I am away." He pointed out "I don't attempt to go out and play Indianapolis tonight and Louisville tomorrow night and that kind of thing. I don't try to do that anymore. That is just too hard. There is nothing resembling normal life in that kind of living." At that point he performed 70 to 75 dates a year.

He had to answer a question about "groupies" who cast their aspirations upon him. The question made him feel awkward and he squirmed, then said, "Awww gee. I'm not in such great demand. Oh, I appreciate the thought, but honestly I lead a very quiet life. I'm even a little surprised when anybody wants to interview me. Because I don't really think I'm news." He admitted there had been some women who "try to take me off stage and take me home. But obviously I've tried to discourage it because I just want to perform. Besides, I know my body is no different from any other man's body."

CHAPTER 58

In his personal life, the first half of the 1980s were pretty good to Eddy Arnold. He liked the fact that he was "ordinary" but lamented that, in the fast-paced world of show biz, he was a bit "boring" compared to some other performers.

He noted, "Entertainers are nothing special. Maybe we have a talent for singing a song, but other people have talents. I wish fans would just come up and say 'hello,' before asking for an autograph. I wish they would just say, 'Hello, I'm so and so, and I just want to shake your hand.' I'm impressed when I find people like that. Most people just say, 'Sign here,' and treat you like a statue.'"

An article in the *Boston Globe* by Steve Morse quoted Arnold saying, "I'm a cornball, I don't know any better. That's why I stay so happy." The writer commented about "the ageless, fit-looking crooner, who paved the way for Nashville pop by introducing violins and orchestral arrangement to country music during the 50s" and stated "His inimitable soothing voice has lost a touch of its strength, but he continues to entrance his diehard listeners with a blend of unabashed sentimentality and boyish naivete."

Arnold told reporter John Fisher, "I'm not an exciting person. Sometimes I'm a little surprised that people even want to interview me, but my strength has been the fact that I can make an album and it will keep selling for years. In other words my catalogue will keep selling and that's where I have gained an awful lot of, what you might say, continued record sales."

Although he was a wealthy man, he declared, "I decided a long time ago I didn't want to make all the money in the world. I want to sing a few songs and pat my wife on her backside and lead somewhat of a normal life."

"I do live a very conservative lifestyle," he said. "My 53-foot Hatteras in St. Petersburg is the only thing I have ever been extravagant on." Arnold loved talking about his yacht: "I'm a pretty good captain," he said. "I polish the chrome and I hose it off. If you came to visit, I'd even pour you a lemonade." On the boat, "I don't have to talk about my latest recording. Most people never say hello. They talk to you as though you were an automatic soft drink machine, push and pick on you and are gone. I love to sit down and talk to somebody and be a human being. I want to know the people I do business with. That's what I like about where I live. There's nothing like living in a place where you know the man who runs the hardware store or the people who work in the supermarket. It's my kind of living."

On his daily life he said, "I stay on the telephone most of the day--talking to either my manager or somebody connected with radio, publishing, or my own little businesses. I have little businesses myself--and I try to stay on top of them. Or I try to help somebody find a job." He also noted that he regularly read the *Wall Street Journal and U. S. News and World Report.*

Arnold said of life with his wife, "Our best times are on the boat or in the car. No phones. No interruptions. These are the happy times." His wife "never misses Las Vegas, likes to play cards." Discussing his marriage he said, "I don't know the secret. We have fought less than most couples. It's not normal not to fight."

In regards to his wife's attitude towards his sex appeal to other women he said, "Well, I'm sure it must have bothered her a little bit and that she had some problems with it. But she certainly lived with it. And I'll tell you what I learned right away, early on. When she was with me in public I had to MAKE them respect her....Many, many times. They would walk on her, step on her, trample on her and ignore her. And I wouldn't let them do that to her. I would take her by the arm and say, 'My good people this is my wife.'"

"When I'm home I go to lunch with a fellow nearby who owns a local hardware store," he said. "We sit there in one of the booths and tell each other stories. That's the way I live, and that's pretty much the way I perform. I haven't been an altar boy all my life [but] suggestive lyrics bother me. When it comes to sex, well, I think a real pretty love song is the answer."

At the end of the year he reminisced about a boyhood Christmas when he was given a toy butterfly that was mounted on wheels so that when he pulled it the wings moved. "It was fantastic," said Arnold. In the RCA Newsletter he was asked what he wanted for Christmas and replied "A case of clam chowder."

He noted that growing up out in the country "you manufacture your own entertainment. We really had no electricity and no plumbing. We used to sing a lot--at school, in chapel, at family gatherings. My mother's side of the family was very musical. All of them played instruments. My dad had a slight interest in music but as far as my immediate family, musically I was it."

He particularly remembered the song, "If You'll Let Me Be Your Little Sweetheart," which, he told an interviewer, "I had the record when I was growing up on the farm there and that's the first song I did on the radio. Strummed the guitar too."

"I was a country boy all my life," said Arnold. "And so I guess that's why I became a country singer--I understand that kind of life. But I've always liked all kinds of music. All I had was a record player when I was growing up, and I listened to everything--everything from Bing Crosby to Gene Autry." Then he added, "Sure, I'm a country boy and I'm proud of it, but that doesn't mean I can't like other things."

He also had ideas about raising children, which came from an experience with his father. In a story he told reporter Mel Shields, Arnold related an incident from his boyhood when his father, who was set to punish him, said, "'Son, hand me that stick,'… 'Uh-uh,' I said. 'Son hand me that stick,' he said again; he had a very strong voice. 'Uh-uh.' My daddy got up, walked over, picked up the stick, turned me across his knee and whipped me. Then he put the stick back and said, 'Hand me that stick, Son.' He whipped me again; and then again after I still refused. But the next time he asked me for the stick, I handed it to him. I was only six or seven then but he never had to whip me again. I have a sort of philosophy about that, despite all the current philosophy about not punishing children: I believe that children lean on authority. I know I did. You can try to reason with a child, but you'll find out quick enough that he doesn't think like an adult. If he's to live in this world, he's got to learn to mind young, just as I did; and he's got to learn to respect his mama's and daddy's authority."

CHAPTER 59

In 1980 Eddy Arnold found a Presidential candidate he was excited about. "Reagan is my man," he said. The excitement generated by Ronald Reagan caused Arnold to become more involved in Republican politics. He liked the way Tennessee and the country were headed; in 1980 the two Senators from Tennessee, Howard Baker and William Brock, were both Republicans and the Governor's race had a promising Republican candidate, Lamar Alexander, who won in November. In September, Eddy and Sally attended a $1,000 a couple Republican fund-raiser at the Hyatt Regency in Nashville. At the event were Senator John Warner and his wife, Elizabeth Taylor. On October 16 he was pictured with Ronald Reagan.

After the election Arnold told Allan Horton of the *Sarasota Herald Tribune* that he was "right of center" in his political ideology and lauded the election of Ronald Reagan for "a healthy return of conservative influence." He liked the fact the new President was "willing to bite the bullet on inflation" and had "the gift of appealing to the same audience which gives country music its strength--the common man." He said Reagan, whom he knew as an actor, "has the same gift of communication which gave Franklin D. Roosevelt's popular 'fireside chats' their common appeal."

At the beginning of May, 1983 Eddy Arnold went to Washington for the 71st Annual Meeting of the Chamber of Commerce USA and entertained. President Reagan delivered the major address to the group. The month before he appeared on the Country Music Association's 25th Anniversary Show. Also in 1983 Arnold went to Fort McHenry in Baltimore to lead the Pledge of Allegiance to the flag along with Maryland Governor William D. Schaefer and Lt. Gov. Joseph Curran.

Arnold was one of the major developers of Brentwood, a subdivision south of Nashville. In early 1981 he sold the utility, the Brentwood Water Company, to the city for $3.2 million. He said of the water company, "It needed money to survive. We took the stock approach, raised the necessary funds and put the company on its feet. Then we were able to meet the water needs of both homes and businesses."

He owned 90 acres on Granny White Pike, 150 acres on Murray Lane and a 52-acre hilltop farm facing Harpeth Hills. He was part-owner of a Buick agency in Davidson Co. and had just sold 17 acres, which was developed as Camelot Estates.

By the 1980s Eddy Arnold had emerged as one of the most articulate spokesmen for country music and its emergence since World War II. He told one interviewer, "In the old days, the better musicians looked down on country music, they didn't think it was respectable. Today, of course, it's a homogenized part of our popular culture, and I think it's good that country is finally getting the respect it should have gotten a long time ago."

In 1980 Eddy Arnold told reporter Barbara Johnson about country music, "I've been there when it wasn't considered popular to like it. And that used to bother me because the music as an art form wasn't respected. I think all music should be respected--even though there's good and bad in all of it. Country music is THE popular music now and all the singers are country oriented. If you stop and think for a moment, you don't have the Perry Comos, Andy Williamses and Eddie Fishers coming along anymore. All are coming out of the country field--like your John Denvers, Kenny Rogers, so forth and so on. Many have come over to the country field because it fills a void. They're looking for a pretty song and that's where they're finding it. Not the nasal kind of country, you understand, but the pretty ballads. If Irving Berlin were writing today, he'd be mighty close to a country boy."

In 1983 he told Stewart Ettinger, "Everybody doesn't like country music you know, but everybody doesn't like chocolate pie either. The more exposure country music gets, the more it moves into the mainstream of music and the entertainment business. Television and movies are part of it and the other part is that radio stations are programming it. I'm talking about stations across the United States. It used to be you didn't even have a small station in the East and North playing it. Now you have plenty of stations playing it 18 to 24 hours a day."

In 1983 there were major changes in the country music industry in Nashville. That year The Gaylord Company, based in Oklahoma City, purchased the Grand Ole Opry and Opryland from American General, the life insurance company that had purchased the National Life and Accident Insurance Company, which had started WSM and the Grand Ole Opry. In March of that year The Nashville Network and Country Music Television both went on the air, bringing country music into homes all across America daily. It was a big gamble that paid off in big dividends; from this point country music joined the growing world of cable television and began to scale new heights never imagined before. Eddy Arnold supported the new ventures and, at the end of the year, wrote a guest editorial in the *Nashville Banner* supporting a cable channel for country music.

Regarding the state of country music in the early 80s, he said, "I think it is very healthy. You have some people out there that are very strong at the moment and its getting pretty much in the mainstream of what you call popular music. Popular music is whatever is popular. Rock still has the edge in overall sales, but the rock artists, bless their hearts, there's no longevity for the most part. You have a group now that is real popular, but in six months they are gone and you have another group. They don't treat their profession as a business. Once you fail to do that you will not stay around for a long time. You must treat it as a business and I mean that as a compliment."

Then he gave some advice: "There is so much more to the music business than just memorizing a song and walking on stage and singing it. There is much more that goes with it." Some of those things included keeping up with "trends and handling your business. Directing yourself, being managed properly, showing up on time, keeping your nose clean."

Finally he appeared to resign himself to the day when he wasn't a superstar any longer. "I won't always do this," he said. "There'll come a time when the people won't want me, and I'm talking about in numbers. There'll come a time when I'll have to hang it up and I realize that, but everything has to come to an end, there is nothing permanent in this life."

CHAPTER 60

The significance of the "Nashville Sound" era, led by Eddy Arnold, was that country music, like the post-World War II population of the United States in general, moved into the middle class. In 1956, for the first time, the United States had more "white-collar" workers than "blue-collar," in terms defined by job description (i.e. management and clerical workers rather than agricultural or assembly line workers). In economic terms, there was a huge shift in the population from "lower" class to "middle class," primarily due to the downward shift in wealth generated by government spending and tax codes. This shift came through an economic definition (an increase in income) although, according to social and cultural definitions of class, these "middle class" white collar workers often remained working class, albeit with higher expectations, more material possessions and more access to upward social and cultural mobility.

By the mid-1980s, sales of the country-pop type sound pioneered by Eddy Arnold declined while country music executives found it increasingly difficult to relate to the core country audience. *The New York Times* published an article by Robert Palmer stating that country music was, effectively, dead. The article noted that sales of country records had suffered a sharp decline and that it was "the end of an era."

The article noted that "It's not just the Nashville Sound that seems to be dying; it's the Nashville dream. For more than four decades, young people with musical talent growing up in the South and the Middle West have dreamed of making it in the big time by singing, playing and making records in Nashville. They're still coming to Nashville, but most of them would like to be rock rather than country stars."

Ironically, the country music industry was rejuvenated by a group of performers labeled "the new traditionalists," led by George Strait, Ricky Skaggs and, beginning in 1985, Randy Travis. When Travis had hit songs on country radio and sold large numbers of albums, it was a shock to many in the Nashville music industry, who were convinced there was no market for a retro old-style country sound. A *New York Times* article noted "the pop-oriented arrangements helped the music attract a mass audience," but that particular mass audience was getting older and not buying records. The Nashville community was concerned about its future, but few thought the "new" country music would be a return to the older sound of country music that Eddy Arnold recorded during the 1940s and early 1950s.

While many viewed this "new" musical trend as a necessary course correction--country music's way of re-connecting with its soul--it could also be viewed in another light because, economically, the American middle class was slipping back to its working class roots instead of continuing on the path of being upwardly mobile. The term "middle class," which used to mean home ownership, vacations in Florida and college for the kids, increasingly meant a group struggling to get by. During the 1980s, as the price of housing and college tuition shot through the roof, the median household income remained where it had been since the late 1970s, at about $30,000 a year.

By the late 1980s there had been a change in image for the term "country." In 1940, when Eddy Arnold joined the Golden West Cowboys, approximately 23 percent of the population lived on farms but by 1950 only 15 percent lived on farms; by 1960 that figure had dropped to eight percent (in 1995 it was around two percent). During the first twenty years after World War II the image of the rural person was that of a country "bumpkin," a "hayseed," "hick," or "rube," as shown by the national media's stereotype of country music and country fans. The image of the city dweller was that of someone cultured and sophisticated, or at least worldly and "streetwise." The term "country" had negative connotations for people who lived in urban areas and those connotations likewise applied to country music.

The income gains from working class families during the 1980s came from working wives whose extra income was increasingly needed to keep their families afloat, or by family members either working overtime or in an extra job. In May, 1989 there were 52.8 million women working, an increase from 28.9 million from 1970.

The struggles of the middle class to make ends meet played a large part in the success of mass discounters like Wal-Mart and K-Mart, developed as contemporary versions of the old style country store which had a little something for everyone, built on a grand scale. The success of those discounters played a direct role in the sales of Country Music.

In 1980 there were 276 Wal-Marts and they sold $1.2 billion worth of merchandise; in 1990 there were 1,528 Wal-Marts and they sold $26 billion worth of merchandise. These facts, in essence, explain the incredible explosion in the sales of country music during the 1980s because mass merchandisers like Wal-Mart sold about 75 percent of all country recordings. Or, to put it another way, Sam Walton had as much to do with country music's explosion in sales during the 1980s as Randy Travis, George Strait, Reba McEntire, Garth Brooks or any other country star.

Sam Walton wasn't the only person who believed big box discount stores were the wave of the future. The same year he opened the first Wal-Mart three other companies began discount chains: S.S. Kresge opened Kmart, F. W. Woolworth started Woolco, and Dayton-Hudson opened Target. Kmart was the most successful from the start; by 1967 it had 250 stores with sales of over $800 million while Wal-Mart had only 19 stores and annual sales of about $9 million.

The mid-1980s and 1990s was the beginning of the era of the large discounter. In 1981 Sears was the country's largest retailer; by the end of the decade Kmart claimed the number one spot. During the 1990s, Wal-Mart surged past Kmart. It was the beginning of the end of the reign of the shopping centers, brought on by shifting consumer buying as well as over development. As the dominant retailers for Americans shifted from shopping centers to the mass merchandising discounters, the sales of rock music--whose strength was in the mall stores--leveled off while the sales of country music--whose sales came from stores like Wal-Mart--zoomed upward. If there had been Wal-Marts and K-Marts stocking Eddy Arnold records during the 1945-1955 period, there's no telling how many records he would have sold!

There was another factor involved in the growth in sales from country music linked to retailing. It came from bar codes and computerized scanners that became an integral part of retailing. Those electronic scanners at check-out counters scan bar codes and automatically record the item purchased, subtract it from the store inventory, tally up the price and show the consumer how much to pay. In addition to having an impact on retailers, who monitor what's selling and what is not, and consumers who spend less time in the check-out lane, those scanners had a tremendous impact on the country music charts published in trade magazines.

The information on the sale of recordings was collected by SoundScan, who relayed this information to *Billboard*, a music industry trade magazine that compiled charts of the top selling songs and albums in all music fields. Retailers and wholesalers used those charts as a barometer for consumer demand and to determine what to stock. SoundScan technology, which was put in place in 1991, gave a quick, accurate reading of what was selling and what wasn't. This differed greatly in the way charts were formerly compiled.

Before SoundScan, *Billboard* and other trades regularly called a pre-selected group of record stores and distributors (called "reporters") around the country and asked a manager or assistant manager (or whoever was in charge of giving the report) to tell them the top sellers in the various categories such as country, rock, rhythm and blues, etc. Specific sales figures were not collected; the stores only gave a relative ranking. Country music suffered from an inherent and willful prejudice; stores regularly underestimated country sales and, since it was stocked in a section outside "pop" or "rock" music, the sales weren't considered comparable. This affected Eddy Arnold, particularly during the 1960s, when he had to be considered a "pop" act in order for his records to achieve big sales. Just being a "country" artist limited record sales and mass market appeal.

With the advent of SoundScan, those prejudices were eliminated; instead, the raw data of unbiased sales figures were reported. When this occurred, it was discovered that country music sales competed with those of pop and rock; indeed, country outsold a number of pop and rock music albums. This had been an open secret within the music industry for a number of years, at least among those in the accounting departments at the major labels. The pop/rock music world was surprised to discover that country music could sell in such huge numbers.

Eddy Arnold's career reflected this. There are books and articles that list the top selling pop artists from the 1940s and early 1950s, but most don't list Eddy Arnold, although Arnold outsold the entire pop division of RCA during 1948 and his records outsold a number of pop artists from the period who are on the best selling lists. "Bouquet of Roses" by Eddy Arnold is not included on any "pop" music collections of the greatest hits from 1948, yet that record outsold almost every recording included on such collections. Such was the plight of being a "country" artist during the years before Soundscan.

Buyers for stores used trade charts as a gauge to determine what they should stock and stores like Wal-Mart, which depended on a quick turnover, routinely bought the top 15 sellers in country, rock and R&B based on the *Billboard* charts. If an album was selling well, it was ordered in larger quantities so it generated larger sales. For country music, which was once happy to collect gold records signifying 500,000 units sold, sales increased to the point that country albums were awarded triple and quadruple platinum plaques (platinum is one million units sold). Stores in malls or free-standing locations began to order more country music because sales figures proved it sold well. Since the purchase of music was often an impulse item, having country albums on hand when consumers were browsing led to more sales.

Another factor integral to understanding the jump in country sales during the 1980s and 1990s is to understand working women. By 1994 almost half the work force (45.6 percent) consisted of women; they made their own money and bought what they wanted; many bought recordings.

Music industry studies during the 1980s showed that

roughly half the country recorded product was sold to men and the other half to women, although that varied from artist to artist; some artists appealed stronger to women while men were dominant buyers of other artists. By 1996 studies showed that women accounted for approximately 65 percent of all country music sales. Country music marketers have sometimes referred to the "nag factor" to demonstrate that up to 80 percent of sales could be traced to women. In other words, a woman will buy albums herself, but will also persuade her husband or boyfriend to purchase others.

The struggles of the middle-class to make ends meet from a combination of stagnant incomes and increased demands for material goods led many to live a middle-class lifestyle through the use of credit cards.

Borrowing has always been part of American economic life. Before World War II people usually had "accounts" at local stores, such as the grocery or general store, which allowed them to go into short-term debt. After World War II, installment loans exploded as people bought homes, cars or appliances such as refrigerators on a monthly or weekly payment plan. Between 1945 and 1960, consumer credit went from $2.6 billion to $45 billion; a decade later it was $105 billion. This reflected optimism that people held that tomorrow would be better than today. For the most part, it was a safe bet. Income improved for most Americans between 1947 and 1959, when the percentage of families earning less than $3,000 annually dropped from 46 percent to 20 percent. Meanwhile, the percentage of families earning an annual income between $7,000 and $10,000, (high middle class income) rose from 5 percent to 20 percent within this same period.

Credit cards and their usage grew: in 1960 there were 233,585 BankAmericards in use; by 1968, there were over a million while credit cards overall accounted for $59 million worth of sales in 1960 and $400 million by 1968. In 1967 there were a total of 32 million credit cards issued and in 1974 there were over 200 million credit card transactions; by 1992 that figure had risen to six billion. There were over 300 million credit cards in circulation by 1993 and 220 million active accounts, or an average of three active credit card accounts for each of the nation's 70 million households.

Just as important as the change in economic well-being and improvement of Americans was the change in attitude towards debt. For those raised during the Great Depression, like Eddy Arnold, a fear of debt haunted them and they studiously avoided financial risk; however, for those who came of age after World War II, debt became the way to a better life. Since income kept growing, debt became a way to quickly acquire the possessions which defined and improved middle class life because what was once unaffordable became obtainable. For the most part, debt after World War II was controlled by others who had to approve a loan or payment. With credit cards there was no one but the customer himself to decide whether or not to borrow to spend. With computers, this decision became easier to make because computer technology reduced credit card approvals from five minutes to fifty-six seconds then, by the 1990s, down to seven seconds.

This directly affected the music industry because people increasingly used credit cards to purchase music; one major chain reported that 22 percent of their music sales came from credit card purchases.

Several other important factors also helped make country music big business during the 1985-1995 period. The introduction of the Compact Disk in 1983 helped create a boon in sales of recorded product because consumers no longer only purchased a current album but also purchased catalog items of past hits. Labels aggressively marketed catalog recordings, repackaging them into boxed sets or compilation albums.

Next, there was a change in image for the term "country." During the first twenty years after World War II the image of the rural person was that of a country "bumpkin," a "hayseed," "hick," or "rube," as shown by the national media's stereotype of country music and country fans. The image of the city dweller was that of someone cultured and sophisticated, or at least worldly and "streetwise." The term "country" had negative connotations for people who lived in urban areas and those connotations likewise applied to country music.

CHAPTER 61

The 1990 census showed the United States to be an urban nation, although more people actually lived in the suburbs that surround a city. Approximately 80 percent of the U.S. population lived in metropolitan areas; by 1990, however, the cities had acquired a negative image and were viewed as areas of widespread violence, rampant crime, crowded living conditions, and--for many inner-city dwellers--hopelessness. Country living, on the other hand, had gained appeal. To live in the "country" meant having fresh air and freedom from inner-city conditions. A home in the country became a status symbol, and country clothing, furniture, and music became increasingly popular.

Helping establish this change of image was largely the work of the media, especially television. The Nashville Network (TNN) and Country Music Television (CMT) both went on the air in 1983 and this brought country music into homes on a regular basis, which altered the old image of country bumpkins in country music. The change also came within the industry as country music executives increasingly looked for good-looking young men and women ("hunks and babes") to sign.

Eddy Arnold had to obtain a spot on network television, competing against every major musical act in all genres, and then travel to New York, Chicago or Los Angeles in order to appear on television in his heyday. By 1985, a country artist in Nashville only needed to make the short drive to The Nashville Network offices at Opryland, where country music shows were broadcast seven days a week. Or, an artist might spend two days shooting a video that was played over and over for a national audience. That was an opportunity artists like Eddy Arnold never enjoyed.

In addition to the increase in regular television exposure, there was a huge growth in radio exposure for country music. In 1961, the first year for which the Country Music Association compiled data on radio stations, and the year that probably marked the low point for country music programming (numerous stations had switched from country to rock'n'roll between 1956 and 1961), there were only 81 stations playing country music full-time. By 1969, there were 606, and during the 1970s that figure grew to 1,434. In 1980 there were 1,534 full time country stations and by the end of that decade there were 2,108. By 1994 that figure had risen to 2,427 radio stations programming country music full time. In order for Eddy Arnold to be a successful artist on the radio he had to obtain exposure on the networks in the 1940s and early 1950s. During the 1960s he had to be a "crossover" act, or get played on pop and rock music stations to achieve mass appeal. By the 1990s, a country artist only needed exposure on country radio in order to achieve a large national audience.

The dominant area for country music radio stations and sales of country records was the South and during the 1980s and early 1990s there was a huge influx of people moving into the South. In 1995 a fourth of the population of Nashville had not lived there a decade earlier. This was indicative of the entire region as people moved from the Northern rust belt into the South in a population shift that was comparable to the Great Migration during and immediately after World War II.

The shift to the South was helped by several factors. By 1980, 80 percent of the homes in the South had air conditioning; without air conditioning widely available, people would not have moved. The hot muggy south of Eddy Arnold's youth was still around, but people didn't notice it as they drove their air conditioned cars to air conditioned offices and then went home to air conditioned houses. Computers transformed businesses, making it possible to do business anywhere so companies could conduct business for less money in the South but with the same efficiency, thus precipitating a number of moves.

The growth of long-distance phone service also increased since World War II. In 1945 only 46 percent of the population had a phone and direct-dialing for long-distance calls did not begin until 1951. When Chicago publisher Fred Forster called Frank Walker at Victor in New York to obtain a recording contract for Eddy Arnold in 1943, or when Steve Sholes in New York called Eddy Arnold in Nashville in 1945 to discuss his recording career, an operator had to place the call. It was not until 1965 that most long distance calls were dialed directly; by the mid-1990s over 150 million calls were dialed directly, a result of technology as well as the breakup of AT&T in 1984, which caused competing phone companies to come into the market and drive down prices. In 1995 Eddy Arnold only needed to punch eleven digits to talk to his manager in New York, and a FAX machine kept Arnold informed of his upcoming concert dates and television appearances.

The growth of interstate highways, which account for 20 percent of traffic in the United States, although they are only one percent of the roads, made it easier to be mobile--and that made it easier for country artists to travel throughout the country on large custom buses. Jet travel also played a role in increased country exposure because it allowed country artists to travel long distances for performances. In 1940 United States airlines transported 3.5 million passengers; by the mid-1990s that figure had increased to over 400 million.

In terms of the country music audience, there were, essentially, two different audiences. First were the record buyers, who were essentially younger (ages 18-45) and that demographic trended younger because of country music videos and a change in the image of country music. The audience for live shows was often older (ages 25-65) and the demand for older country artists--even those who had not had a hit in years--remained strong, giving rise to places like Branson, Missouri which catered to an older audience. A prime reason was Social Security. In 1948 about half the men over 65 worked; by the mid-1990s most of those over 65 were retired on Social Security and private pensions--a number that exceeded 26 million. The idea of a person retiring while in their 60s, still active and potentially productive, was a new idea which came into being in the late 1960s. That audience had the time and money to travel to country music shows, and they did so.

During the 1980s there were a number of corporate mergers: RCA, Eddy Arnold's long-time label, was purchased by the German-based Bertlesman Group (BMG); CBS Records was purchased by the Japanese company, Sony; the Japanese firm Matsushita purchased MCA; Time, Inc. and Warner Brothers merged. The increase in size of these multi-national firms meant that Nashville offices had more autonomy and their own marketing departments. Prior to this, Nashville was a corporate outpost where country music acts were signed and recorded but marketing decisions came from New York and Los Angeles.

The growth of country music can perhaps best be demonstrated in the number of "Gold" and "Platinum" albums awarded for country sales. Since the Recording Industry Association of America (RIAA) instituted the "Gold" record in 1958 to represent a half million albums sold (or one million singles), there was a steady increase in the number of Gold and Platinum awards each year. Before 1968 only a few country albums or singles went "Gold," but in 1968 and 1969 ten albums went "Gold" in each of those years. It dropped to less than ten until 1973, when ten country albums again achieved "Gold" status before dropping below ten again. In 1976 country music received its first Platinum album for *The Outlaws*, a compilation featuring recordings by Waylon Jennings, Willie Nelson, Tompall Glaser and Jessi Colter.

The following year, 1977, there were 14 albums certified gold and two platinum. From this point to the twenty-first century, the number of country albums certified Gold was always in double digits with the high water marks being 1978 (22 gold, 6 platinum), 1980 (22 Gold, 8 platinum), 1981 (30 Gold, six platinum) 1983 (21 Gold, 5 platinum) and 1987 (20 Gold, 9 platinum and 1 multiplatinum). Then, in 1991 when SoundScan, which tracked unbiased record sales with computers using bar codes was used to compiled industry trade charts, there were 28 Gold albums, 22 platinum albums and 11 multi-platinum albums. In 1992, the first full year for SoundScan, country music had 40 Gold albums, 24 platinum, and 20 multi-platinum albums. That number continued to increase throughout the 1990s.

Officially, Eddy Arnold had only a few "Gold" albums, yet is credited with sales of 85 million recordings. His success came at a time when it was much more difficult to sell country music. If Eddy Arnold had his big-selling years from 1985-1995 instead of 1945-1955, there would not have been room enough on his walls to hold all of his Gold and Platinum albums.

CHAPTER 62

The last song by Eddy Arnold as a solo artist that charted in *Billboard* during the twentieth century was "The Blues Don't Care Who's Got 'Em" in 1983. By that time, 145 of Eddy Arnold's single records had appeared on the *Billboard* country chart during his career. That same year he was given the "Pioneer Award" by the Academy of Country Music. Fans continued to purchase his albums; in 1985 *Reader's Digest* presented him with a Gold Album for sales of almost a million copies of a three-CD album marketed through their magazine. Awards regularly came in; in 1987 the Songwriter's Guild gave him their "President's Award."

In 1987 he purchased a get-away place in Punta Gorda, Florida, where he stayed during the winter. Two days before his seventieth birthday he and his close friend, Bobby Campbell, went to Henderson, Tennessee where they visited the farm where Arnold grew up and Pinson Elementary School, where Arnold went to school.

Although he was still active in his businesses, and still performed occasional concerts, his health caused some concern. On March 28, 1990 he underwent double-bypass heart surgery at St. Thomas Hospital in Nashville; he was released on April 6 and began a regimen of walking and exercise. The following year he became a spokesman for the American Heart Association.

Some of Arnold's older recordings were re-packaged on compact disc, although his earliest material--from the 1945-1955 period--remained mostly unavailable. Part of this was Arnold's choice; he preferred the recordings from the 1960s era when he hit his stride as an artist in both the country and popular fields, singing smooth love songs in a lower register than his earlier work of more traditional country songs as a tenor.

In 1995 the United States celebrated the 50th Anniversary of the end of World War II. It was also the 50th Anniversary of the first record released by Eddy Arnold, "Mommy, Please Stay Home With Me," that began his remarkable career. Also in 1995 was a press announcement that Garth Brooks had become the biggest selling country artist of all time. The man he replaced was Eddy Arnold.

At the time of the Garth Brooks announcement, Eddy Arnold was seventy-six years old, living a busy, active life, still going to his office every day. On May 15 he celebrated his seventy-seventh birthday by working in his office, then attended a small birthday party during lunch time at Campbell's Glass Company, owned and run by his best friend, Bobby Campbell. There he ate some barbecue and birthday cake, then went back to his office.

On the wall in Eddy Arnold's office was a typed sheet headlined "The Customer." Under this heading were statements like: "Remember that you are nothing without your customer" and "You must always take care of your customers or they will find someone else who will." This single sheet demonstrated that Eddy Arnold was a salesman and he was proud of it. His ambition had been to sell recordings and he had sold a lot of them.

During the summer months Arnold usually left his office early on Friday afternoons and headed to the lake where he kept his boat. The "Sally K." was a 53-foot yacht where Eddy loved to spend summer weekends, cruising around Nashville area lakes.

In October, 1995 he performed at the Alabama Theater in Myrtle Beach, South Carolina. At 11 a.m. on the morning of the concert Eddy Arnold and the group of musicians who performed with him arrived and began rehearsals. Eddy Arnold did not perform many concerts, only eight to ten a year, so he did not have a regular band, although he kept guitarist Jim Lance on retainer. The hired musicians consisted of an arranger, who played a baby grand piano, two female background singers, two guitar players, a bass player, drummer, and two electronic keyboard players who played the synthesized sound of an orchestra.

During rehearsal he practiced the songs, made sure the tempo was right, became excited when the band got in a groove and even did a shuffle dance step when rehearsing "Mountain Dew." He let the sound man know when he wanted to hear more guitar, or vocals. He asked the musicians to play a song again if it didn't feel quite right. He practiced each one of his stage moves, moving his hands on certain songs. He wanted the fans to get full value for their money;

they paid to hear him sing and he was determined to give them a top notch show.

There was a obvious sense of excitement and energy when a song moved him. He was especially excited about "You Again," a song by the Forrester Sisters that he performed that evening. "I like the love songs," he said. "That's what people relate to." At the concert that evening he gave them an entire range of love songs. "I'm a sentimentalist," he said. "I believe in holding hands."

He remembered the old days with fondness. "I wanted to sell records," he said--and he did! He learned early that he needed to find the best songs. "I never played politics with songs," he said. "I always picked the best I could find and I didn't care who wrote 'em or who published 'em."

The highlight of the concert came when he sat alone with his guitar in front of the closed curtain and sang parts of his old hits: "Lovebug Itch," "I Really Don't Want to Know," "I'll Hold You In My Heart," "Turn the World Around," "What's He Doing In My World," "Bouquet of Roses," and "Make the World Go Away."

When he sang "Cattle Call" there was a collective gasp from the audience. That had always been his trademark song. He paused after the gasp, "You didn't think I could still do it, did you?" he said. The audience laughed.

Eddy Arnold's voice wasn't as strong as it used to be. "I've lost some of my high notes," he confessed. That was not the reason people came to see Eddy Arnold. They went to see him because he was a legend and, somewhere along the line, he touched their lives. It was an audience that was comfortable with him because his performances exuded comfort and geniality.

The other reason people came to Eddy Arnold concerts as he approached 80 was because he was one of those rare, remarkable performers who bonded with his audience. The large theater could have been a living room and Eddy Arnold was an old friend. He sang songs for them, told stories and jokes, and made them feel comfortable. He had a sense of style that came across as both elegant and down home at the same time, the country boy who made it big but never forgot his roots.

He finished the concert with two songs that were autobiographical: "If I Had My Life to Live Over (I'd Still Fall in Love With You)" and "I've So Much to Be Thankful For."

Backstage afterwards he said, "I don't mind telling you I'm tired." Still, he met with fans and old friends. He gave hugs, signed autographs, and talked with fans who had driven a hundred miles just to see him. During the concert one woman wept, and backstage after the show there were men and women of all ages clearly flabbergasted to be in the same room with Eddy Arnold.

During the latter half of 1995 Eddy Arnold went into a studio as a favor for his long-time friend Mike Curb and recorded a duet of "Cattle Call" with a 13-year singer. After the album was released in 1996 LeAnn Rimes became the hottest new story in country music with her song "Blue" and Eddy Arnold became a contemporary "star" all over again.

Suddenly a new group of people became acquainted with Eddy Arnold. Record producer Chuck Howard's young sons pronounced him "cool" and this delighted Arnold, who sent each an autographed picture.

In February, 1995 Arnold performed in Laughlin, Nevada for a week to packed houses. He went back into the studio with guitarist Jim Lance and recorded a number of his old songs acoustically which he hoped would become an album of duets. On his seventy-eighth birthday he spent the afternoon at his office rehearsing songs with Lance that they planned to record. He also picked three Christmas songs to record for a Christmas release.

In May, 1996 Eddy Arnold boarded a plane in Nashville headed for Pittsburgh. He collected the plane ticket at his office from his secretary, Roberta Edging, who had been with him since 1967. At the Pittsburgh airport he met his manager of thirty-two years, Jerry Purcell, and the musicians scheduled to perform with him. They drove to Wheeling, West Virginia, about an hour and a half away, where he appeared at the Capitol Theater, home of the Wheeling Jamboree.

Like the Opry, the Wheeling Jamboree was a live radio program of country music. It was younger than the Opry, having first broadcast on January 7, 1933. Unlike the Opry, the Wheeling Jamboree had not remained at the forefront of country music. A band performed cover songs for about an hour, sang commercials for sponsors, then the thick red velvet curtain was closed and the stage prepared for Eddy Arnold.

Earlier in the day, at 11 in the morning, the band came to the theater to rehearse; they were joined by Arnold at noon and he did a run-through of his show. Around 2:30 everyone took a break and Arnold joined a small group for lunch where he had a steak salad and talked about the National Basketball Association playoffs between the Chicago Bulls and Orlando Magic. Arnold had been watching the games. He was a fan of the Atlanta Braves baseball team as well, and watched their games on television. He talked about Greg Maddux's pitching, "a real artist," he said. Around 3:30 he went back to his room to rest before the concert.

The Jamboree began at 7 p.m. and the first portion ended just before 8. Around 8:15 the curtain opened to an overture of Eddy Arnold's past hits and Arnold walked on stage in a tuxedo with a powder blue jacket. The two thousand people in the audience stood and applauded while Arnold took a bow and began his show. A little over an hour later, he finished.

The next morning, a Sunday, Eddy Arnold, his manager and the group of musicians got in a van and headed back to the Pittsburgh airport where Arnold bought a Pittsburgh newspaper and turned to the sports page to read about the Bulls-Magic game. He had managed to catch a little bit of the action the day before in his hotel room and wanted to read about the game. Back in Nashville, his wife of fifty-four years, Sally, picked him up at the airport and they drove home. A few weeks earlier their son, Dick, had gotten married.

Eddy Arnold was busy and active, in his office every day overseeing his real estate business, recording in the studio, and meeting with a number of people. He spoke with his former steel guitar player, Roy Wiggins, at the funeral of Wiggin's father in May, and had spoken with Tom Parker by phone. He still kept in touch with a number of his old friends and associates.

In August he spent several days with a television crew taping "The Life and Times of Eddy Arnold," a summary of his career that was broadcast over The Nashville Network in the Fall.

He read a biography of Dizzy Dean that spring and then purchased a copy of David Brinkley's memoir for his nighttime reading. Each morning he woke early and walked about two miles at a nearby shopping mall before he drove to the post office, then into his office. He had several concerts scheduled for the Fall.

In many ways Eddy Arnold was the Cal Ripkin of his field, the Iron Man of Country Music. No other country music artist had been so popular for so long and remained so active. He had a new perspective on his recordings and concert appearances. "I used to be so keyed up about recordings," said Arnold. "I was so concerned that if I didn't have a record on the charts, playing on the radio, people would forget me." That, obviously, was not true; whenever he gave a concert, the venue was certain to fill.

The fact that audiences remembered and loved him was obvious on Monday, October 14, 1996 when he appeared on TNN's "Prime Time Country" and received two standing ovations. It had been almost 50 years to the day since his first big hit, "That's How Much I Love You" entered the charts, and that evening he performed "Cattle Call"--a song he first recorded in 1944--with 14-year old LeAnn Rimes.

Sitting in a dressing room backstage before the show, Arnold and Mike Curb, his close friend who had moved to Nashville and established the headquarters for his label, Curb Records, chatted. Curb told how he first thought about LeAnn doing "Cattle Call" in a dream--he had heard her do "I Want to Be a Cowboy's Sweetheart" and searched for a song where she could do a vocal "break." Curb played a tape of LeAnne singing for Eddy Arnold on a car tape player after the two finished dinner at a Cracker Barrel. In the Green Room LeAnn related how Mike Curb had sent her the tape then, before the session, they had all gone out to dinner before they recorded the duet.

The performance on TV came off well and after the show Arnold gathered his belongings to head home and watch the playoff game between the Atlanta Braves and the St. Louis Cardinals. He needed to record more songs for his Christmas album and was concerned time was slipping away. The evening was a mixture of more highlights in the remarkable career of Eddy Arnold, mixed with plans for future projects and activities.

It was a good, full life for Eddy Arnold. There has never really been anyone in country music like him and perhaps there never will be. Perhaps those thousands of young hopefuls who stream into Nashville each year, attracted to the city because it is the magnet for country music hopefuls, may not know all he's done, but if it weren't for Eddy Arnold, there is a good chance that Nashville wouldn't be the center for country music or that country music might not quite be the same as it is today—the music of the American middle class.

CHAPTER 63

In 2001 Eddy Arnold gave a eulogy at Chet Atkins' funeral; it was a moving tribute to his former friend and producer. In 2003 he spoke at Don Gibson's memorial service but declared afterwards that he would no longer speak at funerals; it was too emotional for him. He cried openly.

In 2005 his last album was released. Arnold had made an appointment with Joe Galante, head of RCA's Nashville office, and told him he wanted to do an album; Galante gave him the go-ahead. The album was produced by Jack Clement and Jim Malloy at Jack's studio. Eddy Arnold had practiced singing and his voice had gotten better—but it was a long way from his prime. There was a single released, but it didn't chart. He told me that he knew it was a long shot, but he thought he might "get lucky" and have another hit. He was 87 years old when that album, *After All These Years*, was released. In it he re-recorded "You Don't Know Me," the hit he wrote with Cindy Walker, the Roger Miller classic "King of the Road" and "To Life" written by Dan Tyler and Ken Leray. For that last song, he did a video.

The album was filled with love songs; the kind that Eddy Arnold loved to sing.

CHAPTER 64

Eddy Arnold gave his last performance on May 16, 1999 at the Hotel Orleans in Las Vegas; it was the day after his 81st birthday. Later that year his recording of "Make the World Go Away" was placed in the Grammy Hall of Fame for recordings. In 2000 he was awarded the National Medal of Arts by President Bill Clinton. In 2002 he was given An Honorary Doctorate by Belmont University. In 2003 he donated all of his archival materials—papers, awards, TV show tapings--to the Country Music Hall of Fame.

After the original version of this book was published in 1997, Eddy Arnold and I continued to have lunch regularly; for a while, we had a standing lunch every Friday. We were almost always joined by Bobby Campbell, his best friend.

Eddy Arnold remained active for eight years after his last performance, but by 2008 he was sometimes forgetful and disoriented. On Saturday evening, March 1, I went by his home and we had dinner, then watched the NCAA basketball playoffs. The next day he fell in his driveway and broke his hip; he entered the hospital and never came home again.

His wife, Sally, had been placed in a facility for Alzheimer's patients just before he fell; he was in Vanderbilt Hospital when she died on March 11. They had been married for 66 years. It was several weeks before her memorial service was held because it took that long for Eddy Arnold to be able to attend.

Eddy Arnold was transferred to a care facility in Cool Springs, in Franklin, Tennessee and I visited him regularly. So did his grandson, Shannon Pollard, and Bobby Campbell; Mike and Linda Curb also visited—but visitors were limited. He wanted desperately to see Sally's grave so Shannon and Bobby took him there. He also desperately wanted to go home, but that would not happen.

Early on Wednesday morning, May 8, Eddy Arnold died. He had hoped to live to be 90 but died one week short of that goal. At his death, his former label, RCA released a single, "To Life." The RCA promotion staff, under the direction of Joe Galante, worked overtime to obtain airplay for the song on country radio so Eddy Arnold would have his last chart record. They succeeded; "To Life" entered the *Billboard* country chart on May 31 and reached the number 49 position. It only stayed on the chart for one week, but that allowed him to have the distinction of having a chart record for eight decades: the 1940s, 50s, 60s, 70s, 80s, 90s and in the 2000s. Eddy Arnold would have loved that.

He lay in state at the Country Music Hall of Fame—the first member to be given that honor; the funeral service was held on May 14 at the Ryman Auditorium and was arranged by Shannon Pollard. His former orchestra director, Bill Walker and his wife Jeanine performed "How Great Thou Art,"

Vince Gill sang "Go Rest High On That Mountain" and "You Don't Know Me," the Jordanaires sang "Peace in the Valley" and Jeanine Walker sang "The Lord's Prayer."

I gave the Eulogy and this is what I said:

Those who knew him knew him as the quintessential southern gentlemen. Those who knew him well knew he could be stubborn and when he got tired of somebody or something, he wasn't afraid to let them know.

He was a man who loved to watch the news. Every night at 8 o'clock he watched Larry King, and he loved watching baseball games on TV.

Being with Eddy Arnold had its advantages. Bobby Campbell and I went to an Atlanta baseball game with him and we got to sit in the dugout before the game with all the players, received a personal tour of the clubhouse from manager Bobby Cox and got signed baseballs. It was a great day.

Eddy Arnold knew who he was. I once asked him why he was on the first Board of Directors of the Country Music Association. He said, "They asked me." I said, "Why did they ask you?" He looked straight at me and said, "Because I'm Eddy Arnold."

He told me a very revealing story about himself. He said he was in Fort Worth to do a show and Bob Wills called him up and wanted to go out that night. Bob was a great showman but he had a tendency to go on benders that could last awhile. Eddy Arnold told him "no." He said, "I had a show to do the next day and I needed my rest." He wanted to make sure he was in the best shape he could be when it came time to do his show for people who paid to see him. That was Eddy Arnold.

Someone once asked Yogi Berra why he went to so many funerals. Yogi said, "You have to go to other people's funerals or else they won't come to yours." Eddy Arnold went to a lot of funerals, but he stopped speaking at them because he was a very emotional man—he cried easily. And since his wife Sally's illness and death, he cried often. It was a devastating loss for him.

He had a lot of friends and he cherished them. You knew you were his friend because he was always glad to see you. He'd invite you to have lunch with him and he wanted to spend time with you.

Eddy Arnold also had lots of fans—millions and millions of fans all around the world. They were fans of his recordings and fans of the man himself because Eddy Arnold was worth knowing and worth admiring. He deserved fans.

Today is not a great day for Eddy Arnold's friends and fans but it's a great day for him. The last few years were not all that great for him—a lot of his friends and peers had passed and his wife's illness and his declining health made it difficult at times. He had a lot of pain, physical and emotional. But today we can celebrate because it's a great day for Eddy Arnold.

He received an incredible number of the highest earthly honors that can be bestowed on anyone. Late in life he observed, "They keep wanting to give me 'Lifetime

Achievement' awards. They must think I'm going to die."

He said he didn't want to accept any more honors because whenever he received an honor "They want money."

During his last years he turned down a lot of honors because, really there were no more to give him. It is only fitting that now he is at peace and enjoys an honor and reward that could never be given to him here on Earth.

It's a great day for Eddy Arnold.

After the Eulogy, his grandson Shannon Pollard read a message from Andy Griffith, which stated, "The year was 1954 at the Olympia Theatre in Miami, Florida. I was Eddy Arnold's opening act. I had failed in New York and Eddy gave me my career back." Shannon then talked about Eddy Arnold as a grandfather and head of the Arnold family. It was a moving tribute.

Shannon is the Executor of Eddy Arnold's Estate and it took several years, and some big checks to the I.R.S. before that Estate was wrapped up.

A year or so after Eddy Arnold's death, he received a "Star" in the Music City Walk of Fame. In addition to Eddy Arnold, that day there were stars for Kris Kristofferson, Mel Tillis and Rascal Flatts. I was honored to give the speech honoring Eddy Arnold. Here is what I said:

The story of country music has often been the story of a fight for respect. Eddy Arnold gave country music respect— he put a tuxedo on the music and presented country music to the world with dignity and honor Little Jimmy Dickens.

Eddy Arnold's achievements are longer than the Music

City Walk of Fame itself. I'll only state a few: He had the number one record for 60 straight weeks on the *Billboard* charts in the late 1940s and in 1948 sold more records on RCA than their entire pop division. He had 146 records on the *Billboard* country chart; the first was in 1945 and the last entered the chart in 2008, three weeks after he died. That means he had a record on the country chart for eight consecutive decades.

Eddy Arnold was inducted into the Country Music Hall of Fame in 1966 and it is appropriate that this beautiful park is located in front of the Hall of Fame, where his plaque and archival material are housed. It is also appropriate that Gibson Guitar is a sponsor because Eddy Arnold played a Gibson J-200 during his early career.

When Eddy Arnold started his career, Nashville was not "Music City." The center for country music was Chicago, the most important radio show was "The National Barn Dance" on WLS and there were no recording studios in Nashville. Most of the recording of country music was done by the Singing Cowboys in Los Angeles. Eddy Arnold alone did not make us "Music City," but he was a major player in the evolution of Nashville as a creative and corporate center for the music industry.

During his lifetime, Eddy Arnold honored Nashville and so it seems appropriate that Nashville is honoring him. As an artist he was truly a giant in the world of music, as a businessman and community leader he did gigantic things for this community. When he left this world, one week short of his 90th birthday, he left an enduring legacy.

Eddy Arnold was a star during his lifetime and so it is fitting that he is remembered today by a star here on Earth in the Music City Walk of Fame.

I am honored to present this plaque to Shannon Pollard, grandson of the great Eddy Arnold.

Shannon Pollard accepted the plaque and then made additional comments about his grandfather.

On January 1, 2013, his long-time secretary, Roberta Edging died; she had worked as his private secretary for over 43 years.

In 2012 Shannon Pollard established Plowboy Records to continue the legacy of Eddy Arnold. In 2013, the album, *You Don't Know Me: A Tribute to Eddy Arnold* was released. Artists Bebe Buell, Pokey LaFarge, Jason Ringenwald, Chuck Mead, Sylvain Sylvain, Drivin' 'n' Cryin', Mandy Barnett, Peter Noone, Chris Scruggs, Melinda Doolittle, Mary Gauthier and Cheetah Chrome recorded songs made famous by Eddy Arnold. The Executive Producer for the album was Shannon Pollard and the tracks were produced by Cheetah Chrome and Don Cusic.

That album demonstrated the enduring legacy of Eddy Arnold, a man whose taste in music was impeccable. Like his music, Eddy Arnold was a class act.

ACKNOWLEDGEMENTS

This book was originally published in 1997 under the title *Eddy Arnold: I'll Hold You in My Heart*. *However, the new title, Eddy Arnold: His Life and Times*, reflects this updated version. When Eddy Arnold began recording, there was virtually no recording industry in Nashville and country music was not part of mainstream American music. At the time of his death in 2008, country music was part of mainstream American music and country artists were major stars. Eddy Arnold played a vital role in country music's success during the twentieth century as well as the growth of Nashville to the point that the city is known all over the world as "Music City U.S.A."

During the original period of research and writing Eddy Arnold's biography, I spent many hours with him. Some of that time was spent with interviews where I asked him a set of questions, but a lot of time was spent listening to him reminisce--in his office, on the road during personal appearances and at lunch. A number of the quotes in this book came from Eddy Arnold during those conversations. In addition, he had saved a large number of articles written about him during his career. His wife, Sally, clipped, collected and pasted articles in scrapbooks. During the 1960s he had a clipping agency that collected articles about him. Those articles were in Eddy Arnold's office and I used them extensively. In 2003, at my urging he donated those articles to the Frist Archives at the Country Music Hall of Fame.

The Country Music Foundation is invaluable for those who do research into country music, and I owed them a great debt of gratitude for the original book, especially Ronnie Pugh, Bob Pinson, and John Rumble. Their files on people like Steve Sholes, Paul Cohen, and others involved in the early country music industry were especially helpful.

In addition to Eddy Arnold, I owed a great deal of gratitude to his manager, Jerry Purcell, who was always available to answer any questions and helped immeasurably with the book. I also owed a great debt of gratitude to those who shared their time and thoughts: Mr. and Mrs. Robert Jones (who lived on the farm where Eddy Arnold grew up), Owen Bradley, Bill Denny, Brad McCuen, Chet Atkins, Floyd Cramer, Frances Preston, Joe Talbot, Joe Galante, Charles Brown, Roy Wiggins, Ronnie Pugh, Charles Wolfe, Otto Kittsinger, Keith Bilbrey, LeAnn Rimes, Bobby Campbell, Joe Allison, Vallo Nickalau and Sally Arnold.

Since the original publication, many of those people have died. Between 1997 and Eddy Arnold's death in 2008, he and I spent a good deal of time together. For a number of years we had a standing lunch on Fridays, usually at Sylvan Park Melrose on Franklin Road in Nashville. We were usually accompanied by Eddy's best friend, Bobby Campbell. I attended many events and celebrated birthdays with him, usually during the lunch hour at Bobby Campbell's glass company where the small group included his long-time secretary, Mrs. Roberta Edging, Bobby and Mary Campbell, Sally Arnold and perhaps a few others.

Although he was a "public figure," Eddy Arnold lived a simple, quiet life. His major indulgence was his yacht; otherwise, he tended to go into his office each day, take care of his real estate and other businesses, have lunch with someone and, in the evening, he and Sally went out to dinner. At 8 p.m. he watched "The Larry King Show" on CNN; if there was an Atlanta Braves game on, he also watched that.

After Eddy Arnold's death, I felt I should update this book and include a final chapter on his last years. Additionally, his grandson, Shannon Pollard, found a number of important contracts, letters, pictures and documents after Eddy Arnold's death which were unavailable when the first biography was published and were invaluable in adding new information about Eddy Arnold.

Shannon Pollard is the executor of Eddy Arnold's Estate and wants to perpetuate the life and career of his grandfather. That led him to create Plowboy Records, a label he founded along with former punk rocker Cheetah Chrome and me. In 2013 the label released *You Don't Know Me: A Tribute to Eddy Arnold* which featured a variety of artists singing songs that had been hits for Eddy Arnold. Much thanks must be given to Shannon for remaining active perpetuating the legacy of Eddy Arnold.

The story of Eddy Arnold is not over; his music and his legacy endures. There will be more books, more recordings released and more articles written about Eddy Arnold in the future because he was incredibly important and pivotal to the story of Nashville and country music during the twentieth century.

Upper left: *Eddy Arnold in his 80s.*

Upper right: *Eddy Arnold in performance*

Bottom Left: *Eddy Arnold and biographer Don Cusic in Arnold's office*

Bottom right: *Shannon Pollard, grandson of Eddy Arnold, and his two daughters, Sophie and Rowan at the Music City Walk of Fame induction.*

Upper left: *Eddy Arnold and Minnie Pearl.*
Upper right: *Eddy Arnold with Dave and Sugar (Dave Rowland, Jackie Frantz Cusic and Vicki Hackeman.*
Middle: *Eddy Arnold arrives in Mexico*
Bottom left: *Eddy and Sally Arnold*
Bottom right: *Eddy Arnold during a TV performance.*

Early publicity photos of Eddy Arnold

EDDY ARNOLD BIBLIOGRAPHY

Billboard Chart Singles from Eddy Arnold (Year and highest position)
1945: Each Minute Seems a Million Years (#5)
1946: All Alone in This World Without You (#7)
1946: That's How Much I Love You (A side) (#2)
1946: Chained to a Memory (B Side) (#3)
1947: What is Life Without Love? (#1)
1947: It's a Sin (A Side) (#1)
1947: I Couldn't Believe It Was True (B Side) (#4)
1947: I'll Hold You In My Heart (Till I Can Hold You In My Arms (#1)
1947: To My Sorrow (#2)
1948: Molly Darling (#10)
1948: Anytime (A Side) (#1)
1948: What a Fool I Was (B Side) (#2)
1948: Bouquet of Roses (A Side) (#1)
1948: Texarkana Baby (B Side) (#1)
1948: Just a Little Lovin' (Will Go a Long, Long Way) (A) (#1) (A Side)
1948: My Daddy Is Only a Picture (B Side) (#5)
1948: A Heart Full of Love (For a Handful of Kisses) (A Side) (#1)
1948: Then I Turned And Walked Slowly Away (B Side) (#2)
1949: Many Tears Ago (#10)
1949: Don't Rob Another Man's Castle (A Side) (#1)
1949: There's Not a Thing (I Wouldn't Do For You) (B Side) (#3)
1949: One Kiss Too Many (#1)
1949: The Echo of Your Footsteps (#2)
1949: I'm Throwing Rice (At the Girl I Love) (A Side) (#1)
1949: Show Me The Way Back To Your Heart (B Side) (#7)
1949: C-H-R-I-S-T-M-A-S (A Side) (#7)
1949: Will Santa Come to Shanty Town (B Side) (#5)
1950: There's No Wings on My Angel (#6)
1950: Take Me In Your Arms and Hold ME (A Side) (#1)
1950: Mama and Daddy Broke My Heart (B Side) (#6)
1950: Little Angel With The Dirty Face (A Side) (#3)
1950: Why Should I Cry? (B Side) (#3)
1950: Cuddle Buggin' Baby (A Side) (#2)
1950: Enclosed, One Broken Heart (B Side) (#6)

1950: Lovebug Itch (A Side) (#2)

1950: Prison Without Walls (B Side) (#10)

1951: There's Been A Change In Me (#1)

1951: May the Good Lord Bless And Keep You (#8)

1951: Kentucky Waltz (#1)

1951: I Wanna Play House With You (A Side) (#1)

1951: Something Old, Something New (B Side) (#4)

1951: Somebody's Been Beating My Time (A Side) (#2)

1951: Heart Strings (B Side) (#5)

1952: Bundle of Southern Sunshine (A Side) (#4)

1952: Call Her Your Sweetheart (B Side) (#9)

1952: Easy on the Eyes (#1)

1952: A Full TIme Job (#1)

1952: Older and Bolder (A Side) (#3)

1952: I'd Trade All of My Tomorrows (For Just One Yesterday) (B Side) (#9)

1953: Eddy's Song (#1)

1953: Free Home Demonstration (A Side) (#4)

1953: How's the World Treating You? (B Side) (#4)

1953: Mama, Come Get Your Baby Boy (#4)

1954: I Really Don't Want to Know (#1)

1954: My Everything (#7)

1954: This Is the Thanks I Get (For Loving You) (A Side) (#3)

1954: Hep Cat Baby (B Side) (#7)

1954: Christmas Can't Be Far Away (#12)

1955: I've Been Thinking (A Side) (#2)

1955: Don't Forget (B Side) (#12)

1955: In Time (A Side) (#6)

1955: Two Kinds of Love (B Side) (#9)

1955: The Cattle Call (A Side) (#1)

1955: The Kentuckian Song (B Side) (#8)

1955: That Do Make It Nice (A Side) (#1)

1955: Just Call Me Lonesome (B Side) (#2)

1955: The Richest Man (In the World) (A Side) (#10)

1955: I Walked Alone Last Night (B Side) (#6)

1956: Trouble in Mind (#7)

1956: Casey Jones (The Brave Engineer) (#15)

1956: You Don't Know Me (#10)

1957: Gonna Find Me a Bluebird (#12)

1959: Chip Off the Old Block (#12)
1959: Tennessee Stud (#5)
1961: Before This Day Ends (#23)
1961: (Jim) I Wore a Tie Today (#27)
1961: One Grain of Sand (#17)
1962: Tears Broke Out on Me (#7)
1962: A Little Heartache (A Side) (#3)
1962: After Loving You (B Side) (#7)
1963: Does He Mean That Much To You? (#5)
1963: Yesterday's Memories (#11)
1963: A Million Years Or So (#13)
1963: Jealous Hearted Me (#12)
1964: Molly (#5)
1964: Sweet Adorable You (#26)
1964: I Thank My Lucky Stars (#8)
1965: What's He Doing In My World (#1)
1965: I'm Letting You Go (#15)
1965: Make the World Go Away (#1)
1966: I Want To Go With You (#1)
1966: The Last Word In Lonesome Is Me (#2)
1966: The Tip of My Fingers (#3)
1966: Somebody Like Me (#1)
1967: The First Word (#51)
1967: Lonely Again (#1)
1967: Misty Blue (#3)
1967: Turn the World Around (#1)
1968: Here Comes Heaven (#2)
1968: Here Comes The Rain, Baby (#4)
1968: It's Over (#4)
1968: Then You Can Tell Me Goodbye (#1)
1968: They Don't Make Love Like They Used To (#10)
1969: Please Don't Go (#10)
1969: But For Love (#19)
1969: You Fool (#69)
1970: Since December (#73)
1970: Soul Deep (#22)
1970: A Man's Kind of Woman (A Side) (#28)
1970: Living Under Pressure (B Side) (#28)

1970: From Heaven To Heartache (#22)
1971: Portrait of My Woman (#26)
1971: A Part of America Died (#49)
1971: Welcome To My World (#34)
1971: I Love You Dear (#55)
1972: Lonely People (#38)
1972: Lucy (#62)
1973: So Many Ways (#28)
1973: If the Whole World Stopped Lovin' (#56)
1973: Oh, Oh, I'm Falling In Love Again (#29)
1974: She's Got Everything I Need (#24)
1974: Just For Old Times Sake (#56)
1974: I Wish That I Had Loved You Better (#19)
1975: Butterfly (#47)
1975: Red Roses For a Blue Lady (#60)
1975: Middle of a Memory (#86)
1976: Cowboy (#13)
1976: Put Me Back Into Your World (#43)
1977: (I Need You) All the Time (#22)
1977: Freedom Ain't the Same as Being Free (#53)
1977: Where Lonely People Go (#83)
1978: Country Lovin' (#23)
1978: I'm the South (#91)
1979: If Everyone Had Someone Like You (#13)
1979: What In Her World Did I Do (#21)
1979: Goodbye (#22)
1979: If I Ever Had to Say Goodbye To You (#28)
1980: Let's Get It While the Gettin's Good (#6)
1980: That's What I Get For Loving You (#10)
1980: Don't Look Now (But We Just Fell in Love) (#11)
1981: Bally-Hoo Days (A) (#32)
1981: Two Hearts Beat Better Than One (B) (#32)
1982: All I'm Missing Is You (#30)
1982: Don't Give Up On Me (#73)
1983: The Blues Don't Care Who's Got 'Em (#76)
2008: To Life (#49)

BIBLIOGRAPHY

"A Record Date With Eddy Arnold." *Country Song Round Up*: 1949.

Ambrose, Stephen E. *Eisenhower: Soldier and President*. New York: Touchstone, 1990.

"American Folk Tunes." *Cowboy and Hillbilly Tunes and Tunesters*. April 5, 1947.

Antrim, Doron K. "Whoop-And-Holler Opera." *Collier's*, January 26, 1946. Vol 117, No. 4.

"Arnold Denies He's a Western Singer." *Albuquerque, NM Journal*. Sept. 17, 1968.

"Arnold, Eddy. "My True Romance" in *True Romance*, 1949.

Arnold, Eddy. *It's a Long Way From Chester County*. Old Tappan, N.J.: Hewitt House, 1969.

Barron, Mark. "Eddie Arnold Homesick During New York Visit" by Mark Barron (*Rapid City S.D. Journal* Apr 21, 1949) AP Newsfeature

Barthelme, Don. "Disc Sounds Familiar" in *Houston Post* May 14, 1949

Betz, Betty. "Arnold Gets Marriage Bids in Mail," *Houston Post*, 1949.

Biszick-Lockwood, Bar. *Restless Giant: The Life and Times of Jean Aberbach & Hill and Range Songs*. Urbana: University of Illinois Press, 2010.

Blachar, Ted. Article in *The Ottawa Journal*, August 30, 1968.

Brooks, Tim and Earle Marsh. *The Complete Directory to Prime Time Network and Cable TV Shows 1946-Present*. Eighth Edition. New York: Ballantine, 2003.

"Bull Market in Corn." Time October 4, 1943. Vol 42, No. 14.

Bumpass, Gina. "Eddy Arnold" in *Ft. Worth Star-Telegram* Mar 16, 1948.

Carey, Bill. *Fortunes, Fiddles & Fried Chicken: A Nashville Business History*. Franklin, TN: Hillsboro Press, 2000.

Carr, Patrick. ed. *The Illustrated History of Country Music*, New York: Dolphin, 1980.

Cash, Johnny with Patrick Carr. *Cash: The Autobiography.* San Franciso: HarperSanFrancisco, 1997.

Churchill, Allen. "Tin Pan Alley's Git-Tar Blues." *New York Times* Magazine, July 15, 1951. Sec. 6.

Clark, Roy with Marc Eliot. *My Life: In Spite of Myself!* New York: Simon and Schuster, 1994

Clovis, Kathryn Kirkham. "Radio's Famous "Wranglers' Spread Good Will of Sooner State" in *Clovis (NM) News-Journal*, 1948.

Concert Review from Panama City, FLA., January, 20, 1968.

Concert Review. from Monroe, LA. January 21, 1968.

Coon, Dick. Article in *Great Falls Tribune*, July 27, 1968.

"Corn of Plenty." *Newsweek* June 13, 1949. Vol 33, No. 24.

"Country Disc Craze Grows; Arnold Nabs Another Hit!" *Record Bulletin*, C. M. McClung & Co., Knoxville, TN; May 2, 1949.

"Country Music Goes to Town." *Mademoiselle*, April 1948.

"Country Music is Big Business, and Nashville is its Detroit." *Newsweek*, August 11, 1952. Vol 40, No. 6.

"Country Music Snaps Its Regional Bounds." *Business Week*. March 19, 1966. No. 1907. pp 96-103.

"Country Music: The Nashville Sound." *Time*, November 17, 1964. Vol 84, No. 22 pp 76 and 79.

"Country Musicians Fiddle Up Roaring Business." *Life*, November 19, 1956. Vol 41, No. 21

Crumbaker, Marge and Gabe Tucker. *Up and Down With Elvis Presley.* (New York: G.P. Putnam's Sons, 1981)

Cusic, Don. *Discovering Country Music*. Praeger, 2008.

Cusic, Don. *Eddy Arnold: I'll Hold You in My Heart*. Nashville: Rutledge Hill, 1997.

Cusic, Don. *Elvis and Nashville*. Nashville: Brackish, 2012.

Davis, Louise Littleton. *Nashville Tales*. Gretna, GA: Pelica, 1982.

Dean, Jimmy and Donna Meade Dean. *Thirty Years of Sausage, Fifty Years of Ham: Jimmy Dean's Own Story*. New York: Berkley Books, 2004

Diekman, Diane. *Live Fast Love Hard: The Faron Young Story*. Urbana: University of Illinois Press, 2007.

Doyle, Don C. *New Men, New Cities, New South: Atlanta, Nashville, Charleston, Mobile, 1860-1910*.Chapel Hill: University of North Carolina Press, 1990.

Doyle, Don H. *Nashville Since the 1920s*. Knoxville: The University of Tennessee Press, 1985.

Duff, Morris. "Make Way for the Country Sound." *Toronto Daily Star,* March 21, 1964. Section 2: pp 23-24.

"Eddy Arnold Halts Traffic in Bradenton." Bradenton, FLA Aug 15, 1948

"Eddy Arnold opened record shop in Murfreesboro, TN." *Variety* May 17, 1948

Eddy Arnold's Radio Favorites Song Book No. 1. Adams, Vee & Abbott (1946) Song folio.

Eddy, Don. "Hillbilly Heaven." *American Magazine*, March, 1952. Vol 153, No. 3.

Editors of Country Music Magazine. *The Comprehensive Country Music Encyclopedia*. New York: Times, 1994.

Escott, Colin with George Merritt and William MacEwen. *Hank Williams: The Biography* (Boston: Little, Brown, 1994)

"Fort Knox No Longer Has Exclusive On Pot of Gold; WSM, Nashville, Talent Corners a Good Chunk of It," *Variety*, Oct 26, 1949:

Freda, Michael D. *Eddy Arnold Discography, 1944-1996*. Westport, CT: Greenwood Press, 1997.

Gentry, Linnell. *A History and Encyclopedia of Country, Western, and Gospel Music* (Nashville: Clairmont, 1969.)

Gleason, Ralph J. "Eddy's the Man Who Helped Bring The Country Song to the Big Town," *San Francisco Chronicle*. July 15, 1951.

"Gold Guitars, The." *Newsweek*. April 4, 1966. Vol 67, No. 4.

Goodwin, Doris Kearns. *No Ordinary Time: Franklin and Eleanor Roosevelt: The Home Front in World War II*. (New York: Touchstone, 1994).

Gordon, Jack. "Eddy Arnold, Former Plow Boy, is Visitor." *Fort Worth Press*, March 16, 1948

Graebner, William S. *The Age of Doubt: American Thought and Culture in the 1940s*. Boston: Twyane, 1991.

Gray, Dick. Column in *Atlanta Journal*. Feb 9, 1968.

Green, Douglas B. *Country Roots: The Origins of Country Music*. (New York: Hawthorn, 1976)

Guralnick, Peter. *Careless Love: The Unmaking of Elvis Presley*. Boston and New York: Back Bay Books, 1999.

Guralnick, Peter. *Last Train to Memphis: The Rise of Elvis Presley*. Boston: Little, Brown, 1994).

Hagen, Chet. *Grand Ole Opry: The Complete Story of a Great American Institution and Its Stars*. New York: Owl, 1989

Hall, Wade. *Hell Bent For Music: Pee Wee King*. (Lexington: University of Kentucky Press, 1996).

Hanna, Charlie. Concert review of Portland show in *The Oregonian*, June 6, 1968.

Harris, Roy. "Folk Songs. *House & Garden*, December, 1954. Vol 106, No. 6.

Harrison, Nigel. *Songwriters: A Biographical Dictionary with Discographies*. Jefferson, N.C.: McFarland & Company, Inc.: 1998.

Havighurst, Craig. *Air Castle of the South: WSM and the Making of Music City*. Urbana: University of Illinois Press, 2007.

Hefferman, Harold. "Studio Nips Flight of Lonely Balladeer." *The Detroit News*, 1949.

Hemphill, Paul. *The Nashville Sound: Bright Lights and Country Music*. New York: Simon & Schuster, 1970.

Hicks, Ida Belle. "Eddie's Country Boy, Not Singing Cowboy." *Fort Worth Star-Telegram*. March 16, 1948.

Hilburn, Robert. Article in *Long Island Press*. October 6, 1968.

"Hillbilly Fans, Including Tuck, Acclaim Eddy Arnold's Show." *Richmond Times-Dispatch*. Mar 31, 1948

"Hoedown on a Harpsichord." *Time*, November 14, 1960. Vol 76, No. 20

Horstman, Dorothy. *Sing Your Heart Out, Country Boy: Classic Country Songs and Their Inside Stories by the People Who Wrote Them*. (New York: E.P. Dutton, 1975)

Humphrey, Hal. "Cowpokes Shout 'Boycott," *Oakland Tribune*, Aug 10, 1953.

Ivey, Bill "The Bottom Line: Business Practices That Have Shaped Country Music." in *Country: The Music and the Musicians*. New York: Abbeville Press, 1988.

Jackson, Kenneth T. *Crabgrass Frontier: The Suburbanization of the United States*. (Oxford U P, 1985) HT 384.5 U 5

Jarman, Rufus. "Country Music Goes to Town." *Nation's Business*, February, 1953. Vol 41, No. 2.

Jones, George with Tom Carter. *I Lived To Tell It All*. New York: Villard, 1996.

Jones, Loyal. *Country Music Humorists and Comedians*. Urbana and Chicago: University of Illinois Press, 2008.

Jones, Paul. "Hillbilly Sound Attaining Dignity," October 30, 1968.

Kaliff, Joe. *Brooklyn Daily*, May 29, 1968.

Killen, Buddy with Tom Carter. *By the Seat of My Pants: My Life in Country Music*. New York: Simon and Schuster, 1993.

King, Larry L. "Inside Grand Ole Opry," Reader's Digest, July 1968. (condensed from Harper's July 1968)

King, Nelson. "Hillbilly Music Leaves the Hills." *Good Housekeeping*, June, 1954. Vol 138, No. 6.

Kingsbury, Paul and Alan Axelrod, eds. *Country: The Music and the Musicians*. New York: Abbeville Press, 1988.

Kingsbury, Paul, ed. *The Country Music Reader*. (Nashville: Vanderbilt University Press, 1996)

Kingsbury, Paul. *The Grand Ole Opry History of Country Music: 70 Years of the Songs, the Stars, and the Stories*. New York: Villard Books, 1995

Kittsinger, Otto. Liner notes for Pee Wee King (Bear Family Records)

Kosser, Michael. *How Nashville Became Music City U.S.A.: 50 Years of Music Row*. Milwaukee, WI: Hal Leonard, 2006.

Langdon, Philip. *A Better Place to Live: Reshaping the American Suburb*. University of Massachusetts Press.

Langley, Frank. *Boston Herald*, June 30, 1968.

Lieberson, Goddard. "'Country Sweeps the Country." *New York Times Magazine*. July 28, 1957. Section 6.

MacKenzie, Bob. "On Televison," Oakland newspaper, April 25, 1968.

Malone, Bill C. and Judith McCulloh, eds. *The Stars of Country Music*. (Urbana: University of Illinois Press, 1975.

Malone, Bill C. *Singing Cowboys and Musical Mountaineers: Southern Culture and the Roots of Country Music*. Athens, GA: The University of Georgia Press, 1993.

Malone, Bill. *Country Music U.S.A.* (Austin, TX: University of Texas Press, 1968)

Marek, Richard. "Country Music, Nashville Style." *McCall's*, April, 1961. Vol 88, No. 7.

Marvin, Wanda. "Hillbillies Win in New York: Much Mazuma Found in Mountain Music-Making," July 22, 1944.

Mason, Bobbie Ann. *Elvis Presley: A Penguin Life*. New York: Viking, 2003.

Mazor, Barry. *Ralph Peer and the Making of Popular Roots Music.* Chicago: Chicago Review Press, 2015.

McCloud, Barry. *Definitive Country: The Ultimate Encyclopedia of Country Music and Its Performers.* New York: Perigree, 1995.

McElvaine, Robert S. *The Great Depression: America 1929-1941.* New York: Times, 1984.

Miller, Stephen. *Johnny Cash: The Life of an American Icon.* London: Omnibus Press, 2003.

Montana, Kay. "About Eddie Arnold" in *Silver Star Song Club Bulletin*, Fall & Winter, 1948.

Morris, Edward. "New, Improved, Homogenized: Country Radio Since 1950." in *Country: The Music and the Musicians.* New York: Abbeville Press, 1988.

Nash, Alanna. *Behind Closed Doors: Talking With the Legends of Country Music.* New York: Alfred A. Knopf, 1988.

Nash, Alanna. *The Colonel: The Extraordinary Story of Colonel Tom Parker and Elvis Presley.* New York: Simon and Schuster, 2003.

Nocera, Joseph. *A Piece of the Action: How the Middle Class Joined the Money Class.* New York: Simon & Schuster, 1994.

Oermann, Robert. *America's Music: The Roots of Country.* (Atlanta: Turner Publisher, 1996)

O'Neil, Thomas. *The Grammys: For the Record.* New York: Penguin, 1993.

"Pistol Packin' Mama." *Life*, October 11, 1943. Vol 15, No. 11.

Porterfield, Nolan. *Jimmie Rodgers: The Life and Times of America's Blue Yodeler.* Urbana: University of Illinois Press, 1979.

Portis, Charles. "That New Sound From Nashville." *Saturday Evening Post*, February 12, 1966. Vol 239. pp 30-38.

Pugh, Ronnie. *Ernest Tubb: Texas Troubadour.* (Durham, N.C,: Duke University Press, 1996).

"RCA in Promotion Tie on Arnold Disk for Divorce Squelching."
Variety, December 28, 1949

Reynolds, David. *Rich Relations: The American Occupation of Britain,
1942-1945*. (New York: Random House, 1995).

Rose, Frank. *The Agency: William Morris and the Hidden History of
Show Business*. New York: HarperBusiness, 1995.

Rosenberg, Neil V. *Bluegrass: A History*. Urbana, ILL: University of
Illinois Press, 1985.

Rumble, John Woodruff. *Fred Rose and the Development of the
Nashville Music Industry, 1942-1954*. Unpublished dissertation
from Vanderbilt University, 1980. Ann Arbor, MI: University
Microfilms International.

Rumble, John. "Behind the Board with Bill Porter: Part One." *The
Journal Of Country Music*, Vol. 18, No. 1, 1996. Pp 27-40.

Rumble, John. "Behind the Board with Bill Porter: Part Three." *The
Journal Of Country Music*, Vol. 19, No. 1, 1997. Pp 24-31.

Rumble, John. "Behind the Board with Bill Porter: Part Two." The
Journal Of Country Music, Vol. 18, No. 2, 1996. Pp 20-30.

Sanjek, Russell. *American Popular Music and its Business: The First
Four Hundred Years: Vol III From 1900 to 1984*. New York:
Oxford University Press, 1988.

Scherman, Robert. "Hillbilly Phenomenon." *The Christian Science
Monitor*, March 13, 1948.

Schipper, Henry. *Broken Record: The Inside Story of the Grammy
Awards*. New York: Birch Lane, 1992

Schlappi, Elizabeth. *Roy Acuff: The Smoky Mountain Boy*. Gretna,
GA: Pelican Publishing Company, 1978, 1993)

Sears, Richard S. *V-Discs: A History and Discography*. Westport,
CT: Greenwood Press, 1980.

Singer, Samuel. Concert review of Philadelphia show, April 20, 1968.

Snow, Hank with Jack Ownbey and Bob Burris. *The Hank Snow
Story*. Urbana and Chicago: University of Illinois Press, 1994.

"Songs From Texas." *Time*, Vol 37, No. 12, March 24, 1941.

Stone, Jack. "Millions in Music--Hillbillies in Clover." *The American Weekly*. February 6, 1949

Streissguth, Michael. *Eddy Arnold: Pioneer of the Nashville Sound*. New York: Schirmer Books, 1007.

Streissguth, Michael. *Like a Moth to the Flame: The Jim Reeves Story*. Nashville: Rutledge Hill Press, 1998.

"Strictly By Ear." *Time*, February 11, 1946. Vol 47, No. 6.

Teeter, H.B. "Nashville, Broadway of Country Music." *Coronet*, August, 1952. Vol 43, No. 4.

Terry, Bea. "Folk Music and Its Folks," 1949.

Tichi, Cecelia. *High Lonesome: The American Culture of Country Music*. Chapel Hill: The University of North Carolina Press, 1994.

Tilley, Nannie M. *The R.J. Reynolds Tobacco Company*. Chapel Hill: University of North Carolina Press, 1985.

Tosches, Nick. *Country: The Biggest Music in America*. New York: Delta, 1977.

Turner, Steve. *The Man Called Cash: The Life, Love, and faith of an American Legend*. Nashville: W Publishing Group, 2004.

Vellenga, Dirk and Mick Farren. *Elvis and the Colonel: The True and Shocking Story of the Man Behind 'The King.'* London: Grafton Books, 1990.

Waldron, Eli. "Country Music: The Squaya Dansu From Nashville." *The Reporter*, June 2, 1955. Vol 12, No. 11.

Westbrooks, Bill with Barbara M. McLean and Sandra S. Grafton. *Everybody's Cousin: Cousin Wilbur*. (New York: Manor Books, 1979)

Whitburn, Joel. *Hot Country Albums: Billboard 1964 to 2007*. Menomonee Falls, Wisconsin, 2008.

Whitburn, Joel. *Hot Country Songs: Billboard 1944 to 2008*.

Menomonee Falls, Wisconsin, 2008.

Whitburn, Joel. *Pop Memories 1890-1954*. Menomonee Falls, Wisconsin, 1986.

Whitburn, Joel. *The Billboard Albums: 6th Edition*. Menomonee Falls, Wisconsin: Record Research Inc., 2006.

Whitburn, Joel. *Top Pop Singles, 12th Edition*. Menomonee Falls, WI: Record Research Inc, 2009.

Williams, Andy. *Moon River and Me: A Memoir*. New York: Viking, 2009.

Williams, Roger. *Sing a Sad Song: The Life of Hank Williams*. New York: Ballantine, 1973.

Wilson, Eleanor. "Tennessee Plowboy Plows Right to Top of *Billboard's* Popularity Chart," February 25, 1949

Wiseman, Mac, as told to Walt Trott. *All My Memories Fit For Print*. Nashville: Nova Books, 2015.

Wolfe, Charles K. *A Good-Natured Riot: The Birth of the Grand Ole Opry*. Nashville, TN: Country Music Foundation Press, 1999.

Wolfe, Charles K. *Tennessee Strings: The Story of Country Music in Tennessee*. Knoxville: University of Tennessee Press, 1977.

Wolfe, Charles. "The Triumph of the Hills: Country Radio, 1920-1950" in *Country: The Music and the Musicians*. New York: Abbeville Press, 1988.

Zepela, Monte. "I'm Really a Pop Music Artist" *Charlotte Observer*, December 8, 1968.

Zolotow, Maurice. "Hillbilly Boom." *Saturday Evening Post*, February 12, 1944. Vol 216, No. 33.

Zolotow, Maurice. "Hayride." *Theater Arts*, November, 1954. Vol 38, No. 11.

Zwonitzer, Mark with Charles Hershberg. *Will You Miss Me When I'm Gone?" The Carter Family & Their Legacy in American Music*. New York: Simon & Shuster, 2002.

SONG INDEX

GENERAL INDEX

Made in United States
North Haven, CT
13 January 2022